Metamorphosis Alpha Roleplaying Game

James M. Ward & Jamie Chambers

METAMORPHOSIS ALPHA created by James M. Ward
SYSTEM 26 game rules by Jamie Chambers

Writing & Development Team

Craig Brain, Christy Everette, Sean Everette, Lizard

Project Management: Joie Brown, Jamie Chambers

Editing: Christy Everette ✧ **Development:** Sean Everette ✧ **Typesetting:** Jamie Chambers

Cover Art: Jason Engle ✧ **Starship Warden Art:** Jeff Carlisle ✧ **Lead Interior Art:** Lindsay Archer
Cover Design: Digger Hayes, Lindsay Archer ✧ **Interior Design:** Digger Hayes, Ben Mund
Illustrations: Lindsay Archer, Jeff Carlisle, Josh Harris, Melanie Hayes, Young Kim, Ben Mund
Art Direction: Joie Brown, Renae Chambers

Acknowledgements: This game would not be possible without the support of 447 extremely patient backers via Kickstarter.com. Please see the back page of this book for the credit they very much deserve. Special recognition also to Lindsay Archer and Ben Mund for continuing to step up and assist without even being asked.

Special Thanks: Ann Chambers-Robinson, Ben Dobyns, Nikki Crites, Don Early, Thomas Groomes, Liz Hayes, Tracy Hickman, Roger Robinson, Sarah Supancic, Reanne Yancey, Ken Whitman, Joseph C. Wolf

Jamie's Dedication: This book is dedicated to my favorite little mutants …
Mell, Liz, Chris, Xander, Justin, Piper, and Jensen.

FREE DIGITAL VERSION
Enter the URL below and use the code from the inside cover on checkout to make the item absolutely free. Check out bonus content found on DriveThruRPG.com!
drivethrurpg.com/product/151040/

signal fire studios

2265 Roswell Road, Suite 100, Marietta, GA 30062
www.signalfirestudios.com

CONTENTS

A half-naked barbarian warrior wanders the land with only his brawn, wits, and blade to keep him alive. A feline beast with glowing red eyes prowls the shadows, ready to fight or flee, since she only survives by making quick decisions and acting without hesitation. A living tree shambles from place to place after its original grove was burned, quiet and gentle until its inner rage is unleashed. Their land is a dangerous one, but also filled with tremendous rewards. Artifacts from the old times can be found by those determined enough to look, strong enough to seize them, and clever enough to discover their secrets. There is safety in numbers … if you decide anyone is worthy of trust. It is a world in which survival is no small victory, yet it is never enough.

Something has been forgotten. If it cannot be remembered, perhaps it can be rediscovered.

There is a word. Its meaning is known but within hides a secret. If understood, explored, controlled … the word could change everything:

WARDEN

METAMORPHOSIS ALPHA

Welcome aboard the starship *Warden*! This volume contains everything you need to experience the unique genre-blending adventure of METAMORPHOSIS ALPHA. You can select pre-made characters and jump right into the action or your group can create a collection of mutants and misfits from scratch and write scenarios wholly your own. The game is designed so the basics are quite easy to learn but have enough depth to keep experienced gamers engaged. Exploring the *Warden* offers the action and adventure of fantasy, the environment and technology of science fiction, and the bizarre powers of superhero comics.

Science Fiction

METAMORPHOSIS ALPHA is all about science fiction. Characters can discover suits of powered armor, blaster rifles, and artificial intelligence gone haywire. The action takes place aboard a generation ship carrying thousands of colonists in suspended animation, set to travel for countless years until the ship reaches its destination. Mutagenic energy has given humans, animals, and even plants altered appearances, strange powers, and horrible defects. Creatures run wild aboard the *Warden*, either roaming its decks or staking out territories and defending them without mercy. Computers, robots, and androids all follow programming which may aid or destroy the beings who encounter them. Discovering high-tech artifacts in the bowels of the ship is incredibly rewarding but also fraught with danger.

Exploration & Discovery

METAMORPHOSIS ALPHA is all about exploration. The *Warden* has levels seventeen miles long and up to nine miles wide; some areas are open and vast, while others are crammed with tight corridors and maintenance hatches. Most aboard the ship don't understand the true nature of their world, but for the curious and determined there are countless secrets to uncover and technology to master. Understanding mutant breeds can make the difference between life and death, as can understanding your own mutant powers. In the future the true secrets of the ship will be uncovered and the keys to its control might be mastered.

Action & Adventure

METAMORPHOSIS ALPHA is all about action and adventure. Danger can be found on every deck and around every corner. The small white rabbit in your path could be a tasty morsel; however, it might generate a life-leeching energy field and evade your attacks with mentally-projected illusions. It isn't easy to predict what might happen next or a given enemies' weaknesses. Your group might be running toward something—or just as likely—away from it. Seemingly ordinary situations suddenly present unexpected challenges. Combat is swift, chaotic, and deadly. Life aboard the *Warden* is never dull.

A History of METAMORPHOSIS ALPHA

METAMORPHOSIS ALPHA is the original science fiction roleplaying game, created when DUNGEONS & DRAGONS was still new and growing in popularity. The game was designed by James M. Ward in southeast Wisconsin and published by TSR, Inc. in 1976. The original gamebook was a slim 32 pages and packed with information. It enjoyed support from the fans and in early issues of *Dragon* magazine, eventually inspiring an entire world filled with mutants and technology. In the 1990s, TSR published *Metamorphosis Alpha to Omega*, marrying the concept to a new set of game rules.

In 2002, the Starship *Warden* was launched again with its original creator at the helm. Fast Forward Entertainment published a third edition in hardcover, which marked a return to a system closer to its original game rules. Those ideas were pushed forward in 2006 with the fourth edition published by Mudpuppy Games. Fourth edition pushed the story of the *Warden* forward when the vessel crashed into an asteroid possessed of a fungus-based intelligence, and alien life began to invade the ship.

WHAT YOU NEED

Besides the copy of the game you're reading right now, you only need a few things to get started. Roleplaying games are a hobby that need only some basic investment and offer years of fun! Be sure to have:

⊛ **A group of friends to play.** One takes the role of the referee—the person who will describe the action and encounters and is the final judge of the rules in a given situation. Everyone else is a player, taking the role of one character each. The ideal group size is three to six players and one referee.

⊛ **Six-sided dice.** The dice can show pips or actual numbers—it doesn't really matter. While a group could theoretically make due with a single die, it is really best if there is at least a big handful to share if everyone doesn't have their own.

⊛ **A play space.** A big table often works best, but anywhere that is comfortable, offers a place for dice to be rolled, and is reasonably free of distractions will do the job.

⊛ **Odds and ends.** Character sheets (which can be downloaded and printed from our website or photocopied from the back of this book) or at least blank sheets of paper are a must, as are writing utensils. Other game enhancers—such as caffeinated drinks, pizza, and chips—are completely optional.

What's In This Book?

While you may read this book cover-to-cover if you so choose, you can also jump to whatever chapter you need. This is a reference volume and set of tools for you to have fun with your friends. Here's what is waiting for you:

⊛ **Chapter One** introduces the starship *Warden* and provides the kind of information that characters will most likely know. It gives an idea of the tone and theme of a typical METAMORPHOSIS ALPHA game.

⊛ **Chapter Two** offers the basic rules, so you'll know what dice to roll and how to understand the results when your character performs actions.

⊛ **Chapter Three** teaches you the steps to create a character in the game—whether it is a human, mutated human, mutant animal, or mutant plant.

⊛ **Sample Characters** show you the kinds of characters you can generate and offers some pre-made if you want to start playing right away!

⊛ **Chapter Four** defines traits and qualities, so they can be referenced easily.

⊛ **Chapter Five** lists the many beneficial and debilitating mutations that can be found among the life on the *Warden* and offers detailed descriptions of how they all work in the game.

⊛ **Chapter Six** presents some of the gear characters might possess and tech they may acquire—everything from a dull knife to a laser pistol.

⊛ **Chapter Seven** is the meat of the game—the rules. While it's useful for players to be familiar with this material, it's important for the referee to be able to quickly reference this section during play.

⊛ **Chapter Eight** details the role of the referee and offers advice on how to run everything from one-shot adventures to full-length campaigns.

⊛ **Chapter Nine** contains some of the mutant and artificial life that might aid, or more likely endanger, a group as it explores the *Warden*.

⊛ **"The Petting Zoo of Death"** is an introductory adventure for METAMORPHOSIS ALPHA. It offers a great starting point to get a group of diverse characters together and shows how scenarios are presented in the game.

WARDEN ▷◁   ▷PULL HA

The shaman told Scar-lock that to prove his worth as future leader of the tribe, he must journey far—past the wolfoid packs, through the field of leechvines, and risk unknown dangers—to reach the Great Eye. Looking into the Eye is to risk madness as a price for wisdom. Scar-lock was young, brave, and foolhardy; of course, he agreed. He only needed to know where it was he could find this Great Eye. The shaman gestured with withered, webbed fingers and said in a harsh whisper, "At the wall at the end of the world."

The world of METAMORPHOSIS ALPHA is the starship *Warden*, or at least what's left of it. Constructed and launched as a vast colonization ship, the *Warden* left Earth in search of a new planet. With all environments and life of Earth held inside its hull, the *Warden* was ready to populate a new world full of hope and promise. However, something happened. Something bad. Perhaps no one truly knows the answer, or maybe the secret is hidden somewhere within the ship waiting to be found. Whatever disaster befell the *Warden* killed many of the humans, plants, and animals living on its many decks. Of those who survived, most were forever mutated, with each subsequent generation evolving stranger and stranger. While horrible defects continue to crop up, many mutations offer fantastic powers that help the mutants survive on a tiny world of decreasing resources and increasing danger.

The disaster left the computer systems malfunctioning and the *Warden* adrift. Artificial intelligence still maintains the primary life support and auxiliary systems aboard the ship, but it is unable to properly identify mutant life—making encounters with robots and androids unpredictable at best and a brush with metallic, laser-wielding death at worst.

Somewhere within the bowels of the ship, military personnel and supplemental crew are held in cryogenic stasis, intended to be awakened in the event of emergency. If those systems were damaged or mishandled by the computers, the humans inside could be dead or suffer serious problems when roused from their long slumber.

This is the world of the starship *Warden*. Within its walls are all the hopes, dreams, and wonder of mankind and life on Earth. However, danger, madness, and death are dealt with equal measure.

Introducing the Warden
by James M. Ward

Far from being just a science fiction experience, a METAMORPHOSIS ALPHA campaign is a combination of the future and the past. Primitive tribes with bone spears and mutated turtle shell shields live alongside advanced robots with integrated blaster rifles and laser welding torches.

Players must solve puzzles as they explore a gigantic environment. Each of the ship levels has unique dangers and encounters. As a colonization ship, there were many ecological levels vastly transformed by the terrible accident that stopped the starship in its path to an Earth-like planet many light years from home. Learning that the characters aren't on a normal world is the first of many surprises. After years of exploration they might learn a bitter truth: Something happened to the *Warden*, and they have no idea or control over where they are going until the ship is repaired.

Players usually start as primitive tribesmen, exploring the ship and learning how to use the fantastic technology they find all around them. Experienced groups can start out as military personnel coming alive from a cryosleep, as they were put to sleep only be used in case of deadly emergency. Other player groups may begin as robots or androids with their own unique agendas, options opening up in future supplements for this core game.

On reading this for the first time, a player might not realize that discovery and exploration are key features to playing METAMORPHOSIS ALPHA. The game may begin in the strict confines of the walls and floors of a spaceship, but there is a huge campaign's worth of enjoyment to be had by players and referees alike in playing this game.

LIFE ON THE WARDEN

Warden, the first colonization starship, left the Trans-Plutonian Space Yards with tremendous fanfare. The biggest structure ever built in space, the enormous vessel was hailed throughout the solar system as an achievement equal to the pyramids on Earth.

At the beginning of its voyage, the starship *Warden* perfectly reproduced life on Earth. Many of the ship's levels duplicated environments found on the home planet. There were areas for forests, plains, swamps, mountains, deserts, and an ocean, as well as a large city area, a huge section dedicated to the vessel's massive engines, and other levels for engineering. The *Warden* originally had supplemental ships attached to be used as needed—a battleship, three destroyers, a battle cruiser, and five frigates. If those vessels are still functioning after all this time, much information and equipment might be recovered from them or even a means of escape.

Many colonists, military personnel, and crew were placed in cryosleep. Robots and androids helped with the daily operation and maintenance of the ship. A series of artificial intelligence modules linked to the central computer system, independently running the operation of each deck of the ship.

There were large numbers of Earth animals placed on board the *Warden*, and each was treated to be extremely fertile. When the cataclysm struck, the atmosphere of the ship was radically changed. The fertility of all creatures on the ship was increased an even greater amount, and massive mutational forces changed the animals forever. Some wolves became eight foot tall, intelligent humanoid creatures retaining a savage nature. Simple robins became large savage killers, striking from the ceiling and swooping down to attack with surprise. Many plants became mobile and predatory, some fully sentient and highly dangerous. Small venus fly-traps grew to massive killers, able to scoop up human-sized victims and dissolve them in caustic acid-pods, turning the bodies to mush in short order. Dandelion weeds grew to tremendous heights, and each leaf became a razor sharp cutting machine suitable for spilling blood.

When the reactors malfunctioned, high intensity radiation leaked on to different areas of the ship. Automatic safety protocols turned off the systems, but

the damage was done; pools of steaming, hot liquid burned through the decks and splashed into many levels of the ship.

Survival is the first order of business on the *Warden*, as the ship is filled with vicious and powerful potential enemies. Some are feral and attack only by instinct, while others might prove valuable as allies, if you can break through barriers of paranoia and xenophobia.

Tribes of mutants and even rare, pure humans have carved out small territories on the different levels of the ship. There is little communication and trade, as hostilities and the needs of day-to-day survival have long ruled. However, some have realized the value of discovery. The secrets, technology, and other forms of life out there are prizes waiting to be claimed by the daring, strong, and clever. A rare few have realized that knowledge is power. The unknown represents terrifying potential danger, as isolated tribes and bands of explorers never know if powerful enemies might be around the next corner until they dare to step around it.

Safety

In brief, the *Warden* is <u>not</u> a safe place, but it was designed to be. Much like the *Titanic* of long-ago Earth, the colony ship was purported to be impervious to the dangers and energies of interstellar space. And like the mighty ocean-going vessel, pride in mankind's achievements is always trumped by the forces of nature. Like the *Titanic*, the *Warden* was doomed to suffer tragedy that no planning committee or engineer could have foreseen.

While a cataclysm did kill most life aboard the ship and forever mutate the rest, the *Warden* did fulfill its purpose to keep the cargo inside its massive duralloy walls alive and maintain its own crucial systems to sustain that life.

Though filled with danger, there are pockets of respite and safety on the ship. Some compartments designed for storage have remained sealed, and clever explorers might discover the secrets to unlocking them. Friendly tribes could be bartered with for shelter and sustenance, though explorers must guard against deception. Powerful tech can be uncovered and deciphered, giving adventurers access to sturdy protection, portable shelter, and devastating weapons that would deter all but mindless foes.

Artificial life maintains the ship and guards protected sections. These systems recognize humans and respond to them according to their primary programming, though mutant life is not in the computer's data banks. Robots and computer systems might react in unpredictable ways.

Some sections of the ship were flooded with radiation, gaining reputations as zones of death. Sometimes these areas clear on their own or because of long overdue robotic repair, leaving areas feared by most to be quite safe—assuming a party is daring enough to confirm these facts for themselves.

Risk & Reward

A character may well begin as a tribesman from a dirt-hut village, ignorant of the dangers and treasures awaiting discovery. As he explores his own level, he will encounter wonders he cannot possibly understand. He may fight monsters and mutants firing weapons

Tech
by James M. Ward

If the characters are pure strain humans, robots and androids are often respectful and very willing to help, so there is little risk. If the characters are mutants of any type, the robots and androids can be deadly and instantly attack, so there is great risk. Either way, new weapons must be found or taken from others who clearly don't need them enough.

One of the great fun elements of the game is learning how to use ultra powerful weapons and equipment. Clearly a primitive tribesman doesn't know how to use a self-contained toaster, and they may end up believing this toaster is a deadly heat ray device. The same situation can happen as a character picks up a powerful fusion blaster rifle. Taking a risk on learning how to use this weapon can have the adventurer shoot himself in the chest or have him figure out a way to send a beam of energy through a twelve inch wall of steel.

Even when the tribesman has learned how to use the most dramatic of power armor with massive energy weapons, it may not be enough. In METAMORPHOSIS ALPHA, you could be destroying whole jungles full of creatures and be instantly laid low by a seven foot tall rabbit that turns all of your armor and fine equipment to soft gray rubber.

that can only be magic and deal with powers he is ill-equipped to face. His flint-tipped spear may not keep him alive past the next hill.

Through discovery, trade, combat, and sheer luck, a character might acquire fantastic tech weapons and the know-how to use them properly. As she advances in skill and equips herself for exploration and battle,

she might become just as feared as that first pack of wolfoids. But one should never get cocky, for the next mutant could have powers that reduce her mighty arms to rubber and leave her mind a quivering mass of jelly. Sometimes the smartest thing to do in a fight is to turn and run hard and fast in the opposite direction.

Adventuring

For those with the ambition and fortitude required to journey beyond the safety of their own village, tribe, pack, or grove, the dangers ahead are almost always beyond the scope of any individual. Friends, or at least allies, are needed to watch your back, guard your sleep, and fight at your side. Trust is established, earned, and easily broken.

Exploration will reveal new habitats, frightening enemies, puzzling mysteries, dark secrets, and incredible treasures. You only have to decide which direction you wish to go and temper inquisitiveness with caution. A simple field of mushrooms might pose horrible risk, while a giant tusked sloth may be a tough but ultimately gentle creature—though it would be dangerous indeed to assume this fact from the start.

Artificial life is not well understood by most, and it is also unpredictable and often frought with danger. A robot may ignore or assist a human while attempting to cage or kill a mutant animal. Approach with caution.

New tech may present powerful possibilities, but unlocking its secrets may involve a fair bit of danger or leave you completely clueless as how to turn the damn thing on. Some folk aboard the ship have learned much tech lore and are valuable in dealing with the many artifacts found on the *Warden*'s levels.

Where To Next

It's recommended that you learn the basic nuts and bolts of the SYSTEM 26 rules to help you understand what's found in the rest of the book, so proceed to **Chapter Two: Basic Gameplay**. If you'd like to understand more about the setting and the role of the referee, check out **Chapter Eight: Storyteller & Referee**.

You want to fire a laser pistol at the charging wolfoid and use your mutant levitation ability to escape before the rest of the pack tears you to bloody shreds. Action is often fast and furious aboard the *Warden*, and the SYSTEM 26 game rules are designed to reflect that. The basics of the game are easy to learn, and it doesn't take long to resolve actions quickly and get on with the adventure.

Whether the actions are taken during the heat of combat, the tension of negotiations, or the frustration of puzzling out tech artifacts, the basic rules of the game are the same. You'll be grabbing some dice and using the rolls to determine success or failure. In a moment you'll know whether you blasted your enemy's face off, won over a potential ally, or accidentally detonated an explosive. Uncertainty is part of the fun, and failure can often be as interesting—and potentially hilarious—as success.

Only one person at the table is required to have a detailed knowledge of the rules, the Referee. While being a game guru is never a bad thing at the table (unless you try to be an obnoxious know-it-all), if you learn the material in this chapter you'll be prepared to adventure aboard the *Warden*.

The main elements to learn are how to interpret the information on your character sheet, how many dice to roll for an action, and how to read success or failure so the referee can tell you what happens next. Once you learn the basic game rules, you can either jump right into playing with your friends or read other sections of the book. If you want to create your own character, that information is in the next chapter.

PLAYERS

There are central characters at the heart of any good movie, television show, or book—the people that the audience is following and rooting to succeed (or at least survive) against all odds. In our game, these are the **player characters** and, like the name suggests, these are the characters controlled by the players. Their decisions, successes, and failures are what drive the story and keep the group entertained. If they screw up, the characters are the ones who will have to live with the consequences.

In the METAMORPHOSIS ALPHA RPG, the player characters are humans, mutated humans, mutant animals, or mutant plants with a variety of skills, special powers, and acquired tech artifacts. They survive the dangers of the starship *Warden* while exploring its mysteries and uncovering its secrets. They win by surviving and succeeding in their goals as a group, as well as individual agendas, and lose when they are defeated or even die facing the many hazards aboard the ship.

REFEREE

While each player usually has only one character, the **referee** plays literally everyone and everything else—including the environment the player characters are exploring and every living and nonliving thing they run into along the way. He has to know the rules well enough to both explain and arbitrate them for the players, be able to adjust the ongoing story to react to new decisions and situations, and bear the responsibility for keeping the game fun for everyone.

The referee may feel like an adversary to the players, since he spends a lot of time throwing enemies and danger their way, but it's ultimately a referee's job to keep things fun and fair—or at least as fair as things get aboard the *Warden*.

Anything a player character sees, hears, or even perceives through mutant powers comes from the descriptions of the referee. Whether he's got a detailed adventure plan or is making things up as he goes along, the referee must think on his feet and keep the action moving. The referee interprets the game rules for the entire table and is the ultimate authority on how things resolve.

DICE

The SYSTEM 26 rules that power the METAMORPHOSIS ALPHA RPG use six-sided dice, the kind you can pull out any family board game or purchase from a hobby game store. It doesn't matter if the dice have pips or actual numbers, so players should use whichever they prefer. While a desperate group could share one die and roll it repeatedly, that would be time-consuming and slow down the pace of the game. Also, players tend to get picky and even a bit superstitious when it comes to their dice. There are smartphone apps to simulate dice, and chits of paper in a jar can substitute in a pinch.

The shorthand for rolling dice in this game puts the letter **d** behind the number of dice rolled. Therefore …

2d

…indicates rolling two dice. The dice you roll to generate results in the game are called a dice pool, even if you only use one die for a particular action.

Basic Roll

2d is incidentally the default roll that a player uses for character actions during the course of the game. If a character is neither good nor bad at something, the roll is assumed to be 2d. It allows the information on the character sheet to focus on strengths and weaknesses instead of spelling out every possibility and allows everyone to focus only on the most interesting details about any given character.

If any circumstances reduce the number of dice rolled to less than one, the action is an automatic failure or cannot be attempted, as determined by the referee. And for standard actions attempted by a character, the number of dice cannot be greater than five—though it can go as high as six dice if advanced tech or mutations are involved.

While dice are usually rolled in multiples, the results are not added together to create a total. Instead, each die is compared to the level of difficulty (defined as Easy, Average, or Hard), and achievements are counted to determine success. All of this is explained in greater detail below.

RULES, ACTION, AND RESULTS

This is a game of fast-moving action, combining elements from science fiction, sword-and-sorcery tales, and superhero comics. In order to keep that kind of excitement and pacing, the rules provide enough structure to resolve actions but enough freedom to keep games from becoming bogged down in endless details and constant page-flipping.

Most Important Rule: Keep things moving. If the rules don't seem to cover it, make it up. The firm-yet-loose structure of our game is designed to handle just about anything and make it easy for the referee to improvise. However, no game mechanics can cover every conceivable situation, nor are they meant to do so. If a situation comes up and you can't find it in the rules, the referee is encouraged to improvise and move on. The referee is the final word on rules in the game.

CHARACTER SHEET

We talked about characters a bit by discussing players and the referee above, but now we'll show how characters are defined in the game. The character sheet holds all of the game information and other notes about your character handy for reference during a play session. It can be the official sheet in this book or just a piece of paper with some handwritten notes.

Characters are defined by how they are special. A character is probably "normal" when attempting most types of actions, so rather than list everything, your character sheet only shows where she differs from the norm.

Stock

Usually, a character's **stock** can be determined at a glance. A pure human is easy to distinguish from a mutated human, which is even easier to tell apart from a mutant aardvark or pine tree. The stocks available to player characters are the following:

- **Human**
- **Mutated Human**
- **Mutant Animal**
- **Mutant Plant**

Traits

Now we learn what kinds of actions your character is good at and the tasks that should probably be saved as last resorts. **Traits** combine natural ability, aptitude, and training to highlight the actions in which a character varies from the norm. The actions defined by traits can be physical, mental, or social—almost anything a character can attempt.

Traits are listed as a modifier to the basic roll (2d), so traits listed as good (+2d) mean that 4d are rolled for that particular action. Traits in a character's weak (–1d) areas leave him with only one die to roll for an action; any that are hopeless (–2d) are automatic failures under most circumstances, since there is no chance of success with no dice to roll.

If it seems like too many traits to keep track of, keep in mind that most traits are assumed to be the average of 2d, so the only ones that need listing are the traits that are either better or worse.

Example: Scar-lock, a human, has amazing Discipline (+3d), good Leadership (+2d), competent Brawn (+1d), and weak Alertness and Dexterity (–1d).

Mutations

The starship *Warden* is an environment in which the vast majority of people, animals, and even plants are mutants. While some breeds of mutated life have established themselves over generations, there is no telling what strange powers or defects any given character might possess. **Mutations** generally break the standard rules, giving characters actions they could not normally attempt or situational bonuses. If the mutation is a **defect**, it's just the opposite and makes life a bit more interesting for the character—and by interesting, we mean difficult.

Mutations do not have a standard format, since they cover a wide range of possibility. Each mutation lists how it works in the game.

Example: Lock-scar, a mutated human, has Poison Bite (2d) and Regeneration (4d), which grant him advantages in battle. Unfortunately, he has defects in the form of Diminished Sense: Sight (1d) and Energy Sensitivity: Cold (2d).

Traits

Alertness, Artistry, Athletics, Brawn, Constitution, Crafting, Deception, Dexterity, Discipline, Influence, Leadership, Medicine, Melee Weapons, Performance, Ranged Weapons, Stealth, Survival, Tech, and Unarmed Combat.

Qualities

Your character could have a talent or liability in a particular area, a bad temper, or some other defining characteristic. Features such as these make each character unique. We call them **qualities**, and they generally offer action modifiers based on the situation.

A good quality that helps a character in certain situations is known as a **talent**, while one that's more of a disadvantage is called a **liability**.

Example: Scar-lock is particularly handy in dealing damage with his sword, so he has a +2d talent in Weapon Attack. Unfortunately he suffers from bad vision, and lists the –1d liability of Near-Sighted.

ACTIONS

Whether you're swinging an axe at a mutated razorback, trying to decipher the workings of a strange artifact, or using a mutant power to heal your own wounds, it's called an **action**. Most of the game is your character trying to accomplish things or, at the very least, survive them. The game would be tedious and boring if you had to roll for each and every mundane task over the course of your character's day. Most actions are automatically successful, so you don't have to roll to walk across the room. However, the moment there is both a chance of failure and consequences either way, the dice come into play. For example, walking across a minefield would be worthy of some dice-rolling.

Action Points

Characters possess action points to help them succeed, fail less spectacularly, and reduce damage to keep them alive. Every player character begins an adventure with 2 points and spends them as chosen during play. They can be earned during an adventure by succeeding at impressive actions, coming up with crazy plans, great roleplaying, and other rewards as determined by the referee.

Traits & Dice Pool

When you declare an action, the referee determines if your character has any traits that apply to the situation. If so, you add or subtract the appropriate number of dice from the basic roll (2d). The referee might determine the situation warrants a bonus or penalty, further modifying the number of dice you have for the action. Once you have your fistful of dice, roll 'em!

Example: Spike has been cornered by a jackaloid, so she decides to take a swing at it with her heavy wrench. Spike is Good (+2d), but the wrench is not intended for combat; the referee penalizes her for the improvised weapon (–1d). Since everything modifies the basic roll, it comes out as 2d (the default roll) + 2d (for being good with melee weapons) – 1d (for the wrench as an improvised weapon). Spike's player rolls 3 dice for the action.

Difficulty & Achievements

Sad but true: Nothing is equal, let alone fair. Depending on the nature of the action and the surrounding circumstances, it could be a cake walk or nigh impossible. Slipping out of a loosely-tied rope is one thing, while escaping from a pair of plasteel handcuffs is another. The game has three levels of difficulty: **Easy**, **Average**, and **Hard**.

The difficulty is what sets the range of numbers needed on each die to score an achievement. The more achievements rolled for an action, the more successful.

Easy: 3+

Average: 4+

Hard: 5+

If the action is easy, any die roll above a 2 (i.e. 3 or higher) scores achievements. If it's average, a 4, 5 or 6 earns them. A hard action only scores achievements when a 5 or 6 is rolled.

Example: Randall, a mutant wolverine, is attempting to rip open a secured door. Good thing he has amazing Brawn, granting him 5 dice for the attempt. The referee determines this to be a hard action, so at least one of those dice must roll a 5 or 6 for Randall to get the door even partially open. The dice comes up 2, 4, 4, 5, 6 — two earning achievements for the action.

Success & Failure

It only takes one achievement for an action to be at least somewhat successful, but the more achievements rolled, the higher the level of success. A pile of achievements from a roll means the action went very well! As a general rule, here is how the number of achievements measures an action's success:

1 Achievement: Minimum Success
The action is successful but just barely, and the results may be only temporary.

2 Achievements: Modest Success
It's nothing to write home about, but it gets the job done.

3 Achievements: Good Success
The action is handled successfully, even impressively.

Enhancements

Sometimes you do better than good—you succeed and then some. You don't just kick the ursoid, you strike with bone-crunching force that throws him back five feet and knocks over his denmate as well. These benefits of extraordinary success are called **enhancements**, and they occur when your action scores more than 3 achievements. Each achievement above 3 is an enhancement. They are counted separately and allow you to add additional effects to your planned action, effects that range from on-going conditions to bonuses on follow-up actions.

The referee determines the precise results of any enhancements rolled, but as a player you may give suggestions as fits the action. Here are some game guidelines:

1 Enhancement

☉ Your opponent is penalized (–1d) on its next action.

☉ You receive a bonus (+1d) on your next roll for a similar action.

2 Enhancements

☉ Your opponent loses its next action, is disarmed, or is moved against its will.

☉ You gain a temporary bonus (+1d) while continuing with a type of action.

3 Enhancements:

☉ Your opponent gains a debilitating condition (dazed, blinded), or your attack also affects its allies or impacts the environment in your favor.

☉ You make a discovery or change the situation significantly in your favor.

Sound vague? This is where the referee shines by interpreting the situation. It should never come out so dull as a mere game bonus or clinical status update. Enhancements are satisfying and fun, if they are delivered descriptively. In a fight, you might have delivered a wicked cut above an enemy's eyes, temporarily blinding him. When trying to decipher a keypad code for a door lock, you might stumble upon a passkey that works for the entire area. When negotiating with a potentially hostile mutant, you might say just the right thing to gain her trust and a potential new ally.

Some enhancements are specific to the environment, and pre-written adventures might have notes for possible enhancements based on the situation.

Botching

Sometimes you kick ass and take names, other times you just embarrass yourself. Sometimes the dice roll high, other times you get snake eyes. When this happens in the game, it's called a **botch**. A botch happens whenever all the dice you roll for an action come up as 1. You not only fail, but do so in spectacular fashion. Your blade slips from your fingers; you fall on your backside; you break the tech artifact you're trying figure out. The referee will describe your exact misfortune, though you can use an action point to turn your botch into plain old, mediocre failure. Note that

botching is far more likely when you are rolling only one or two dice, which make legendary goofs more of a habit when you attempt actions at which your character isn't very talented.

Complex Actions

Most of the time you're trying to do something relatively simple: hit a foe over the head, kick down a door, or fry a control panel with energy emanating from your mutant eyes. However, sometimes the action is more complicated, like performing battlefield surgery on a badly-wounded friend, solving a complicated puzzle, or figuring out whether a tech artifact was meant to project your thoughts into moving pictures or toast bread on both sides. Sometimes, the action may involve different steps, allowing for different traits to come in to play.

For a **complex action**, it's often an issue of how long something takes rather than if you will succeed or fail. You will eventually close your friend's wounds, but if she's bled to death that won't be very helpful. You make a series of rolls over a period of time to figure out just how long it takes for you to succeed. Take too long and the point may be moot, or you could screw up so badly that you're forced to give up.

The **threshold** is the number of achievements necessary to complete the complex action. Once the threshold has been reached, the action succeeds—assuming you made it in time.

An **increment** is determined by the referee and represents how much time elapses with each roll. The increment could be a combat turn (3 seconds), a minute, an hour, or even longer for something truly complicated. Difficulty and the dice pool are determined the same way as with simple actions, but now achievements are tracked and accumulate with each increment.

If you botch during a complex action, your entire attempt is a failure. The referee will let you know the consequences and if starting over is even an option. Just like normal botching, an action point can transform the roll into ordinary, boring failure for that increment.

STAYING ALIVE

The starship *Warden* is a dangerous place. Fire, radiation, flooded areas, and malfunctioning robots are as dangerous as mutants battling over territory or just plain spite. The rules offer two ways to track damage, so you know when your character is down for the count or pushing up daisies.

Fatigue is a combination of bumps and bruises, exhaustion and stress, as well as luck being pushed to its limit. When a character suffers fatigue damage equal or greater than her limit, she falls unconscious. Fatigue recovers relatively quickly. Once per day a character may use an action to get her second wind and recover 1d fatigue immediately.

Wounds represent cuts, trauma, internal bleeding, and other serious injuries. If a character suffers wound damage equal or more than his limit, he is dying—unconscious and must make rolls just to cling to life in hopes of receiving aid. Wounds recover slowly on their own, but the process can be accelerated through medical care, mutations, and specialized tech.

NUTS & BOLTS

The basic gameplay here is just enough to get you started as a player with pre-made characters. The referee is the only one at the gaming table expected to have a thorough understanding of the rules, so don't sweat it if you only have the basic dice-rolling concepts down. The important thing is to have fun and be ready to figure out just how your character will survive the group's latest scrape.

Where to Next?

If you want to get started with creating a character, keep reading through **Chapter Three: Mutants & Mankind**. If you want a more thorough explanation of the rules and mechanics, flip ahead to **Chapter Seven: Rules**.

The *Warden* is an enormous and thrilling place for adventure—filled with mysteries to be solved, mutants to be befriended or beheaded, challenges to overcome, and powerful artifacts to be recovered. Your character is a window into the environment and the vehicle through which you enter the story. Whether you play an ordinary human scrabbling to survive using only brain and blade or a shambling giant cactus who can shoot beams of deadly radiation, all player characters in METAMORPHOSIS ALPHA can be created using one of three methods and are defined in the same ways.

Most of the time a player will hold the reins of only one character, making decisions and rolling the dice to see if outcomes will end with the triumph of victory or the squishy agony of defeat. While characters can be played purely for the strategy and action offered in the game, they can also be infused with as much personality, backstory, and drama the player cares to muster.

If you're just getting started and want to grab a ready-made character to play, or want to see some examples of characters completely finished, just flip to the end of Chapter Six to see a batch of completed sample characters.

Character Building

There are five primary steps involved in creating (and defining) a character:

- ◉ **Stock** - Basic Type: Human, Mutated Human, Mutant Animal, Mutant Plant
- ◉ **Traits** - How good (or bad) a character is at different types of actions.
- ◉ **Qualities** - Situational talents, quirks, and flaws.
- ◉ **Mutations** - Special powers or unfortunate defects.
- ◉ **Gear** - Weapons, equipment, and whatever odds and ends a character drags around.

Once each of these elements are defined, a character can be transferred from whatever scratch paper on which he started to a character sheet, finishing notations and and filling out derived information. The character is now ready to play!

Remember: Your referee has final approval on your character creation methods and choices.

Note that the following methods are used to create a relatively inexperienced character who's just getting started. We call this type of character "green." The referee might offers methods to create a more advanced and powerful character.

Stock

The *Warden* is home to a staggering variety of life, from unaltered humans to shambling shrubberies. The first step in the character creation process is to determine a character's stock: human, mutated human, mutant animal, or mutant plant. Either choose or roll randomly, then proceed to the appropriate section to learn more about just what your character's stock means for her lot in life.

3.1 - Stock

d6	Type
1	Human
2-3	Mutated Human
4-5	Mutant Animal
6	Plant

Humans

Hardy and adaptable, humans can survive the most hostile environments and rise to every challenge.

Some humans managed to survive aboard the *Warden* without succumbing to mutation. They have reverted to an almost barbaric state, and the knowledge they may have once possessed about technology has faded to folklore and superstition—though it's enough of that they possess more of a knack for tech than other types of life.

Human Basics

15 feet standard movement
No Mutations
Qualities: Struggling to survive alongside mutant life, humans have developed an edge in other areas. All humans are gifted (+1d) in Radiation Resistance and Tech Lore and possess +2d talents chosen by the player. See Qualities later in this chapter and in more detail in Chapter 4.

Physical Characteristics

Pure humans lack the physical diversity of their mutated brethren, but they reflect the many races of the forgotten ancient world. However, there has been so much interbreeding that most humans are a mix of the ethnicities of old. The constant struggle to survive leaves most humans in excellent physical condition, if sometimes a bit undernourished. Most humans wear a mix of scavenged or hand-me-down clothes of ancient days along with more primitive homespun additions.

Playing a Human

Humans carry with them a cultural memory of disaster and fighting against those who are different. Many grew up with tales about how they were once the masters of their world, and the mutated humans, animals, and plants rose against them. This leads to many humans acting both arrogant and suspicious of other character types, some showing undisguised disgust at mutated humans with obvious physical deformities.

Most humans grow up with stories and lore about technology that make them more adept and comfortable with it than others, and shipboard systems and robots treat humans with a preference and deference that no other types enjoy.

Mutated Humans

Marked as different from birth, mutated humans use their unusual powers to surprise their enemies.

Most humans died during whatever crisis changed life aboard the *Warden*, but some survived and were forever changed—passing on the capacity to mutate to their children. Each is completely unique, both in appearance and potentially dangerous powers. Sometimes a mutated human crops up among the pure humans, but it is rare for such an individual to survive.

Mutated Human Basics

15 feet standard movement
Physical and Mental Mutations

Physical Characteristics

Mutated humans resemble their pure counterparts, except each carries the mark of mutation. Some are grotesque with asymmetrical features or exaggerated characteristics (over-large eyes or extra digits on the hands and feet). They are often more primitive than human characters, with a greater amount of mismatched and scavenged clothing and gear.

Playing a Mutated Human

There has been so much death and chaos among the mutated humans that there is not much sense of history or culture. They are much more a people who live in the present, struggling to survive and understand the world and their place in it. There is perhaps greater room for variety in terms of appearance and personality among mutated humans than any other character type.

Mutant Animals

Whether shy or ferocious, big or small, mutant animals carry over the powerful survival instincts of their ancestors.

The crisis left many animals dead, and others forever changed. Most grew in intelligence and understanding of their environment. Many grew in size and developed ways to handle and manipulate objects as needed. But within those standard changes, mutant animals reflect the incredible variety of animal life derived from the ancient world. Reptiles, birds, mammals, and arthropods are mutant animals.

All mutant animal characters are able to move about and handle objects with the same ability as human characters. Like all life on the *Warden*, they can understand speech, but they cannot speak unless they possess the Quality to do so.

Mutant animal characters are created by either choosing an example Breed (which overrides the Basics, below) or by coming up with a basic animal type and reflecting it with a mix of mutations and qualities. When creating a new mutant animal, the choices must be approved by the referee.

Mutant Animal Basics

15 feet standard movement (+1d Qualities by reducing to 10 feet, –1d Qualities by increasing to 20 feet)
Physical and Mental Mutations

Creating a Breed

With the referee's approval, new breeds can be created using the examples below as templates. Each breed will have a standard base movement and assumed mutations and qualities for all starting characters.

Sample Breeds

The following are just a few examples of specific breeds that can be created to generate a consistent type of mutant animal. No one is required to create a character the falls into the rules of a given breed, but it can be a good starting point. Other breeds are presented later in the book primarily as opponents (the Wolfoid being a prime example), but a breed could easily be created from those descriptions as well.

Felinoid

Evolved from great cats, felinoids combine deadly speed and fury with inborn grace.

Deadly hunters capable of surprising speed and agility despite their size, felinoids stalk their prey with slow patience before delivering a lightning-quick strike. They roam either alone or in prides, preferring to conserve their energy until the chase or battle begins.

Felinoid characters tend to have high Athletics, Dexterity, and Stealth traits. They are often deficient in Deception, Discipline, and Influence.

Felinoid Basics

20 feet standard movement
Breed Mutations: New Body Parts (claws, teeth).
Breed Qualities: Agile Combatant, Restless

Physical Characteristics

Felinoids resemble great hunter-cats, but they can vary greatly in size and appearance—averaging 6½ feet in height and weighing around 180 pounds. Their hands and feet bear the sharp claws of their cat ancestors, and their eyes immediately identify them as felinoid. Felinoid bodies are covered in short fur that ranges from simple colors to elaborate patterns.

Most felinoids walk and run on all fours, though they can comfortably walk upright whenever necessary. Their movements seem slow—even lazy—until the need for haste arises, and they burst into amazing speed.

Playing a Felinoid

Felinoids usually share similar personality traits with other cats. They sometimes seem lazy (sleeping whenever the opportunity for a nap presents itself), but it is their nature to wait until action is required. They enjoy the hunt, stealth, stalking their prey, and pouncing at the moment of maximum advantage.

Survival and comfort are usually top concerns of felinoids. They look for cozy, safe places to sleep, take their meals whenever they can, flee without shame when faced with danger, but fight without fear when cornered. Humor is rare for felinoids but comes across as perverse to others when it arises.

In addition to practical and predatory instincts, felinoids are often intensely curious. Mysteries, whether they are strange sounds in the distance or the origins of a mysterious relic, beg to be investigated. This generally applies to the outside world only though, as the personal lives and relationships of companions are so much trivial minutiae as far as most felinoids are concerned. Their own relationships are generally more pragmatic, and genuine emotional attachments happen only a handful of times in the course of their lives—but once those relationships are established, the felinoid is fiercely loyal until death or serious betrayal.

Felinoids are happy to accept companions of any race in typical pragmatic fashion, but appreciate those who provide amusement or distraction while showing patience for their true friends.

Musteloids

Evolved from the likes of badgers, weasels, and wolverines, they combine cunning and tenacity to survive in a hostile world.

Clever survivors who can thrive even in extreme conditions, musteloids are often underestimated but are extremely adaptable. They roam from one place to the next, managing to succeed when others fail. In battle, they rely on maneuverability or sheer toughness to see them through. While the breed example here focuses on weasels and badgers, this group also includes otters, raccoons, and skunks, which is easily reflected through appropriate description and mutations.

Musteloid characters tend to have high Brawn, Constitution, and Survival traits. They are often deficient in Alertness, Deception, and Influence.

Musteloids Basics

15 feet standard movement, **1 foot burrow** (granted by quality)

Breed Mutations: New Body Parts (teeth)
Breed Qualities: Burrower, Specialties (Fortitude +2d, Emotional Control –2d)

Physical Characteristics

While musteloids can differ widely in appearance, they share some general qualities. Their bodies are covered with thick fur that offers protection from the elements and allows them to swim comfortably even in ice-cold water. The color of the fur and fur patterns range across a broad spectrum. They have short limbs that are surprisingly strong and nimble. Their round ears can rotate to catch far-away sounds.

Musteloids generally walk upright, though they are capable of bounding on all fours to go over treacherous terrain. The claws on their hands and feet are small, but they have strong teeth and jaws that are as effective crushing bone as they are crunching open shellfish. They hiss or growl when threatened, and when in a defensive posture their fur bristles sharply—signaling they are either fearful or ready to attack.

Badger musteloids have more compact, sturdy features and bodies that are far more broad than their heads. Weasel-based musteloids have longer, almost serpentine bodies and long necks.

Playing a Musteloid

Musteloids often have their next meal on the mind; weasels are especially fond of eggs, while badgers have a sweet tooth for honey and sugar. While they are physically capable hunters, both use their wits to gain an edge as predators or to gain access to hidden sources of food. Musteloids accept allies who help them achieve their goals, though adult badgers show little tolerance for their own kind when not actively seeking a mate.

Badgers are stout-hearted combatants who often show foolhardy levels of bravery—ready to charge in and take on a dangerous foe. But even while brave and vicious, a badger keeps his wits about him even while his powerful jaws are locked on the base of a victim's skull.

More nimble than other types of musteloids, the weasel usually favors maneuverability and strategically placed strikes to weaken and wear down the enemy before going in for the kill. Even while darting about the battlefield, the weasel is always mindful of the terrain and uses it to best advantage.

All musteloids demonstrate great adaptability and will wander to find promising areas with a defendable den and a reliable food source. The badger is almost always alone if not with his mate or young, while weasels often band together in packs called *boogles*.

Raptoroid
Evolved from predatory birds, they descend on their enemies with calculated precision.

Graceful creatures at home on the ground or in the air, raptoroids use their freedom of movement to avoid danger or attack with maximum advantage. They keep their wits about them during combat, making calculated strikes and avoiding confinement.

Raptoroid characters tend to have high Alertness, Dexterity, Discipline, and Performance traits. They are often deficient in Brawn, Leadership, and Stealth.

Raptoroid Basics
10 feet standard movement, **30 feet flight** (granted by mutation)
Breed Mutations: New Body Parts (wings, claws).
Breed Qualities: Far-Sighted, Speech

Physical Characteristics
To other races, raptoroids appear to be large, slightly humanoid birds. Their heads, wings, and clawed feet strongly favor the avians from which they evolved—with wings that usually end with clawed hands to allow manipulation of objects. Individual appearance may vary widely, with some specimens strongly resembling specific birds (eagles, hawks, owls) while others don't much look like anything found in nature.

Playing a Raptoroid
Predatory birds like to stay on the move. They don't enjoy staying in one location very long, and if circumstances force this, they become agitated and irritable. Raptors do not appreciate being stuck in vulnerable places and prefer perches where they can observe the surrounding terrain and approaching enemies. They will gladly dine on a fresh kill but are usually happy to devour any available food without discrimination—including things that would make other creatures ill.

To other races, a raptoroid may seem aloof, cold, or distant. They communicate verbally, but it's a forced process and difficult for any bird. As such, they do not typically engage in idle chatter. Raptoroids generally only speak when they have a specific purpose, and they choose their words carefully. Internally, though, raptoroids feel intense emotions and have vivid imaginations. When they display their feelings, whether love, anger, or joy, it's often surprisingly powerful to the few who are allowed to witness.

Raptoroids are usually distrustful of others—whether from another race or their own kind—but are relatively equal in that attitude toward everyone. Those who travel or live with others require occasional solitude, even a simple stolen hour within sight and hearing of their group.

Plants
Mobile and intelligent vegetable life, their motivations are wholly alien to creatures of the animal world.

Vegetable life that has developed intelligence and mobility, sentient plants perceive the world in ways animal life cannot possibly understand. They do not possess the same need for food and shelter as other creatures, and so their motives are often misunderstood by friends and enemies alike.

Plant characters have the same five senses as other character types, even if there is no obvious source for the sensory information, and they can manipulate objects as easily as a human character. They may communicate with other nearby plants without difficulty and can understand speech, but they require the Plantspeak mutation or must use a form of sign language to properly communicate with non-plants. The appearance of a plant character is up to the player and the referee, with lots of room for variety—trees, bushes, vines, and the like are all possibilities. Plants are inherently adept in the natural world but bad with technology. The are often distrusted by humans and animals and usually ignored entirely by artificial life.

Plant Basics
10 feet standard movement
Physical, Mental, and Plant Mutations

Basic Needs: Sentient plants have no need of food, requiring only four hours worth of bright light per day. If deprived sunlight, the sentient plant must make Endurance checks as if starving. A sentient plant's air requirements are measured in hours instead of minutes. Its water requirements are normal.

Taking Root: Rather than sleep, sentient plants anchor themselves in place for at least one hour to gain the nourishment required for the day. The plant is fully aware of its surroundings and requires only one turn to unroot itself and return to normal activity.

Physical Characteristics

There is incredibly diversity within the plant world, and so it is with sentient plants. Some resemble walking trees, others thorny tangles of vines, and still others great mounds of moss. They are usually green in color, though some go through seasonal changes in which they display reds, golds, or other colors. Some are flowering, some bear cones, others fruit.

All plant characters are mobile, though the method of movement differs between variety. One might have a set of "legs" at its base, while others might move by means of a strange shambling or slither along like a snake. They usually communicate with the animal world through gestures and rustling, though some are capable of speech.

Sentient plants are usually indifferent to the presence of other creatures as long as they do not threaten it or its goals. It will work with others for mutually beneficial reasons but will leave when the reasons no longer exist—though a group that has established teamwork and problem-solving might keep a sentient plant's loyalty for a long time indeed. It has no preference between animal- or plant-kind, and because reproduction is handled through pollination, it does not require the company of its kind even to produce young. Plants might be male, female, or hermaphroditic—though the difference will be lost on everyone except other plants.

Seeds, cones, or pods are usually dropped in a suitable place, and the young left to grow and survive on their own. The immature plant is able to free itself and become fully mobile within a few months and is physically mature within a year. The lifespans of sentient plants differ by variety, but some can potentially thrive for hundreds of years.

Playing a Plant

While humans and other animal-based life have long had a higher understanding of the world around them, plants are only newly a part of the higher-thinking world. They do not share the same instincts as animals, and their survival needs are quite different, which makes each pursue highly individual goals. One sentient plant might have a burning desire to solve a particular mystery, while another might seek to further the cause of its species by establishing a well-defended grove. Others might try to defend other types of plant-life from destruction by the animal world. However, one instinctive terror shared by all is a fear of fire.

Because their anatomies are so different and movements so alien, most foes are continually surprised by a sentient plant's attacks. Enemies are caught off-guard, not knowing which way to face the sentient plant or where its weak points may lie. Artificial beings, such as robots and computers, are usually not programmed to recognize or properly deal with mobile, intelligent plant life.

SIZE MATTERS

Characters are generally assumed to be roughly the size of adult humans, or Medium in game terms. But the size of animals, plants, mutants, and robots can vary greatly—meaning that size can be an issue. The following are the sizes used in the game, in order of smallest to largest, with examples:

- **Tiny:** Cockroach, Mouse, Orchid
- **Small:** Skunk, Human Toddler, Shrubbery
- **Medium:** Bear, Human Adult, Elm Sapling
- **Large:** Elephant, Giraffe, Adult Oak
- **Huge:** Whale, Apatosaurus, Sequoia

See Chapter Seven, Size for more information about how size effects characters specific situations.

TRAITS

A character's natural aptitude, talent, training, schooling, weaknesses, and ineptitudes are summed up by Traits. In short, traits define what your character can or cannot do. If it's an action, it will almost always be represented by a trait that will tell you if the character is exceptionally good or hopelessly bad at the particular activity.

The game doesn't distinguish why your character is amazing or embarrassing at a particular task, allowing the player to represent it through roleplaying. Low Influence? Your character may be awful in social situations or has a universally-repulsive face. High Brawn? The character might be naturally big and strong or perhaps spends every free hour exercising and pushing her body to the limits. The reasons can be thought out ahead of time or made up on the fly during play.

Traits are listed as headers on the master list at the end of the chapter, and represent broad categories of action. The list of words below each trait are Specialties—which both detail the kinds of actions that fall under the main trait and also more specific actions that could be modified by Qualities (see below). For more detailed descriptions of traits and specialties, see Chapter Four.

At first glance, it appears there are far too many traits to easily keep track. Remember, however, that characters in the METAMORPHOSIS ALPHA RPG are only defined by the ways in which they are exceptional. Most traits will default to the standard roll (2d) and don't need to be listed at all.

Questionnaire Trait Selection

When building a new character, think about the character concept you have in mind, then answer the following questions:

What is the character best at?
Pick one trait at Amazing (+3d)

What is the character worst at?
Pick two traits at Hopeless (–2d)

What is the character good at?
Pick two traits at Good (+2d)

What is the character weak at?
Pick three traits at Weak (–1d)

What is the character competent at?
Pick two traits at Competent (+1d)

Custom Build Trait Selection

This method takes longer but allows for a more customized character. All traits begin at 2d. Starting characters begin with 2 additional dice to add to the overall trait selection—meaning that a valid character would Good (+2d) in one trait and no others.

You may subtract up to 2d per trait to gain extra dice for others—modifying no more than ten traits in all. No trait may go above Amazing (+3d) or below Hopeless (–2d).

Random Trait Selection

Selecting random traits will create unusual characters! It's recommended that if the random method is chosen, it is used for all characters in the game. Go through the Questionnaire method, but instead of making an active choice, roll and check against the tables below.

3.2 - Trait Categories

1d	Category
1	Creative
2	Physical
3	Social
4	Combat
5	Mental
6	Preservation

3.3 - Creative Traits

1d	Type
1-2	Artistry
3-4	Crafting
5-6	Performance

3.4 - Physical Traits

1d	Type
1	Brawn
2	Dexterity
3-4	Constitution
5	Athletics
6	Stealth

3.5 - Social Traits

1d	Type
1-2	Deception
3-4	Influence
5-6	Leadership

3.6 - Combat Traits

1d	Type
1-2	Melee Weapons
3-4	Ranged Weapons
5-6	Unarmed Combat

3.7 - Mental Traits

1d	Type
1-2	Alertness
3-4	Discipline
5-6	Tech

3.8 - Preservation Traits

1d	Type
1-3	Medicine
4-6	Survival

QUALITIES

A trait is all about how good (or bad) you are at a particular type of action—whether it's throwing a punch or performing battlefield first aid. A trait is static. Qualities are conditional. They often modify the dice pool of traits when the particular situation arises.

A positive quality is a **talent**. A negative quality is a **liability**. A starting character has 2 dice to use for talents and may take 2 dice worth of liabilities to gain more. These should be chosen, not picked at random. See Chapter Four for detailed descriptions of Qualities.

Specialties

Many of the qualities available define your character's talents in a more specific type of action. They can go up to +2d / −2d but no higher or lower.

MUTATIONS

With the exception of humans, all characters aboard the *Warden* have at least one mutation. These give characters unique abilities, unusual attacks, and special powers outside the scope of traits and qualities. One never knows whether or not the large mushroom on the floor has the power to dominate your brain and force you to attack your allies.

Defects

Sadly, not all mutations are about bursts of super-strength or shooting death rays from your eyes. Some are unfortunate evolutionary drawbacks with which characters must suffer. They can range from strange physical characteristics that only get in the way to radiating a strong aroma that makes the mutant smell like a tasty meat snack to any predators nearby.

Choosing Mutations

If your group is building custom characters, the standard method is to choose up to 6d worth of mutations from those available to your character's stock, optionally choosing up to 4d worth of defects to acquire more mutations.

Random Mutation Selection

Your group may choose that all mutations are chosen at random instead of being hand-picked. After all, who gets to choose their own DNA? Random mutations may also crop up during the course of play if a character is exposed to potentially lethal doses of radiation (see Chapter Seven, Specialized Damage).

See Chapter Five, Random Mutations to determine mutations by roll of the dice.

GEAR

Domars are the old-world currency aboard the *Warden*, but items are either scavenged, stolen, created, or obtained through barter. The referee can go over the items listed in Chapter Six with the players and grant them anything that seems reasonable based on their character concept with the following guidelines:

Most characters will have only primitive gear and generally only carry armor and weapons if they are superior to those granted by stock or mutation. Human characters may start with one tech item, either chosen or rolled at random at the referee's discretion. (See Chapter 6, Table 6.2: Human Starting Tech).

DERIVED STATS

If you've made it this far through the process, you're done making choices! There are just a few quick pieces of bookkeeping to make the play of the game go faster. These derived stats define some important elements about your character: Initiative, Dodge, Radiation Resistance, Fatigue, Wounds, and starting Action Points (2).

Note that mutations and qualities might have a direct affect on your derived stats, so double-check as you note each on your character sheet.

Initiative

In high-pressure situations during which every moment counts and it's important to know who acts first (see Chapter Seven, Initiative). Initiative is based on Alertness and the Responsiveness specialty.

Dodge

The need to dodge might be either a defensive action or a reaction to an unexpected situation. Dodge is a specialty of the Dexterity trait and should be noted for easy reference.

Radiation Resistance

The crisis that changed life forever aboard the *Warden* also created the hazard of radiation in different areas around the ship, as well as nasty weapons and dangerous mutations that make use of it. Radiation Resistance is a specialty of the Constitution trait. Note human characters are gifted (+1d) in this specialty.

Fatigue

One of two types of damage a character can suffer, Fatigue represents strain, exhaustion, bruises, scrapes, and other types of minor injuries that might not bother a character individually but when accumulated will knock him down for the count. The good news is that Fatigue damage recovers quickly with simple rest.

Fatigue Capacity is a flat number that starts at 10 and adds in the total number of dice for the Athletics and Discipline traits. The starting value of 10 represents a minimum, so characters have *at least* 10 Fatigue. A strictly average character would begin with 14.

Fatigue = Athletics + Discipline + 10

Example: Gnarl has competent Athletics (+1d for a total of 3d) but is strictly average in Discipline (2d). 3 + 2 + 10 = 15 — indicating his Fatigue capacity.

Wounds

While Fatigue represents minor problems that can go away after a long nap, Wounds are more serious. Broken bones, deep cuts, internal trauma, and every other injury your character hopes won't ever happen but will anyway.

Wounds Capacity is a flat number that starts at 10 and adds in total number of dice based on Brawn and Constitution. The starting value of 10 represents a minimum, so characters have *at least* 10 Wounds. A strictly average character would begin with 14.

Wounds = Brawn + Constitution + 10

Example: Gnarl is a beefy individual with Good Brawn (+2d for a total of 4d) and an Amazing Constitution (+3d for a total of 5d). 4 + 5 + 10 = 19 — indicating his Wounds capacity.

WHERE TO NEXT

If you want to better understand traits and qualities, continue reading the next chapter. If you want to study mutations, jump ahead to **Chapter Five: Mutations & Defects**. When you want to learn about equipment and tech items, head over to **Chapter Six: Gear & Tech**. If you're ready to dive into the full rules of the game, skip to **Chapter Eight: Storyteller & Referee**.

TRAITS

ALERTNESS
Awareness, Observation, Responsiveness, Searching

ARTISTRY
Cooking, Painting, Sculpture, Writing

ATHLETICS
Climbing, Jumping, Running, Swimming, Throwing

BRAWN
Grappling, Lifting, Pushing, Smashing

CONSTITUTION
Endurance, Fortitude, Radiation Resistance

CRAFTING
Breaking, Fixing, Making

DECEPTION
Disguise, Feinting, Subterfuge

DEXTERITY
Acrobatics, Contortion, Dodging

DISCIPLINE
Concentration, Emotional Control, Memory, Mental Resistance

INFLUENCE
Conversation, Empathy, Negotiation, Persuasion, Seduction, Social Defense

LEADERSHIP
Command, Morale, Presence, Social Endurance

MEDICINE
Dentistry, First Aid, Poison Knowledge, Surgery

MELEE WEAPONS
Melee Weapon Attack, Melee Weapon Defense, Melee Weapon Knowledge

PERFORMANCE
Acting, Dancing, Musical Instrument, Oratory, Singing

RANGED WEAPONS
Ranged Weapon Attack, Ranged Weapon Knowledge

STEALTH
Hiding, Moving Quietly, Pickpocketing

SURVIVAL
Camouflage, Handling Animals, Scavenging, Shelter, Tracking

TECH
Computer Use, Tech Infiltration, Tech Lore, Tech Repair

UNARMED COMBAT
Biting, Clawing, Striking, Unarmed Defense

While stock provides a first glance at a character, it doesn't tell us much. We have no idea if she's good with a sword or deft in the art of diplomacy, or whether she is clumsy and graceless or a horrible shot with a pistol. It also provides no hint as to her background, personality, or special skills. **Traits** and **qualities** define a character, making her interesting and fun to play.

TRAITS

Traits are all about action, defining what characters can do and whether or not they can expect impressive success or humiliating failure. Characters default to the standard roll of 2d for unspecified traits, with anything listed on the character sheet showing to what degree they are outliers.

Note the game doesn't distinguish whether a character's knack for a type of action comes from raw ability, inborn talent, extensive training, or implanted muscle memory from an advanced tech facility—those are the kinds of details a player can decide before the game begins or even make up on the spot. All that matters in game terms is whether or not traits vary from the norm and to what extreme.

Remember that the modifiers listed below are always applied to the assumed 2d average, so a sentient fern with Good Discipline would roll 4d for those actions.

Competent (+1d)
You've got natural ability in this area or you've had enough practice to get the job done.

Weak (–1d)
While not an utter failure, you're perfectly aware that these actions aren't your strong suit.

Good (+2d)
If the task is easy, it's all but a sure thing, and even if it's hard, you've got a fair chance at success.

Hopeless (–2d)
You've failed before you start. Unless you have some edge to give you a fighting chance, the effort is doomed.

Amazing (+3d)
You're better at this type of action than almost anyone, with failure being the exception instead of the rule.

Specialties

Traits cover broad categories of action, and many times that's all we need to know in order to determine just how good or bad actions are likely to go. Specialties perform double-duty in the System 26 game; they tell us what types of specific actions fall under the more general umbrella of each trait and also allow some characters to be better or worse in that area than they are for other types of actions. (A character who is strong or weak in a specialty is defined by his qualities, as described later in this chapter.)

ALERTNESS

You are sharp, aware, and responsive … or you are often clueless and constantly surprised. Alertness is used to search for visual cues or find hidden objects. It's also used to determine a character's awareness of her surroundings and how swiftly she reacts to a surprise.

Related Mutations & Tech

Mutations that deal with new or enhanced senses (infravision, sonar) work with Alertness, as well as those that rely on being able to properly observe a target (molecular disruption, pyrokinesis). Tech that enhances any of the five senses or requires attention to detail will enhance or make use of Alertness actions.

Specialties

✣ **Awareness** is often a reaction roll to see if a character notices a clue or otherwise hidden detail.

✣ **Observation** is usually an active roll to see if a character's study of person or object gleans specialized information.

✣ **Responsiveness** is called upon to determine how quickly a character reacts to sudden danger or a changing situation—though it's about mentally processing the danger rather than measuring physical response time. Responsiveness is used to determine a character's initiative.

✣ **Searching** is rolled when a character is actively looking for something in the area, be it a needle in a haystack or hidden hatch in the floor.

ARTISTRY

You are creative and capable of making things to delight and inspire … or you are dull and unimaginative. Artistry is used for inspiring endeavors, for creating things either temporary or permanent. This trait could add any number of specialties related to a creative field or undertaking.

Related Mutations & Tech

Mutations that use creativity or expression (Blinding Pattern) make use of Artistry. Some tech artifacts are sophisticated tools that could allow a character to synthesize meals in moments, creative vivid three-dimensional pictures, or otherwise enhance an artistic ability to make use of the trait.

Specialties

⚕ **Cooking** is used to make the most horrid scavengings palatable or to prepare extraordinary cuisine. It might also be used to hide the taste of drugs or poison in food or drink.

⚕ **Painting** also covers drawing and similar techniques that put pictures on paper, canvas, etc.

⚕ **Sculpture** can either be carving images from stone or using soft clay to create pottery or statues from the ground up.

⚕ **Writing** covers the ability to convey printed information efficiently, as well as craft a moving story or structure a convincing argument.

ATHLETICS

You are fit and physically prepared for almost any terrain or situation … or you are slow and challenged when the going gets rough. Athletics is most often related to movement when things aren't as simple as walking across a room. This trait could add specialties related to specific sports or other modes of movement (flying for winged mutants, etc.).

Related Mutations & Tech

Some mutations modify physical traits or offer new modes of movement that relate to directly to Athletics. Some tech artifacts offer assisted movement or enhance physical performance.

New Specialties

Most of the situations that crop up on the *Warden* are covered by the traits and listed specialties. However, a player or referee may feel there is a need for a new specialty to match a particular situation or allow a character to shine in a previously unexplored area. That's fine! If the referee agrees that a player's specialty suggestion isn't already covered on the list, it can be added and modified with a character's qualities like any other.

Specialties

⚕ **Climbing** covers ascending ropes, scaling walls, or going up a tree.

⚕ **Jumping** is used for vertical leaps or long, running bounds.

⚕ **Running** is rolled for bursts of top speed or maintaining speed while avoiding obvious obstacles, opposed against other characters for races and chase situations.

⚕ **Swimming** comes into play when the character is in water or similar liquids, whether slicing through with skilled strokes or diving below to search the bottom.

⚕ **Throwing** involves lobbing, hurling, or tossing an object toward a general area or specific target.

BRAWN

You are powerful and able to exert your might on the physical world … or you're a puny specimen who has difficulties opening normal doors or lifting small objects. Brawn comes into play when a character needs brute strength to accomplish a task without skill being much of an issue.

Related Mutations & Tech

There are mutations modifying physical traits or enhance physical strength, which tie in to Brawn. Tech artifacts might offer increased physical performance or assist with Brawn-related tasks.

Specialties

⊕ **Grappling** is rolled when attempting to grab or hold the unwilling or engaging in some form of wrestling.

⊕ **Lifting** is used to halt a descending gate, raise a fallen object, or pick up an injured comrade.

⊕ **Pushing** is for heaving a dense object or shoving an opponent off his feet.

⊕ **Smashing** is for slamming something with pure violence, breaking down a door, or knocking someone's teeth out with no self-defense.

Brawn in Combat

Skilled hand-to-hand combat makes use of the Unarmed Combat trait and related specialties, while wrestling and grabbing maneuvers use Brawn and the Grappling specialty. For a character who wishes to rely on physical strength to smash his enemies with little thought to personal safety, he may use Brawn (Smashing) at a –1d penalty to all defensive rolls until his next turn.

CONSTITUTION

You are hale and hearty, able to shake off physical punishment, endure hardships, and resist disease … or you're anemic, fragile, and get sick each time someone sneezes. Constitution becomes an issue when determining a character's ability to resist exhaustion, fight against disease or poison, and resist the effects of radiation.

Related Mutations & Tech

Mutations that channel energy through the body often rely on Constitution. It's used to resist many forms of damage or outside influences and is a trait enhanced by mutations that toughen a character. Tech that enhances a character's ability to endure a heavy load or artificially strengthens immune response tie into Constitution.

Specialties

⊕ **Endurance** is called upon for staying awake when exhausted, to keep moving while carrying a heavy burden, or pushing through pain to slog on.

⊕ **Fortitude** reflects the body's natural defenses against disease, toxins, and infections, and its ability to recover from injury.

⊕ **Radiation Resistance** is a character's ability to reduce or avoid the damage and possible mutations caused by exposure to certain types of harmful energy.

Constitution & Damage

With Wounds Capacity partially derived from a character's Constitution trait (along with Brawn) as well as rolls to resist poison and mutation, it's especially relevant in determining just how much punishment a character can take. Powerful, tough characters intended to take a beating will have a high Constitution.

CRAFTING

You work well with your hands (or paws, tendrils, what have you), able to build, repair, and even strategically break things … or you're hopeless with even the simplest of tools and can't remove a loose screw without help. Crafting is used for repairing, breaking, or creating simple objects and structures. This trait could add specialties related to a specific discipline, from stone mason to carpenter.

Related Mutations & Tech

Mutations rarely interact with crafting, though the complex actions that often go with building or repair projects might make use of mutations that make the work go easier. Technology has always been the friend of the crafter, and advanced tech includes tools to make the work faster and more precise, as well as true miracle gadgets that can create components on the fly.

Specialties

⊕ **Breaking** isn't about smashing something (that falls under Brawn), but rather disassembling or breaking something with strategic precision, as well as bypassing mechanical locks or simple devices.

⊕ **Fixing** covers quick battlefield jury-rigging, as well as intensive repair and improvement projects.

⊕ **Making** is the art of creating new structures or items from raw materials, usually a complex action.

DECEPTION

You can lie like an old rug, bluff your way out of danger, and disguise yourself as another gender or species … or you've got a hopelessly honest face and obvious nervous tick when you try to deceive. Deception is all about a character creating convenient and believable fiction to achieve a goal, whether faking out an enemy in a fight, cosmetically altering his appearance, or telling a whopper of a lie.

Related Mutations & Tech

Mental mutations that plant false information in the receiving brain often rely on Deception. Advanced tech can be used to alter appearance, change voice pitch, or even plant subconscious suggestions by sound.

Specialties

✪ **Disguise** can be a thrown-together change, small cosmetic alteration, or an elaborate costume with all the embellishments.

✪ **Feint** does not only reflect a dirty maneuver in physical combat, but any use of body movement or language with the intent to deceive the viewer.

✪ **Subterfuge** is the art of the lie, including verbal trickery and simple bluffing.

DEXTERITY

You are nimble and limber, able to avoid danger, flip over obstacles, and squeeze through a tight spot … or you can barely walk through a door without bumping into it and often trip over your own laces with the grace of a three-legged cow. Dexterity measures the finesse of the body, how well and how fast it can be bent to the needs of the moment.

Related Mutations & Tech

Some mutations enhance physical prowess or increase a mutant's speed or reflexes, which interact with Dexterity. Tech can assist in gross and fine motor control or speed up a character's physical reactions.

Specialties

✪ **Acrobatics** is used to dive, roll, flip, or properly land a jump—maneuvers that come in handy during the heat of combat.

✪ **Contortion** involves bending the body in non-standard ways, whether to escape confinement, get through a narrow opening, or some other purpose.

✪ **Dodging** is often used in combat as a defensive measure to avoid an attack, but it can also be used to evade danger in other situations.

DISCIPLINE

You can focus your mind with laser-like precision, keep your emotions in check while you handle a situation wisely, are able to recall tiny details from long ago, and defend yourself from psychic attack … or you're easily distracted, emotionally unstable, can't remember breakfast, and are wide open for mental possession. Discipline is about mental self-control and all that goes with it.

Related Mutations & Tech

Discipline is a paired trait with many mental mutations or used to extend psychic effects. It is very often the defensive trait against mental mutations. Some tech can stimulate appropriate areas of the brain related to concentration, mental balance, and memory, while other devices can shield the mind from outside influence.

Specialties

✪ **Concentration** is mental focus, keeping the mind from wandering away from the matter at hand.

✪ **Emotional Control** prevents pain, anger, pity, or other pesky feelings from overwhelming a character.

✪ **Memory** is used to recall important pieces of information or events from long ago.

✪ **Mental Resistance** is used against psychic assaults, to overcome possession, and dispel other cerebral influences.

INFLUENCE

You're able to win friends and sway crowds, easily talking and reading the intentions of others, haggling and getting your way, convincing another to give into your desires, and standing up for yourself against accusation or insinuation … or you're dull and offensive, mystified by contextual clues in conversation, and make your listener want to either leave the room or slap your face. Influence is a social trait used to achieve goals through diplomacy or personal manipulation.

Related Mutations & Tech

Mutations that make the mutant more likable might pair with Influence. Certain drugs can make their users more susceptible to Influence, and some tech might improve personal characteristics with which Influence interplays.

Specialties

✪ **Conversation** covers one-on-one interactions and larger social engagements in which you attempt to steer a topic or pursue a subtle agenda.

✪ **Empathy** is the art of reading social cues to understand someone's feelings and intentions, and it is also the ability to project the sense that the character sympathizes, whether it is true or not.

✪ **Negotiation** might be high-level diplomacy, haggling a simple deal or a complicated barter, or a situation of give-or-take and trying to get the better half.

✪ **Persuasion** is used to convince an individual or audience of a point of view or course of action.

✪ **Seduction** is not just about convincing another to give into carnal desires, but it also involves any act of convincing another to surrender higher principles in the name of baser instincts.

✪ **Social Defense** is necessary to maintain one's reputation or standing when honor, trustworthiness, or dignity is called into question.

LEADERSHIP

You command respect, boost flagging spirits, intimidate with a glare, and have the social staying power that works in politics and political structures … or you inspire derision, make others feel worse about themselves, and don't have the backbone to handle a group vote. Leadership determines whether your character is a social sheep or the leader of the pack.

Related Mutations & Tech

Some mutations that are about asserting one's will on another living creature make use of Leadership. There isn't much tech to improve an inherent social trait such as Leadership, though some devices might alter a character's voice to be more powerful and commanding, change the appearance of the eyes to be more intimidating, etc.

Specialties

✪ **Command** is used to convince a weak-willed individual to obey, at least in the short term, or for determining the effectiveness of control.

✪ **Morale** is rolled when attempting to keep an ally's confidence up or maintain the positive attitude of a group.

✪ **Presence** is about having "it"—a bearing that stands out in a crowd or a quality that demands attention, and it is also used for subtle intimidation.

✪ **Social Endurance** is used to defend against social slander that threatens a character's command structure or damages his reputation as a leader.

Medicine

You understand the workings of living bodies, able to perform emergency first aid, check for signs of toxin, or even perform surgery on grievous wounds … or you are hopeless with the sight of blood, unable to distinguish medical problems or evaluate pain, and would only kill someone with a surgeon's blade. Medicine is a healer's trait, one used to keep living things in fighting form.

Related Mutations & Tech

Mutations generally don't directly interact with Medicine, though many that deal with healing can work in concert with a healer's talents. Tech can provide almost anything a Medicine practitioner could ask for, from surgical tools, fast-healing devices, helpful pharmaceuticals, or cellular regeneration artifacts that revive the recently dead or re-grow a severed limb.

Specialties

⚜ **Dentistry** is called upon when the problem relates to the mouth or teeth.

⚜ **First Aid** is short-term measures to keep someone alive or to keep an injury from getting worse.

⚜ **Poison Knowledge** offers a chance to detect harmful toxins and what countermeasures can neutralize them.

⚜ **Surgery** is the art of cutting up a living creature to help it recover from injury or serious ailment.

Use of Medicine

The use of Medicine in helping characters heal their injuries is covered in Chapter Seven, Recovery & Healing. More information about poison can be found in Chapter Seven, Specialized Damage.

MELEE WEAPONS

You are deadly in hand-to-hand combat, able to block incoming strikes and discern quality weapons from the inferior … or you tend to drop handheld weapons and are only barely able to avoid holding the sharp end of a blade. Melee Weapons is used in close combat for attack and defense, or outside of combat for general knowledge about these types of death-dealing implements.

Related Mutations & Tech

Mutations that simulate handheld weapons pair with the Melee Weapons trait. There are many tech offerings of sophisticated and terrifying murder instruments, from vibroblades to laser saws.

Specialties

⚜ **Melee Weapon Attack** is rolled when attempting to slash, stab, bludgeon, or otherwise harm with a handheld weapon.

⚜ **Melee Weapon Defense** is used to parry, block, or disarm using a held weapon.

⚜ **Melee Weapon Knowledge** is used outside of combat to appraise a weapon's quality or recall useful information on the subject.

PERFORMANCE

You come alive for an audience, bringing nuance to a character, dancing with meaning and beauty, playing music that moves the soul, delivering rousing speeches, or singing with the voice of an angel … or you fumble your lines, move without grace, are a wretched speaker, or are completely tone-deaf. Performance is about putting on a show and giving your audience something to remember.

Related Mutations & Tech

Some mental mutations tie into a character's ability to move and inform a viewer or listener, making use of Performance. Tech might be used to magnify or improve the quality of a character's voice, to extend her image larger than life, or allow her to project the music of an entire symphony straight from her mind.

Specialties

⚜ **Acting** is used to portray a believable character, whether in personal situations or in front of an audience.

⚜ **Dancing** is used to move the body in rhythm and time, with or without music.

⚜ **Musical Instrument** allows the the character to use one or more specialized tools to make pleasing sounds.

⚜ **Oratory** is the art speech, using the spoken word to stir emotions.

⚜ **Singing** is used to convey the beauty of music using only the tools with which the character was born.

RANGED WEAPONS

You are an excellent shot who can shoot the wings off a gnat … or you couldn't hit the broadside of a bulkhead. Ranged Weapons covers hitting something that's too far to stab, using bow, gun, or thrown rock.

Related Mutations & Tech

Mutations that simulate or augment ranged weapons pair with the Ranged Weapons trait. There are many horrible ranged tech weapons, from lasers to disruptors.

Specialties

⊛ **Ranged Weapon Attack** is used to pick off an enemy without getting one's appendages dirty.

⊛ **Ranged Weapon Knowledge** is rolled to determine knowledge about non-tech weapons, other than perhaps which way to point the thing. (Tech is used for all advanced technology, including weapons.)

STEALTH

You're able to vanish into the shadows, walk with silent steps, and have nimble fingers able to pluck a small prize without notice … or you're a clod who has trouble hiding behind a wall, walks with heavy footfalls, and is burdened with fingers made of butter. Stealth is a method of avoiding detection, sometimes (and especially) when engaged in a clandestine activity.

Related Mutations & Tech

Some mutations enhance physical traits or aid in stealth by making a character less noticeable. Tech can aid in Stealth by providing camouflage, muting localized sounds, or assisting in cutpurse activities.

Specialties

⊛ **Hiding** is rolled when a character attempts to use the concealment of darkness, terrain, or whatever large object is nearby to stay out of sight.

⊛ **Moving Quietly** is used for not alerting or alarming those within earshot.

⊛ **Pickpocketing** is used to deftly snatch small objects unnoticed, and other feats of sleight of hand.

SURVIVAL

You stay alive using cunning and scavenged resources, remaining hidden from enemies and predators, calming and taming animals, grabbing whatever food is available, constructing a temporary refuge, or following the tracks of potential prey … or you have a hard time finding your next meal, can barely use ready-made shelters, and have a hard time finding your way home. Survival is about the mundane-yet-essential tasks that keep an individual or group alive on a day-to-day basis, making sure that essential needs like food, water, and shelter are covered.

Related Mutations & Tech

Mutations that summon or control other creatures sometimes use Survival, while others might aid in specific Survival-related tasks, such as group camouflage, noticing details that aid in tracking, etc. While tech rarely aids in Survival in the broader sense, many artifacts might assist with specific needs, such as synthesizing food or water, a collapsable tent or shelter, or scanning for tracks.

Specialties

⊛ **Camouflage** is about creating a way to hide in plain sight using the surrounding background, though it's usually less effective at close range.

⊛ **Handling Animals** is used to calm, tame, train, and befriend creatures of lower intelligence.

⊛ **Scavenging** is about finding whatever food is most readily available, be it plants, discarded waste, or the recently dead.

⊛ **Shelter** is used to either find a suitable place to rest or to construct one from available materials.

⊛ **Tracking** is used to follow a specific target over a long distance, terrain permitting.

Notes on Performance

More than any other, the Performance trait is rather broad and covers more ground than might be considered realistic. It's a very rare character that would be an effective public speaker, graceful dancer, and a master on the flute, after all. However, it's useful shorthand for the game, and since it covers limited situations, there is little harm in leaving things as-is and roleplaying out a character's talents in these areas.

Alternately, if the referee and group want more believability, these specialties can all be treated as separate traits that do not overlap with new specialties specific to those areas. And perhaps the group may want to make a character with a high Musical Instrument choose specifically in which type of instrument her talents lie.

Alternate Rule: Weapon-Specific Specialties

The listed rules make characters equally deadly or useless with all weapons based on their traits and specialties. If the group and referee prefers, instead of having separate specialties for attack and defense, they can refer to types of weapons: Blades, Bludgeons, Staves, etc. In this method, it's familiarity with the weapon that can be improved as a specialty, not just one facet of hand-to-hand fighting. Both attack and defense would be rolled equally with the type of weapon being used. For Ranged Weapons it would be Bows, Slings, Pistols, Rifles, etc.

TECH

The use of tools and technology comes instinctively to you, allowing you to interface with mysterious computer terminals, bypass locking mechanisms, use your extensive knowledge to identify the purpose and use of artifacts, and repair broken technology … or you're unsure and uncertain how these complicated devices are supposed to work and descriptions of them sound like an alien language. Tech is about the understanding of items created before life reverted to simple savagery, artifacts with purposes ranging from the mundane to the spectacular.

Related Mutations & Tech

Mutations almost never directly interact with tech, though some that assist in memory or the gaining of knowledge might help indirectly. This trait is all about the use of technology of any kind, and it is used to help identify and figure out unknown tech artifacts.

Specialties

⚙ **Computer Use** is rolled when a character attempts to use a computer terminal or remote device to gain information or accomplish some other goal.

⚙ **Tech Infiltration** is used to disable electronic locks and security systems that usually require a color band, passcode, or special key.

⚙ **Tech Lore** is used to identify the purpose and use of an unknown tech artifact, preferably without melting one's face off. Use of this facet of Tech is covered in detail in Chapter Six.

⚙ **Tech Repair** is for that sad day when a valuable tech item breaks and needs to be fixed.

Character Tech Knowledge

The understanding and use of technology is an especially important place to distinguish between a player's knowledge and that of the character. Most aboard the *Warden* have reverted to a primitive tribal state with a bizarre mix of hunter-gatherer knowledge and confused lore about robots, lasers, and rooms that move with the push of a button. At the basic 2d level, a character knows that buttons and switches might do something, but most clues as to an artifact's purpose are completely lost on them. Each higher level in Tech indicates more talent and grounding when dealing with technology, but even the most advanced character has a primitive understanding of how things work and what they mean, with less understanding of technology than her player.

UNARMED COMBAT

You require no weapons to be dangerous, able to lash out with fist or foot, tooth or claw, vine or branch … or you're awkwardly terrible at hand fighting, telegraphing your attacks and striking ineffectively. Unarmed Combat is used for personal violence with no implements, just fists (or paws) and fury.

Related Mutations & Tech

There are mutations that create or enhance a creature's natural weaponry or physical savagery, making them never truly unarmed in a fight. Tech items can enhance hand combat, such as powered gauntlets, retractable claws, and more.

Specialties

- ☸ **Biting** is most often used by mutant animals with the teeth for the job, though in the right brawl even a human can find a good place to clamp down with painful effect.
- ☸ **Clawing** is most often the domain of mutant animals or humans who've evolved talons, giving them an inborn weapon to slash a target to ribbons.
- ☸ **Striking** is rolled for punching, whether precise jabs or wild haymakers.
- ☸ **Kicking** includes stomping and other violent use of leg and foot.
- ☸ **Unarmed Defense** is a block rather than a dodge, effective unless the enemy is using a weapon.

Unarmed Defense vs. Armed Attack

When fighting unarmed against a foe using a melee weapon, it's usually best to dodge, but if that's not an option or less than effective, a character may still block. If the defense is successful, he has canceled out the opponent's achievements, but he is still subject to the bonus damage for that weapon.

QUALITIES

Traits are all about action, defining what a character can do in broad strokes. Qualities define a character in a more specific way — either by focusing on a more tightly-defined type of action or a situation in which he might excel or struggle. Talents are qualities that provide an advantage; liabilities are those qualities that present a disadvantage.

Qualities can be a great source of inspiration for roleplaying, offering a glimpse into the personality or personal history of a character. Players should consider these smaller details when deciding just what makes a character tick.

Characters start with 2 dice worth of talents and can take up to 2 additional dice worth of liabilities to get an equal number in additional talents (so a character could possess a maximum of 4d of talents, 2d of liabilities).

Stock-Specific Qualities

While most qualities are available for any character, others are available only for characters of particular stock, as noted in the description. One of the most basic examples of this is Speech — which is assumed for human and mutated humans but must be taken as a talent for mutant animals. Otherwise, those characters must rely on non-verbal forms of communication.

Compatibility

Some qualities just don't go together. One cannot have Speech and be Mute at the same time, for example. Others might seem to disagree but could work in concert with some creative thinking. As with so much else, the referee is the final word if there is a question on whether qualities are compatible or might require some reselection.

SPECIALTIES

Are you a fast runner but awkward swimmer? Do you possess focused concentration but a terrible memory? Is the skill of negotiation a snap for you but you are inept in the arts of seduction? Specialties are the subset of traits that cover a more narrow range of action and define a character's skills and abilities more specifically.

Specialties can be found under their respective traits earlier in this chapter. A specialty cannot be modified more than 2d either to the positive ("talented at" as descriptive shorthand) or negative ("inept at"), and the normal rule of dice pools not going higher than 5d under normal circumstances still applies.

Examples

Gnarl has Brawn at 4d, meaning with actions such as Lifting, Pushing, and Smashing, he rolls four dice. He is talented at Grappling however, with that specialty receiving +1d for a total of five dice for wrestling, grabbing, and related actions.

Iyam has a normal Discipline, the default 2d all characters have with undefined traits. However, he is inept at Emotional Control, suffering a –2d penalty and suffering automatic failure (as zero-dice actions generally do) in situations where he might let his instincts and feelings get the better of him.

TALENTS

While not the more extraordinary abilities granted by mutations, talents are nonetheless significant and important abilities a character might use to survive and thrive in a dangerous environment. They represent situational advantages that fall outside of traits (often affecting or interacting with them) but could otherwise be the result of an inborn proclivity or constant training. The window dressing of the whys and hows of a talent are a decision for the player in the portrayal of a character.

Agile Combatant (2d)

Focusing on movement as part of combat, the character does not suffer a multi-action penalty if moving and attacking at once. (The benefit does not apply if the character attacks more than once or takes other actions in a turn.)

Note: This ability only works with either Melee or Ranged attacks, one of which is chosen when the talent is acquired.

Ambidextrous (1d)

The character can use any limb equally well and does not suffer an off-hand weapon penalty.

Brutal (1d)

Talented at dealing damage, the character may reduce 1d from the dice pool of an attack, then add 1 Wound to the damage inflicted if the attack is successful.

Burrower (1d)

Energetic digging grants the character an additional movement type: burrow. Soft earth is the norm, and the base speed is 1 foot per turn. Hard earth allows only half-movement, and harder terrain may not allow burrowing at all.

Stock: Mutant Animal. (Certain animal types are adept at digging, making this talent available at the referee's discretion.)

Defensive (1d)

Better at avoiding damage than dealing it out, the character receives a +1d bonus to all defensive actions (blocking, dodging, etc.) but receives an equal penalty to all attack actions.

Determined (2d)

The character is able to focus through pain and wounds, not suffering a penalty for injured actions (see Chapter Seven, Consequences of Damage).

Driver (1d – 2d)

Skill with vehicles and controlled pieces of tech come naturally to the character, who receives the quality level as a bonus to actions when behind the wheel.

High Tolerance (1d – 2d)

When imbibing alcohol or another ingested toxin, the character receives a bonus to any roll to resist its effects equal to the quality level.

Intuitive (1d – 2d)

Talented at connecting seemingly unrelated ideas, the character receives a bonus equal to the quality level to actions related to speculation or understanding the unknown. (The referee must approve when this quality is applied before the roll is made.)

Knowledgeable (1d – 2d)

Always one to know a fact or piece of history, the character receives a bonus to any related trait roll for simply knowing something rather than taking an action. If no related trait applies, assume the default (2d) value before applying the quality.

Light Sleeper (1d)

Waking up at a moment's notice, the character may roll Alertness checks to detect and respond to an unexpected presence while unconscious.

Stock: Any non-plant. Mutant animal breeds that do not require sleep also may not take this quality.

Literate (1d)

The character is able to understand written language enough so as to easily understands signs, simple directions, etc. More complicated written material might require an action (Tech or other trait, depending on the source) or simply be beyond the character's basic understanding of writing.

Lucky (1d)

When an action point is spent to reroll an action, the character gains +1d to the second roll.

Mobile (2d)

The character is able to move up to 5 feet without it counting as an action. This may be used in conjunction with movement, attack, or other types of actions.

Resilient (2d)

The character rolls 2d to determine recovered Fatigue when performing a Second Wind (see Chapter Seven, Recovery & Healing).

Robotic Empathy (1d – 2d)

Possessing a knack for understanding and communicating with robots, the character receives a bonus for related actions equal to the quality level.

Stock: Humans, Mutated Humans

Speech (1d)

The character has developed the ability to speak, despite others of the species being unable to do so. It might sound like a normal voice and speech or something so alien and stilted that it takes careful listening to understand.

Stock: Mutant Animal. (Human and mutated human characters are assumed to be able to speak without taking a quality. Plants must take the Plantspeak mutation to verbally communicate.)

Sprinter (2d)

Adept at running short distances, the character adds 5 feet to base movement whenever going faster than walking speed.

Tough (2d)

The character adds +2 to total Wounds capacity.

Unyielding (2d)

Unwilling to drop even when mortally wounded, the character rolls an Average Constitution (Fortitude) check when dying and remains conscious for a number of turns equal to the achievements earned.

Vigor (1d)

The character adds +2 to total Fatigue capacity.

LIABILITIES

Everyone has characteristics that get in the way of a job well done, whether related to personality or just a minor quirk from birth. Liabilities are situation-specific hindrances that usually impair an action or a specific element of a character. While not the level of impairment as a defective mutation, liabilities can nonetheless make a difference—in a bad way.

Combat Rage (1d – 2d)

Damage makes the character lose self-control, and he must succeed an Easy (1d) or Average (2d) Discipline (Emotional Control) check or must use the next available action to attack or move toward the source of the damage.

Delicate Stomach (1d)

Disgusting sights and horrible smells distract the character, causing a –1d penalty to all actions for 1d turns.

Far-Sighted (1d – 2d)

Best able to see things far away, vision becomes blurry, and the character suffers a –1d penalty on vision-dependent actions for anything within 10 feet (1d) or 20 feet (2d).

Fixated (2d)

Suffering from a one-track mind, the character suffers an additional –1d penalty for multiple actions.

Flustered (2d)

Stymied by failure, the character cannot take any actions the turn after a botch is rolled (in addition to other penalties).

Fragile (2d)

The character reduces total Wounds capacity by –2.

Heavy Sleeper (1d)

Difficult to rouse, the character suffers a –1d penalty for all checks to detect and respond to an unexpected presence while unconscious.

Stock: Any non-plant. (Mutant animal breeds that do not require sleep also may not take this quality.)

Hesitant (2d)

Slow to react to danger, the character suffers a –2d penalty to any action taken the very first turn of combat or other situation in which initiative is determined.

Low Tolerance (1d)

When imbibing alcohol or another ingested toxin, the character receives a penalty (1d) to any roll to resist its effects equal to the quality level.

Mute (1d)

Whether the character never learned to speak or lost the ability due to injury or mutilation, she is unable to make use of verbal communication. The character must rely on other methods to convey ideas and plans to others.

Stock: Human, Mutated Human. (Mutant plants and mutant animal characters are able to communicate with others of their kind, but are essentially assumed to be mute in terms of human speech and language.)

Near-Sighted (1d - 2d)

Best able to see things close up, vision becomes blurry and the character suffers a –1d penalty on vision-dependent actions for anything more than 20 feet (1d) or 10 feet (2d).

Restless (1d)

The character becomes frustrated and unpleasant with unchanging scenery, suffering a –1d to all social actions if contained to the same general area for more than six waking hours.

Shy (1d)

Uncomfortable around unknown individuals, the character suffers a –1d penalty to all social actions for the first day in their presence.

Slow Runner (2d)

Inept at running long distances, the character reduces base movement by 5 feet whenever going faster than walking speed.

Sluggish Combatant (2d)

Reluctant to move while in a fight, the character suffers an additional –1d multi-action penalty if moving and attacking in the same turn.

Unfocused (2d)

Easily distracted or possessing a short attention span, the character suffers a –1d penalty for all complex action rolls.

Unhelpful (1d)

Not much of a team player, the character may offer a maximum of +1d when offering assistance to another (see Chapter 7, Group Efforts and Assistance).

Unlucky (2d)

When an action point is spent to reroll an action, the character suffers a –1d penalty to the second roll.

Weak (1d)

The character reduces total Fatigue capacity by –2.

Wounded Impairment (2d)

The character is not able to focus through pain and wounds, suffering –2d penalty for injured actions instead of the standard penalty (see Chapter Seven, Consequences of Damage).

WHERE TO NEXT

To understand mutations and how they can impact a character, keep reading in **Chapter Five: Mutations & Defects**. If want to know all about equipment and advanced technology, head over to **Chapter Six: Gear & Tech**. To learn how traits and qualities impact the rules in-depth, read **Chapter Seven: Rules**.

A bear can be frightening all on its own. Combined with razor-sharp spines and the ability to generate a field of life-draining energy, you meet the stuff of nightmares. Fortunately for your life expectancy, the beast has an extra set of limbs that only slow it down as the ursoid terror gives chase.

Mutations are a major element in keeping residents of the *Warden* on their toes, as you never know what to expect and two creatures rarely have exactly the same mutations. (And some mutants may not have toes at all.) However, mutant creatures might also be plagued with defects that only make their lives more difficult.

In game terms, a **mutation** is always beneficial, while a **defect** is always detrimental, though everything described in this chapter is technically a mutation. We've listed them separately for ease of reference.

Chapter Three details how mutants (everyone in the game except humans) acquire their mutations and defects during character creation. Mutations might also crop up during play through exposure to radiation or technology aboard the *Warden* and will be rolled randomly. You never know what might happen!

ACQUIRING MUTATIONS

Unless you're playing a pure, unadulterated human, your character is a mutant of some kind. Most mutations are acquired during the character creation process as described in Chapter Three.

If the referee is allowing players to choose mutations for new characters, they must first check the characters' stock. Mutated humans and mutant animals have access to physical and mental mutations—along with their related defects. Mutant plants also have access to a small group of mutations available to only them.

If playing a mutant animal with an established breed, check to see which mutations you are required to select as part of that breed. Those must be picked (and "paid" for) like any other, even if the rest of the mutations are determined randomly.

Starting mutant characters receive 6d worth of mutations. Optionally, they may take up to 4d worth of defects to acquire an equal number of beneficial mutations. (For example, a player might decide to take 2d of defects to start the game with 8d worth of beneficial mutations.) Defects are <u>not</u> required for starting characters.

Radiation Exposure

Mutations might be acquired during play if a mutant character is exposed to a lethal level of radiation. Before acquiring the damage, the mutant rolls an Average Constitution (Radiation Resistance) check. If successful, the character does not take the damage and instead develops a new, random mutation that manifests in 1d days from the time of exposure.

Random Mutations

If you are building a character with randomly determined mutations, use the tables below; however, you still may choose the mutation power level of the listed mutation or defect. If you cannot afford the listed mutation, simply choose the lowest mutation power level available for that mutation.

If the strength of a mutation must be determined randomly, roll on Table 5.1 and choose the lowest, closest match to what's available for the listed mutation.

5.1 - Random Mutation Power Level

1d	Mutation Power Level
1-2	1d
3-4	2d
5	3d
6	4d

If the character is a mutated human or mutant animal, determine his mutations using Table 5.2.

5.2 - Human / Animal Mutation Determination

1d	Type
1	Defect (1d: 1-3 Mental, 4-6 Physical)
2-3	Mental Mutation
4-5	Physical Mutation
6	Special

If the character is a mutant plant, determine its mutations using Table 5.3.

5.4 - Physical Mutations

dx	Mutation	Levels
11	Biped/Quadruped	1d
12	Extra Eyes	1d
13	Smaller	1d
14	Water Adaptation	1d
15	Allurement	1d - 2d
16	Chameleon Power	1d - 2d
21	Dual Brain	1d - 2d
22	Energy Absorption	1d - 2d
23	Toxin Resistance	1d - 2d
24	Hands of Power	1d - 4d
25	Healing Touch	1d - 4d
26	Heightened Speed	1d - 4d
31	New Body Parts	1d - 4d
32	Disease Immunity	2d
33	Elongated Limbs	2d
34	Infravision	2d
35	Larger	2d
36	Metamorphosis	2d
41	Multiple Limbs	2d
42	Rapid Recovery	2d
43	Sonar	2d
44	Universal Digestion	2d
45	Life Leech	2d - 4d
46	Bodily Control	2d - 4d
51	Electrical Generation	2d - 4d
52	Gas Generation	2d - 4d
53	Heightened Physical Trait	2d / 4d
54	Kinetic Absorption	2d / 4d
55	Poison Bite	2d / 4d
56	Energy Metamorphosis	3d - 4d
61	Energy Reflection	3d - 4d
62	Heat Generation	3d - 4d
63	Density Control, Self	4d
64	Regeneration	4d
65	Shapeshift	4d
66	Sonic Blast	4d

5.5 - Mental Mutations

dx	Mutation	Levels
11	Direction Sense	1d
12	Telekinetic Hand	1d
13	Empathy	1d - 2d
14	Fear Generation	1d - 2d
15	Intuition	1d - 2d
16	Mental Blast	1d - 4d
21	Mental Defense Shield	1d - 4d
22	Mental Reflection	1d - 4d
23	Molecular Disruption	1d - 4d
24	Telekinesis	1d - 4d
25	Thought Imitation	1d - 4d
26	Pyrokinesis	1d - 4d
31	Displacement	2d
32	Levitation	2d
33	Precognition	2d
34	Telekinetic Claw	2d
35	Teleport Object	2d
36	Will Force	2d
41	Force Field Generation	2d - 4d
42	Mental Invisibility	2d - 4d
43	Stunning Blast	2d - 4d
44	Death Field Generation	2d / 4d
45	Heightened Mental Trait	2d / 4d
46	Illusion Generation	2d / 4d
51	Magnetic Control	2d / 4d
52	Psionic Healing	2d / 4d
53	Confusion	4d
54	Density Control, Others	4d
55	Devolution	4d
56	Mental Control	4d
61	Mental Paralysis	4d
62	Repulsion Field Generation	4d
63	Symbiotic Control	4d
64	Telekinetic Flight	4d
65	Telepathy	4d
66	Teleportation	4d

5.3 - Plant Mutation Determination

1d	Type
1	Defect (1d: 1-2 Mental, 3-4 Physical, 5-6 Plant)
2-3	Plant Mutation
4	Physical Mutation
5	Mental Mutation
6	Special

Special: If this mutation is acquired during play, the referee might assign a specific mutation to the character. Otherwise, the player may choose his mutation from any available or strengthen an existing mutation to a higher mutation power level.

Two-Digit Dice Rolls (dx): Note that when rolling on the two-digit tables, you will roll two dice, with one die chosen to represent the "tens" and the other the "ones." For example, if the first die roll is a 4 and the second is a 2, the result would be 42.

If determining mutations randomly, roll on the appropriate table. Mutations and defects are listed by category, alphabetically, later in this chapter.

5.6 - Physical Defects

2d	Defect	Levels
2	Diminished Sense	1d - 2d
3	Allergy	1d - 3d
4	Achilles' Heel	2d
5	Energy Vulnerability	2d
6	Hyperactive Metabolism	2d
7	Nocturnal	2d
8	Poor Respiration	2d
9	Body Change	2d / 4d
10	Skin Alteration	2d / 4d
11	Seizures	3d - 4d
12	Doubled Pain	4d

5.7 - Mental Defects

1d	Defect	Levels
1	Phobia	1d - 2d
2	Weakened Mental Defenses	1d - 4d
3	Mental Block	2d
4	Stress-Induced Amnesia	2d
5	Multiplied Damage	2d / 4d
6	Boomerang	4d

5.8 - Plant Mutations

1d	Mutation	Levels
1	Plantspeak	1d
2	Berries	1d - 4d
3	Thorns	1d / 3d / 4d
4	Cones	2d / 4d
5	Hardened Bark	2d / 4d
6	Vines	2d / 4d

5.9 - Plant Defects

1d	Defect	Levels
1-2	Water Dependent	2d
3-4	Attraction Odor	2d / 4d
5-6	Photodependent	4d

PHYSICAL MUTATIONS

Whether subtle (like immunity to disease) or dramatic (such as blasting bolts of energy from outstretched fingers) physical mutations represent changes to a character's physiology. Most physical mutations manifest in obvious ways, though sometimes the changes go down to the cellular level or only reveal themselves when an ability is called upon.

Allurement (1d - 2d)

The mutant may emit a pheromone or attractive energy that affects one chosen target within sight. If the mutant succeeds the target is compelled to take actions to move adjacent to the character and will do no harm to the mutant (though his allies are fair game). If the target is attacked or takes damage, the influence is broken. Artificial lifeforms (computers, robots, androids) are immune to this ability, along with one other category of creature chosen at random (1d) when the mutation is taken: 1 - Plants, 2 - Mammals, 3 - Reptiles, 4 - Arthropods, 5 - Amphibians, 6 - Fish. This ability may also be used in a subtle manner outside of combat, granting the mutation power level as bonus dice for social actions, performances, etc. when another character or audience is being swayed.

Frequency: At will.

Paired Trait: Influence or Performance (chosen when the mutation is taken), defended by Discipline (Mental Resistance).

Manifestation: Normally, this mutation is a subtle perfume, but it can be hypnotic skin patterns, alluring music, or a psychic call not easily resisted.

Biped/Quadruped (1d)

This mutation permanently alters the standard mode of locomotion for the type of creature. It changes quadrupedal animals into bipeds or bipedal animals into quadrupeds. The mutation does not remove the creature's hands, but they will be integrated into its new mode of locomotion. For birds and bats, this means their wings have evolved into strangely shaped walking limbs.

Manifestation: The physical change is obvious.

Bodily Control (2d - 4d)

By using this mutation, the character can enhance one physical trait temporarily, adding dice equal to the mutation power level for a number of turns equal to Discipline (Concentration). Physical traits include Athletics, Brawn, Constitution, Dexterity, and Stealth.

Frequency: Once per hour.

Manifestation: This often has obvious physical effects while active, such as bulging muscles, distorted limbs, etc. The alteration reverts to normal when the enhancement ends.

Chameleon Power (1d - 2d)

With only a moment's concentration, the mutant can cause his skin to take on the background color and patterns of the area. This is not a perfect disguise, but it makes the mutant much harder to spot in most situations. The mutation does not affect clothing or armor, so the mutant must travel light or lose any benefit. The mutation power level is added to any actions that benefit from the power, and those characters farther away than 20 feet suffer a –1d penalty on attempts to spot the character.

Manifestation: Even when not actively using the power, the mutant's skin will often slowly shift to take on the colors and patterns of whatever she is sitting on or standing near.

Density Control, Self (4d)

With this potent ability, the mutant can control the spacing of the atoms in her own body! There are two ways to use this power.

☣ *Compression*: The mutant may compress her body, shrinking to half normal size but hardening his flesh and providing Armor 2 protection (see Chapter Six, Armor and Chapter Seven, Damage for more information on such protection). Base movement is reduced by 5 feet and a –2d penalty is imposed on any physical actions that take place in water.

☣ *Expansion*: The mutant may expand her body, doubling in height. The mutant's base movement is increased by 5 feet and gains an additional reach of 5 feet, but she suffers a –2d penalty to Brawn-based actions. The expanded mutant is also more buoyant and can walk on water if not weighed down by too much gear.

Frequency: Up to three times per 24 hours with each use lasting for a number of minutes equal to Discipline (Concentration).

Manifestation: Until the mutant uses this power, there are no obvious signs. When used, the mutant's proportions tend to compress or expand slightly, along with size.

Disease Immunity (2d)

The mutant's immune system is hyper-aggressive, making him completely immune to infection and disease. The referee may designate adventure-specific pathogens (an unknown or genetically-engineered virus, some alien infection, etc.) an exception to this mutation.

Manifestation: Other than the character's exceptional health, there is no obvious outward sign.

Mutation Entries

Mutations and defects are presented in a standardized format for easy reference. Note not all entries have every subsection listed below:

Name (Mutation Power Level)

In addition to providing the name of the entry, there is also a die level presented in parentheses—the mutation power level. The die level defines the mutation's relative potency. Sometimes the mutation power level is purely for purposes of game balance and reference, while often it represents dice that will be rolled or added to a dice pool when the mutation or defect comes into play.

Next is a written description of the mutation, summarizing its nature and providing any relevant rules for its use.

Frequency: How often a mutation or defect occurs. Permanent mutations will omit this entry.

Paired Trait: A mutation's power is sometimes used with an action associated with a particular trait. For example, if a mutant character is using Allurement in combat, she might roll her Performance trait (2d) plus the mutation power level of 2d, giving her 4 dice in the pool to attract and pacify a dangerous enemy.

Manifestation: This entry describes how the mutation can be detected by others, whether it's a permanent change or only occurs when the mutation or defect is activated.

Special: Any other rules or requirements for what types of characters can acquire a mutation or defect are listed here.

Dual Brain (1d – 2d)

The mutant develops a second brain, though not a second head. The secondary brain acts as a backup system, constantly mirroring the character's primary brain for thought and memory. This grants a bonus equal to the mutation power level for any attempt to recall a pertinent fact, as well as to resist mental attacks. However, the real utility of this mutation occurs when she is stunned, mind-controlled, mentally paralyzed, or otherwise loses control. After one turn the secondary brain becomes the primary and the mutant is able to resume normal actions. (If the second brain is itself subject to attack, it is handled and tracked separately.) As long as at least one of the brains is uncontrolled, the character may act normally.

Manifestation: The character might possess a grossly enlarged cranium, though it's possible for the second brain to be in an enclosed hump on the spine, in the chest cavity, or another logical place. It will usually be visible as a growth or protuberance, which might be hidden under loose clothing.

Electrical Generation (3d – 4d)

The mutant's body generates and can discharge a shocking amount of electricity. He may either use it as reaction to anything that comes into physical contact (most often an attacking enemy) or as an attack against an Easy target with the mutation power level rolled as bonus Fatigue electricity damage. Alternately, the mutant may release a bolt in a straight line up to 60 feet as a ranged attack with the mutation power level as bonus electrical damage. At the referee's discretion and the character's understanding of tech, he might be able to recharge electrical devices by using the mutation. The mutation grants a constant resistance to electrical damage equal to the mutation power level.

Frequency: Once every four hours.
Paired Traits: Constitution (Endurance) for discharge; Alertness (Awareness) for bolt.
Manifestation: When using the power, the mutant is crackling and glowing with energy. When passive, the mutant still has a powerful static field that causes harmless electrical shocks but might have minor effects on tech.

Elongated Limbs (2d)

The character's limbs (arms or legs, chosen when the mutation is acquired) are elongated, and the muscle and bone structure have altered to compensate. Elongated legs increase base movement and overhead reach by 5 feet. Elongated arms grant an additional reach of 5 feet and a bonus to grappling actions equal to the mutation power level.

Manifestation: The oversized arms or legs are obvious and difficult to disguise.

Energy Absorption (1d – 2d)

The mutant's body hyper-metabolizes or otherwise absorbs a particular type of damage chosen when the mutation is acquired (cold, electricity, fire, radiation, sonic) and has a constant resistance to that damage type equal to the mutation power level.

Manifestation: The mutant often displays a subtle hint as to the type of energy she is resistant to, such as being cool or warm to the to the touch, has oddly textured skin, etc.

Special: If circumstances allow this mutation to increase in power level, the mutation shifts to Energy Metamorphosis or Energy Reflection using the same type of energy. If a mutant already has Energy Metamorphosis and this is chosen or rolled, the mutation must use a different type of energy.

Energy Metamorphosis (3d – 4d)

The mutant's body hyper-metabolizes or otherwise absorbs a particular type of damage chosen when the mutation is acquired (cold, electricity, fire, radiation, sonic) and has a constant resistance to that damage type equal to the mutation power level. In addition, he may recover Fatigue as a reaction to contact with the listed energy type, equal to achievements rolled with a dice pool equal to the mutation power level.

Frequency: Fatigue recovery once every four hours.
Manifestation: The mutant often displays a subtle hint as to the type of energy he is resistant to, such as being cool or warm to the to the touch, has oddly textured skin, etc. He radiates a strangely-colored aura (indicative of the energy type) when recovering fatigue.

Energy Reflection (3d – 4d)

The mutant's body hyper-metabolizes or otherwise absorbs a particular type of damage chosen when the mutation is acquired (cold, electricity, fire, radiation, sonic) and has a constant resistance to that damage type equal to the mutation power level. In addition, she may discharge the energy type as a bolt in a straight line up to 60 feet on her next turn immediately after the resistance was applied.

Frequency: Whenever the energy type is resisted; however, using it as a ranged attack is an action and only possible on the following turn.

Paired Traits: Alertness (Awareness) for the bolt attack.

Manifestation: The mutant often displays a subtle hint as to the type of energy he is resistant to, such as being cool or warm to the to the touch, has oddly textured skin, etc. She radiates a strangely-colored aura (indicative of energy type) just before releasing a bolt.

Extra Eyes (1d)

The mutant has a pair of eyes in the back of his head—or a strange pair of eyes that are out of place for a plant character. This allows a character to see in all directions at once and makes it impossible for others to use facing as an advantage for sneaking. The character also gains a bonus to avoid blinding attacks equal to the mutation power level.

Manifestation: The extra eyes clearly visible, though they might be disguised without difficulty.

Gas Generation (2d – 4d)

The mutant exudes a cloud of gas, the type chosen when the mutation is acquired (chosen at random on 1d when the mutation is taken: 1 - Sleep, 2 - Corrosive, 3 - Obscuring, 4 - Blinding, 5 - Hallucinogenic, 6 - Toxic), which spreads out in a sphere centered on the mutant. The cloud has a radius of 10 feet per die of the mutation power level. For example, if the character has the mutation at 3d, the cloud of gas would be a 30-foot sphere. The cloud remains stationary once generated. The mutant who generated the cloud is immune, but otherwise it affects friend and foe alike.

Sleep: This gas must be inhaled to be effective. Anyone breathing it must fight to stay conscious as if they were at zero Fatigue (see Chapter Seven,

Consequences of Damage), though no actual damage is taken. Any damage will immediately wake those unconscious in the cloud, and the effects are negated if physically removed from the area. Plants and artificial life are immune.

☣ *Corrosive*: This is a cloud of acid. It affects organic and inorganic beings and it does not need to be inhaled. Anything inside the cloud takes 1 Fatigue acid damage on the first turn of exposure as if a successful attack was rolled. This damage repeats and increases by one step each continuous turn inside the cloud (see Chapter Seven, table 7.4 - Damage), reaching a maximum at the mutation power level. The damage stops immediately once outside of the cloud.

☣ *Obscuring*: This is an opaque gas that obstructs vision. Anything more than five feet away is difficult to see, making attacks and other actions requiring sight Hard. The cloud does not obscure other types of vision (heat signatures, echolocation, etc.).

☣ *Blinding*: This gas directly affects exposed eyes, and any vulnerable characters are blind while inside the cloud (see Chapter Seven, Conditions). Those who leave the cloud suffer a –1d penalty to all vision-based actions for one minute. Plants (unless they have an eye mutation) and artificial life are immune.

☣ *Hallucinogenic*: The gas disrupts the ability to interpret sensory information, causing an affected being to see anything moving as an immediate threat. An affected character must succeed a Hard Discipline (Emotional Control) check or attack the closest moving thing. The effects of the gas continue 1d turns after exposure ends. Artificial life is immune.

☣ *Toxic*: The gas is a lethal airborne contact poison. This is identical to the effects of a neurotoxin (see Chapter Seven, Toxins). Artificial life is immune.

Frequency: Once every 8 hours, the gas cloud lasting for a number of minutes equal to Constitution (Fortitude).

Manifestation: All of the gasses are clearly visible when emitted. The mutant's gas generation organs are fairly small and obscure, but they can be found on close inspection.

Hands of Power (1d – 4d)

The mutant can shoot a bolt of damaging energy from her extremities, firing in a straight line up to 60 feet as a ranged attack with the mutation power level as bonus dice in the attack (and may exceed the normal maximum of 5d). The type of damage caused by this mutation is chosen when the power is acquired (cold, electricity, fire, radiation, sonic).

Frequency: Once per hour.

Paired Traits: Alertness (Awareness).

Manifestation: The character's hands display unusual growths that are the source of the energy used for attacks.

Healing Touch (1d – 4d)

The mutant may channel powerful bio-energy by touch that heals another living being in an instant. The target rolls Constitution (Fortitude), healing both Fatigue and Wounds equal to achievements rolled. The healing is applied as if time had passed (meaning fire damage only heals half and other modifying conditions apply). The mutation can only be used on others and has no affect on artificial life.

Frequency: A number of times per day equal to the mutation power level. A recipient may only be healed by this power once per day.

Manifestation: The mutant is surrounded by a momentary halo of bright light during use. Otherwise, the mutation is not readily detectable.

Heat Generation (3d – 4d)

The mutant can raise his body temperature to extreme levels. The heat builds each turn, starting at 1d and raising to a maximum equal to the mutation power level. The mutant can hold the heat generated for up to ten minutes or can be ended early at will, cooling down at the same rate. He may use it as a reaction to anything that comes into physical contact or as an unarmed attack. As a reaction it counts as an automatically successful attack with a number of achievements equal to the mutation power level. As an attack the mutation power level is added as bonus achievements to a successful attack. All damage caused by this mutation is fire damage. At the referee's discretion, the mutant may be able to focus the mutation into a useful noncombat purpose (boiling water, melting soft metals, etc.), but such use might require the use of an appropriate trait. The mutation grants constant resistance to fire damage equal to the mutation power level.

Frequency: Once every four hours.

Paired Traits: Unarmed Combat (for use as an attack).

Manifestation: Even when calm, the mutant's body temperature is very high relative to his stock (around 110 degrees for a mutated human). When the power is active, the mutant glows with an aura of intense heat, and flammable gear in contact with his body may ignite.

Heightened Physical Trait (2d or 4d)

The mutant receives a permanent enhancement to a physical trait equal to half the mutation power level, with the trait chosen at the time the mutation is acquired (Athletics, Brawn, Constitution, Dexterity, or Stealth). For example, if a character receives heightened Brawn at the 2d power level, her trait would increase by 1d. Increases from this mutation can go beyond the normal dice pool limit of 5d, and all derived stats are changed as well.

Manifestation: The character's body physically changes to reflect her enhanced status (lean muscle for Athletics, thick build for Constitution, large muscles for Brawn, cat-like movement for Dexterity or Stealth).

Heightened Speed (1d – 4d)

The mutant's base speed increases by 5 feet per die of the mutation power level and gains an equivalent dice pool bonus for reactions involving fast movement or avoiding attacks. At the referee's discretion, this benefit can also translate into quickly finishing tasks that involve repetitive work, either reducing the time required or adding dice for complex actions, though the character will be Weary for an hour afterward (see Chapter Seven, Conditions).

Paired Traits: Alertness (Responsiveness), Dexterity (Dodge), when the mutation is relevant.

Manifestation: The mutant generally moves noticeably faster with inhuman reaction times. He is likely to have an increased appetite and is usually of a lean build.

Infravision (2d)

The mutant can switch her vision into a mode that detects the infrared spectrum. This allows the mutant to essentially see in the dark or detect otherwise invisible beings within 60 feet if their temperature varies from the background. The mutant cannot distinguish fine details, but she will be able to make out size and general shape. Humans and animals stand out brightly with infravision, plants and artificial life less so but still easily detectable.

Manifestation: The mutant's eyes will be strangely colored or oddly reflective, or she may have antennae or skin pits that serve as heat sensors instead of eyes.

Kinetic Absorption (2d or 4d)

Using this power enables the mutant to reduce kinetic energy from physical attacks (punches, bullets, claws, etc.). Wound damage is reduced from physical attacks equal to half the mutation power level, including damage from falling. A character with this power also gains bonus dice equal to the mutation power level on any attempt to resist being pushed or pulled.

Manifestation: The character's skin is often strange and rubbery, and physical impacts sound oddly muted.

Larger (2d)

The character is one size category larger than is usual for his species (Medium becomes Large, Small becomes Medium, Tiny becomes Small) with all the benefits and drawbacks of that size (see Chapters 3, Size and Chapter 7, Attack for more information).

Manifestation: It is often obvious that the character is oversized, such as a wolf-sized raccoon or a horse-sized skunk.

Special: This may be given at no cost to mutant animals of a small species (at the referee's discretion) to make them playable with human-size characters. If it is used to enlarge a Medium-size character to Large, it costs normally.

Life Leech (2d – 4d)

This mutation drains bio-energy from a target. When the mutant touches any living being (including plants but excluding artificial life), she inflicts d6 Fatigue and recovers an equal amount. Wounds are unaffected by this power, and Fatigue cannot recover past normal maximum. Any action that succeeds in direct physical contact with the target may be used for this power. If used in a surprise situation to an adjacent target, no roll may be required. A willing target also negates the need for a roll.

Frequency: A number of times per day equal to the mutation power level.

Manifestation: The mutant often has a sickly or weak demeanor or might be a full albino. In addition, when using the power, there is usually a sign, such as purplish eyes or a necrotic energy field that withers small plants and kills tiny insects nearby.

Metamorphosis (2d)

This potent power allows the mutant to transform into an outwardly identical copy of any being of roughly equal size (up to 25% larger or smaller) he touches (alive, or dead for less than one hour). Her physical traits temporarily alter to match the target, though she does not gain any additional mutations beyond purely physical changes such as wings, teeth, claws, etc. The process takes 1d turns to complete, and the mutant is essentially prone and immobile during the painful process. The metamorphosis lasts until the next time the mutant sleeps, loses consciousness, or wills the process to reverse. The change is only physical and grants no other means to imitate a target or its abilities.

Frequency: Once per day.

Manifestation: This power is only obvious during the time of transformation.

Special: If circumstances allow this mutation to increase, the mutation changes to Shapeshift.

Multiple Limbs (2d)

The character has an extra set of arms or legs (chosen when the mutation is acquired). Extra legs increase his speed by 5 feet and provide a bonus to acts of balance and athleticism equal to the mutation power level. Extra arms do not grant extra attacks, but they do allow for two-handed weapons and shields to be employed with a single set of limbs or allow the character to hold extra items.

Manifestation: The extra limbs are clearly visible.

New Body Parts (1d – 4d)

The character's body has mutated to grant her body parts normally found on other species, chosen when the power is acquired.

☯ *Quills* (1d): The mutant has grown thick quills which inflict 1W to any enemy attempting to grapple. Every four hours, the character may hurl quills up to 10 feet as a ranged attack with +1W bonus damage.

☯ *Wings* (4d): The character has fully-functional wings, granting flight speed equal to twice her normal ground speed. If the character is Injured (suffered more than half possible wounds, see Chapter Seven, Consequences of Damage), she cannot fly.

☯ *Claws* (2d): The characters fingers end in sharp claws, which she can use in unarmed combat with +1W bonus damage.

☯ *Bite* (3d):The character has gained large, sharp, rending teeth or a powerful beak, granting her a fierce bite in unarmed combat with +2W bonus damage.

☯ *Carapace* (2d): The character has a hard, bony shell covering most of her body, granting armor equal to the mutation power level but reducing base speed by 5 feet.

☯ *Gasbag* (2d): The character can inflate like a pufferfish once every four hours, producing a lifting gas. This allows her to float and descend freely, but she is at the mercy of air currents or handholds for locomotion. When partially inflated, the bag allows a bonus on all jumping or swimming checks equal to the mutation power level.

☯ *Antlers* or *Horn* (2d): The character has a bony horn or set of antlers; these can be used as offensive weapons (+1W in stationary combat or +2W when used in a charge).

☯ *Hump* (1d – 2d): This mutation creates a fatty hump, like that of a camel, which can provide all nourishment for three days per die of the mutation power level.

☯ *Pincer* (2d): One of the character's hands is replaced with a large, crab-like claw. This can be used in unarmed combat (+1W) and provides a +1d bonus for actions in which the claw provides an advantage, but the claw cannot be used for fine manipulation in the manner of a hand.

✆ *Tentacles* (1d): This mutation grants two tentacles in addition to the character's arms. They are 10 feet long when stretched out and fully prehensile, though they are too weak to be used as offensive weapons. They may hold small items, reach into confined areas, and deliver the power of touch-based mutations.

Manifestation: Normally, the new body parts are very obvious, but some might be hidden or disguised.

Poison Bite (2d or 4d)

The mutant produces a toxic venom delivered by bite and gains a slightly altered tooth and jaw structure to accommodate if necessary. The turn following the bite the target suffers the effects of the poison, a paralytic at the 2d mutation power level, a neurotoxin at the 4d level (see Chapter Seven, Toxins).

Frequency: Once every four hours.

Paired Trait: Unarmed Combat (Bite).

Manifestation: The mutant might have an unusual colored pattern on its skin or large fangs that secrete venom.

Rapid Recovery (2d)

The mutant recovers from Fatigue far more quickly than others. With light activity, the character recovers 1 Fatigue every minute and is fully restored with one hour of rest. A character with this power may recover Fatigue equal achievements rolled with a dice pool equal to the mutation power level when gaining a second wind. Wound damage is unaffected by Rapid Recovery.

Manifestation: The mutant seems to never be out of breath, while bruises and bumps heal themselves within moments.

Regeneration (4d)

The mutant recovers from Wound damage more quickly than others. With light activity, the character recovers 1 Wound every 30 minutes, and with exertion, he recovers 1 Wound per hour. A mutant with regeneration never needs to roll to recover even if Injured. Fatigue is unaffected by Regeneration.

Manifestation: The rapid closure of wounds is obvious when it occurs. When not actively using the power, the only sign is a lack of even the smallest scars or scratches.

Shapeshift (4d)

The mutant could become the consummate spy, able to take on the physical appearance (but not the traits or mutations) of any being of the same stock and roughly the same size (within 25% of body mass). This disguise includes simulations of physical mutations such as fangs or armor, but they are ineffective if used. The mutant with this power can look like any being they imagine, or like any being they've studied up-close for at least a minute. The process takes 1d turns to complete, and the mutant is essentially prone and immobile during the somewhat painful process. The shapeshift lasts until the next time the mutant sleeps, loses consciousness, or wills the process to reverse. The change is only physical, and grants no other means to imitate a target or its abilities.

Frequency: Once every six hours.

Manifestation: This power is only noticeable during the period of transformation.

Special: If circumstances cause this mutation to decrease, the mutation changes to Metamorphosis.

Smaller (1d)

The mutant is one size category smaller than most members of its species (Large becomes Medium, Medium becomes Small), giving it all the benefits and drawbacks of that size.

Manifestation: It's often obvious that the character is undersized, whether it's a man-sized grizzly bear or a child-sized human.

Special: At the referee's discretion, this mutation may be granted at not cost to mutant animals who would normally be too large to work well with a group of otherwise human-sized characters.

Sonar (2d)

This mutation allows a character to discern images using sonic echolocation, essentially allowing him to see in the dark (or while blinded) or to provide bonus sensory information even under normal circumstances. While sonar cannot offer fine detail, it will show obstacles, terrain features, and beings in a 30-foot radius. Rolls to distinguish things farther away are at the referee's discretion. Sonar provides a 360-degree field of view, so it is very difficult to sneak up on the character. Extreme sound in the area, such as anyone using a sonic attack, will negate the character's sonar for one turn. As a drawback, the mutant suffers a –1d penalty to defense rolls against sonic attacks.

Paired Trait: Alertness (Awareness) for sensing farther than 30 feet.

Manifestation: Usually the character has large ears which catch the sounds, and he emits a hypersonic chirp to generate the echoes he senses. The chirp can be heard by beings with any enhanced hearing.

Sonic Blast (4d)

This mutation allows a character to emit a powerful burst of focused sound in a cone 60 feet long and 30 feet wide at the end. All characters caught in the cone take sonic damage, and any character who takes 2 or more Fatigue are also deafened for 1d turns. Crystalline or metallic structures suffer a –2d penalty to their defense.

Paired Traits: Defended by Constitution (Endurance), attack roll equal to the mutation power level.

Frequency: Once every four hours.

Manifestation: The mutant will often have an enlarged or distorted larynx or have a very strange buzz or twang to her speaking voice.

Toxin Resistance (1d – 2d)

The mutant receives a bonus to all rolls to resist the effects of toxins equal to the mutation power level and gains a resistance to damage from toxins at the same level.

Manifestation: This mutation is rarely obvious; if it is, the mutation takes the form of an additional organ or growth that handles the processing of toxins.

Universal Digestion (2d)

The mutant can eat anything organic—no matter how normally indigestible or disgusting. Bark, leaves, bone, lichen, fur, and hide are just a few examples. This mutation grants immunity to all ingested toxins and any diseases normally caught from consuming rotting meat. It does not allow the character to ingest rocks or metal.

Manifestation: The character's jaw structure is enlarged, and his teeth strangely shaped. Unusual eating habits may leave the mutant's smell offensive, and watching him eat may sicken some observers.

Water Adaptation (1d)

The mutant has gills, usually along his neck or the sides of her face. She can breathe water as easily as air and can see underwater without difficulty. Webbing on his hands and feet grant a bonus to swimming-based actions equal to the mutation power level and a 5 feet increase to base swimming speed.

Manifestation: The gills and webbing of the hands and feet are normally visible, but they can be disguised.

Special: Fish or amphibian mutants might have an equivalent "land adaptation" variation with functional lungs and ability to move on dry ground.

PHYSICAL DEFECTS

The yang to mutation's yin, physical defects represent the downside of DNA going haywire. While they can simply be extreme versions of mundane issues such as allergies, they often represent noticeable abnormalities or significant weaknesses.

Achilles' Heel (2d)

Some location on the mutant's body is especially sensitive and vulnerable, chosen when the mutation is acquired. While the location is Hard for an enemy to target, it causes +1d Fatigue and +1 Wound each time the spot is struck. Anytime an enemy gains 2 or more enhancements on an attack, he hits the weak spot by blind luck.

Manifestation: The target area is usually not obvious to casual inspection, though it may bear the signs of many wounds or scars.

Allergy (1d – 3d)

The character is highly allergic to a common substance chosen when the mutation is acquired, causing the mutant to suffer a –2d penalty to all physical and mental traits for 30 minutes while coughing, wheezing, or dealing with a flaring rash. Details of the allergic reaction are up to the player and referee. At the 1d level, the allergy is to an ingested substance (gluten, nuts, dairy, shellfish, etc.). At the 2d level, the allergy is from touch (plastic, rust, leaves, fur). At the 3d level, the allergy is airborne (feline or canine dander, pollen, mildew and mold, dust mites).

Manifestation: When the defect is active, the character will sneeze, cry, or suffer hideous rashes and boils. Even stranger effects, such as skin color changes, are possible.

Special: Plants cannot have this defect.

Body Change (2d or 4d)

While almost all mutants have some cosmetic indications of their status, this mutation covers those that affect the character's life or ability to perform tasks. Pick the nature of the deformity (having only one cyclopean eye or possessing legs with no knees, for instance), then pick two relevant traits (Alertness and Ranged Weapons for having only one eye, Athletics and Dexterity for having no knees) which each suffer a –1d penalty. At the 4d level, this trait either penalizes four traits at the –1d level or two traits at a –2d penalty. The referee must approve the traits and may impose additional small penalties related to your character's deformity (such a 5 feet penalty to base speed for having no knees).

Manifestation: A deformity of this nature is usually hard to hide and rather obvious, though in some cases, it might be disguised.

Diminished Sense (1d – 2d)

One of the mutant's primary senses, sight or hearing, is in some way limited. Possibilities include no color vision, no night vision, narrow band of hearing, or no ability to gauge the direction of sound, chosen when the mutation is acquired. The character suffers a penalty to Alertness when relying on either sight or hearing (depending on which is affected) equal to the level of the defect. The penalty doubles when the specific limitation applies to an action or reaction.

Manifestation: The affected organs are likely to be smaller, misplaced, oddly colored, or otherwise indicate that they're the focus of mutation.

Doubled Pain (4d)

The mutant's nervous system is over-sensitive to painful stimuli, making the smallest bump feel like a sledgehammer smash. The character suffers +1 Fatigue anytime damage is suffered, and she suffers the penalty of being Injured (see Chapter Seven, Consequences of Damage) if she has taken any Wound damage at all.

Manifestation: The mutant quickly learns to walk carefully and gingerly, lest she stub a toe or scratch a finger. She will tend to overreact to very small injuries, such as touching a hot surface or nicking her finger with a knife.

Energy Vulnerability (2d)

The mutant is particularly vulnerable to one category of energy (cold, electricity, fire, radiation, sonic). An enemy's attack gains an additional achievement every time the character is injured by this energy type.

Manifestation: Attacks of vulnerable energy leave nasty scars, larger wounds, or otherwise show more damage than they should.

Special: It is possible to possess this defect in addition to Energy Absorption, Energy Metamorphosis, or Energy Reflection, as long as the types of energy affected are different.

Nocturnal (2d)

The mutant normally functions best during night cycles, sleeping during the day. This can cause scheduling problems with daytime allies and lead to loss of sleep. If forced to operate during the day, especially in bright sunlight, he is Weary (see Chapter Seven, Conditions) as if having gone 24 hours without sleep, and the character is drowsy and lethargic. Extremely bright light makes the mutant temporarily Blind (see Chapter Seven, Conditions). Plants cannot take this defect.

Manifestation: The mutant will usually show obvious signs of his nocturnal status, such as pale skin, larger eyes, aversion to bright light, etc.

Hyperactive Metabolism (2d)

The mutant's internal system inefficiently burns off energy at an extraordinary rate, increasing her need for food with no offsetting benefits. She must eat at least one normal meal every 8 hours or becomes Starving (see Chapter Seven, Conditions) with additional penalties occurring every two hours thereafter.

Manifestation: The mutant is noticeably thin despite eating often and is constantly thinking about food.

Special: Mutant plants cannot receive this defect.

Poor Respiration (2d)

The mutant suffers from undersized lungs or some other physical deformity that makes breathing difficult. Every ten minutes of hard physical exertion makes the character Weary (see Chapter Seven, Conditions) as if he had gone 12 hours without rest, though 30 minutes of low activity restores the character to normal. The intensity of combat, even for a shorter amount of time, counts as ten minutes of exertion, though the effect does not occur until combat is concluded.

Manifestation: The mutant is constantly wheezing and short of breath, and even minor physical activity is tiring.

Seizures (3d – 4d)

When the mutant takes damage he might suffer a fit. At the 3d level, this only occurs if the mutant takes Wound damage; at the 4d level seizures are a possibility if he suffers any type of damage. He must make a Constitution (Fortitude) check or fall prone, twitching uncontrollably for 1d turns. The check is normally Easy but becomes Average if the mutant is Injured (see Chapter Seven, Consequences of Damage).

Manifestation: None until a triggering incident occurs.

Skin Alteration (2d or 4d)

The mutant's skin has changed in a detrimental manner, chosen when the defect is acquired.

☣ *Water-soluble* (4d): The mutant takes 1 Wound for each turn she is submerged or doused in water. Heavy rain or the equivalent causes 1d Fatigue per turn. Any dampness on the skin causes so much pain the mutant is penalized as if Injured (see Chapter Seven, Consequences of Damage).

☣ *Photosensitive* (4d): Exposure to bright light causes 1d Fatigue per turn. Exposure to bright light from a more limited source (a fire or a beam of light) inflicts 1 Fatigue per turn. Only dim light or darkness is tolerable, but this defect grants no vision powers to compensate.

☣ *Inflexible* (4d): The mutant's skin is thick and inflexible but provides no additional protection. Base speed is reduced by 5 feet and affected actions (including those using Athletics and Dexterity) suffer a –1d penalty.

☣ *Anti-Chameleon* (2d): The mutant's skin shifts color and pattern in a way to make her extremely obvious—becoming bright red against a white backdrop, for example. This makes the character Easy to see under such conditions.

Manifestation: The character's skin will have a strange texture or coloration and feel unusual to the touch.

MENTAL MUTATIONS

Often thought of by humans as psychic phenomenon, mental mutations expand the mind beyond its normal evolutionary limits and manifest as subtle gifts or extraordinary powers. Generally speaking, they are less obvious than physical mutations, though their effects can often be impossible to ignore. Some groups and individuals become suspicious or even paranoid of telepaths or mental manipulators, leading some mutants to work hard at concealing their abilities from others.

Blinding Pattern (1d – 4d)

The mutant creates fields of flashing multicolored light within a 30-foot radius. He may create one field per mutation power level, each for a specific target. If the attack succeeds, the target takes 1d Fatigue psychic damage and is blind (see Chapter Seven, Conditions) as long as the pattern is maintained. Maintaining the patterns counts as one action per turn, but any or all may be released at will—though all of the patterns still count as one action to maintain. This is a psychic attack, and an enemy closing his eyes will not defend it against the effect.

Frequency: Once every six hours.

Paired Trait: Artistry or Performance (chosen when the mutation is acquired), defended by Alertness (Awareness).

Manifestation: Those not explicitly targeted detect faint lights and colors but suffer no ill effects. Those targeted see an all-consuming, ever-shimmering, eternally fascinating kaleidoscopic array and nothing else.

Special: Plants and artificial life are unaffected by this mutation, along with any other creature lacking standard animal visual centers in the nervous system.

Confusion (4d)

A pulse of psychic energy disrupts the target's ability to perceive and respond to stimulus, causing her to act somewhat randomly. If the psychic attack succeeds, the target suffers 1d Fatigue psychic damage, and for 1d plus the mutation power level in turns, she acts randomly, based on rolling at the beginning of each turn and subject to the referee's interpretation.

1d	Confused Action
1	Takes no meaningful action.
2	Retreats in a random direction.
3	Attacks nearest creature.
4	Drops anything held.
5	Attacks the mutant who used this mutation.
6	Acts normally for one turn.

Frequency: Once every eight hours.
Paired Trait: Discipline (Concentration), defended by Discipline (Mental Resistance).
Manifestation: There is no visible manifestation of this mutation other than the behavior of the target.

Death Field Generation (2d or 4d)

This dread power allows the mutant to emit a blast of energy that kills living cells. The blast has a 50-foot radius and causes psychic damage to anyone within that area, including the mutant himself. The damage is Wounds rolled at half the mutation power level (1d Wounds at the 2d power level, 2d Wounds at the 4d power level). Weaker creatures and non-sentient plants die instantly and noticeably wither and decay when the power is used.

Frequency: Once per day.
Manifestation: The area ravaged by the psychic blast is filled with the corpses of small creatures and insects. Those still alive after the blast appear unhealthy and withered until they recover.

Density Control, Others (4d)

This power allows the mutant to alter the density of other beings, by telekinetically expanding or compressing the atomic structure of their bodies. An unwilling target may defend with an opposed Constitution (Fortitude) roll against the mutation's power level to avoid the effects entirely. There are two ways to use this power:

☣ *Compression*: The mutant compresses the target's body, shrinking it to half normal size but hardening the flesh and providing Armor 2 (see Chapter Six, Armor and Chapter Seven, Damage for more information on such protection). Base movement is reduced by 5 feet, and a –2d penalty is imposed for any swimming-based actions.

☣ *Expansion*: The mutant can expand the target's body, doubling in height. The target's base movement is increased by 5 feet, and she gains an additional reach of 5 feet; however, the target suffers a –2d penalty to Brawn-based actions. The expanded mutant is also more buoyant, and she can walk on water if not weighed down by too much gear (referee's discretion).

Frequency: Up to three times per day, each use lasting for a number of minutes equal to the Discipline (Concentration) trait of the mutant using the power.
Manifestation: This power is not detectable until used.

Devolution (4d)

Through processes not clearly understood, the mutant temporarily reverses changes to a target's genetic makeup, removing mutations and reverting the target closer to an ancestral form. The power requires physical contact, necessitating a touch attack for a non-willing target. If the target is a mutant (human, animal, or plant) and fails his check, he loses access to his most powerful mutation. If the target has more than one mutation at the highest power level, one is selected randomly. Humans suffer a –1d penalty to all mental traits and gain a +1 penalty to all physical traits. Physical changes related to those affected by this power are determined by the referee, which may include additional game effects. The changes reverse after 1d days.

Paired Trait: Defended by a Hard Constitution (Fortitude) check.
Frequency: Once per day.
Manifestation: The loss of mental or internal mutations is not always obvious, but the loss of physical mutations is sudden and dramatic.

Direction Sense (1d)

The mutant always knows which way she is facing, even without any signs or landmarks. The mutant can always find north (the prow of the ship) by instinct. In addition, she can mentally anchor a location or a number of locations equal to Discipline (Memory) dice, and she always knows the precise direction to each of them. She can choose to forget one location to anchor another. The mutant also gain a bonus to checks and actions related to directions, avoiding getting lost, etc. equal to 1d plus the mutation power level.

Paired Trait: Discipline (Memory).

Manifestation: The mutant may feel a slight tingling, sense of warmth, or just a gut feeling that tells her when she is facing the correct direction.

Displacement (2d)

When the mutant is facing deadly danger (can survive 3 or less Wounds in further damage and still in combat, falling, suddenly exposed to lethal radiation or toxic gasses, etc.), his subconscious automatically teleports him to the nearest safe location, if such a spot exists within 300 feet. The destination need not be visible to the mutant; the mutation (and the referee) select it. The mutation only affects the mutant and items in his physical possession. Displacement works to safeguard the mutant even when unconscious and sometimes against his will. The final determination of when it activates is at the referee's discretion.

Frequency: Once every six hours.

Manifestation: None until the mutant suddenly vanishes.

Empathy (1d – 2d)

The mutant can read the emotions of one chosen target, even feelings the target wishes to conceal. The mutation is extremely useful for bargaining, manipulation, and other social situations. The mutation power level adds to any action in which the ability to understand the target's feelings and intentions come into play, as well as learn general feelings and responses (anger, pain, lust, sorrow, etc.). The alien mind of sentient plants and fungi are impossible to read, leaving them completely immune to this mutation.

Manifestation: The mutant sees the emotions of the target as colored auras that she instinctively understands as emotional states. Other than noticing how attentively the mutant is watching a target, there is no outward sign of this ability.

Fear Generation (1d – 2d)

The mutant stimulates survival reflexes in a target, often causing it to flee for a number of turns equal to the roll of the mutation power level. If the psychic attack is successful, the target retreats in the least obviously dangerous route possible—considering the mutant the largest threat. If anything blocks the target's retreat, it will fight with ferocity until it can escape.

Frequency: A number of times per day equal to the mutation power level, but only affects a single target once per day.

Paired Trait: Deception (Subterfuge), defended by Discipline (Emotional Control)

Manifestation: The fear generated by this power is primal—the flight side of the fight-or-flight reflex. There is no obvious cause for the fear perceived by the target, though the target's escape is seen by all.

Force Field Generation (2d – 4d)

This mutation allows the user to create a transparent ellipsoid barrier of protection. While active, the force field prevents the mutant from making any attacks (physical or mental) and movement is limited to half walking speed. The force field ignores Fatigue damage and can absorb up to 15 Wound damage per turn, resetting each turn it is active. If damage exceeds the protection, the mutant receives a backlash of 1d Fatigue electrical damage and the force field does not reset until the beginning of the mutant's next turn. The force field lasts for 30 seconds (10 turns), and may be maintained with a Discipline (Concentration) action for each turn after 10, with any failure ending the force field.

Frequency: A number of times per day equal to one less than the mutation power level (2d meaning once per day, 4d indicating 3 times per day) and never more than once per hour.

Manifestation: The field is a transparent bubble that flickers with energy, though if the mutant chooses, it can be colored or more visible. When the field absorbs damage or backlashes against the user, there is a loud crackling and a flash of light.

Heightened Mental Trait (2d or 4d)

The mutant receives a permanent enhancement to a mental trait equal to half the mutation power level, with the trait chosen at the time the mutation is acquired (Alertness, Discipline, Tech). For example, if a character receives heightened Discipline at the 4d power level, his trait would increase by 2d. Increases from this mutation can go beyond the normal dice pool limit of 5d, and all derived stats are modified as well.

Manifestation: Unless the mutation pushes a trait over the normal maximum, the mutant just seems smart. If the increase goes beyond normal limits, the mutant might have a distinctly alien air, drawing conclusions out of thin air and having seemingly impossible insights.

Illusion Generation (2d or 4d)

The mutant may create visible illusions (2d) or visible and audible illusions (4d) within line of sight that observers might easily believe are real. Use of the mutation counts as an action each turn it is active and allows the mutant to create an illusion in a radius of up to 5 feet times the mutation power level. Simple illusions (a stationary object) are automatically believable, while more complex ones (a specific living creature) might require a check. The illusion will be seen as real by all observers unless there is a logical reason to doubt, such as fire that does not burn or a wall one can pass through, allowing a check to disbelieve and cancel the illusion. Illusions affect robots, sentient plants, and any being with the power to see and/or hear. The illusions cannot cause physical harm. They last for up to 30 seconds (10 turns) and can be maintained longer by making a check each turn without incurring an extra action.

Frequency: Once every 12 hours.

Paired Trait: Deception (Subterfuge), maintained by Discipline (Concentration), disbelief attempts use Alertness (Awareness).

Manifestation: The mutation affects anyone who can observe its effects unless he has successfully disbelieved it.

Intuition (1d – 2d)

The mutant picks up on tiny psychic clues that allow him to sense enemy actions before they begin. The mutation power level applies as a bonus to all defensive actions to avoid conscious attacks and to any checks to avoid surprise, ambush, etc. It does not apply to any offensive actions, mechanical traps, or the attacks of artificial life (robots, armed computer systems, etc.).

Manifestation: The mutant's ability to know exactly when to step, duck, or dodge quickly exceeds anything that can be explained by simple training, especially when attacks come from behind or from hidden foes.

Levitation (2d)

The mutant may float slowly, ascending or descending at half normal speed with no forward or backward movement. There is no limit to the duration of levitation, but if the mutant takes any damage, she must succeed a Discipline (Concentration) check or fall. This mutation may also be used as a reaction to an unexpected fall, requiring an Alertness (Responsiveness) check to activate in time.

Manifestation: There is no obvious manifestation until the power is activated.

Special: If the mutant has the power of flight through stock (a bird-based mutant animal, for instance) or another mutation (New Body Part: Wings), the mutation power level can be added to actions related to ascending quickly.

Magnetic Control (2d or 4d)

This mutation allows a character to move or manipulate metal objects within 100 feet and in line of sight. At the 2d power level, the mutant may only focus on one object at a time and uses Discipline (Concentration) in place of Brawn or Dexterity in terms of controlling the object in question, which must be large enough to be easily visible yet have a total mass no more than twice the mutant's own. At the 4d power level, the mutant may either split between two metal objects as described or one object up to four times the mutant's own mass. A mutant with this ability may also damage a robot or cyborg as if performing an unarmed attack, one that cannot be dodged or defended against, using the mutation power level as the trait.

Paired Trait: Discipline (Concentration).

Manifestation: The powerful magnetic fields this mutant generates when using his power can sometimes be felt and might cause mild headaches or dizzy spells to those nearby. Sometimes the mutant's power is visible, appearing as lines of force that stretch to the objects he controls.

Mental Blast (1d – 4d)

The mutant attacks a target within line of sight with a blast of psychic energy, attacking with the mutation power level and is automatically defended if the target is aware of the attacker. Bonus damage is half the mutation power level (rounded down) as Wounds of psychic damage. For example, at the 3d level, this mutation would grant a 3d dice pool on the attack action with +1W psychic damage if successful; at 4d level, it would be a 4d dice pool and +2W as the bonus damage. Enhancements on such an attack often stun or otherwise mentally incapacitate a target.

Paired Trait: Defended by Discipline (Mental Resistance)

Frequency: Once every 5 turns (15 seconds).

Manifestation: This power usually appears as a visible bolt of psychic energy with the specific color, shape, and form determined by the mutant's subconscious preferences.

Mental Control (4d)

This powerful ability allows the mutant to completely control a living creature's body. The mutation is activated by focusing on a target within 50 feet and in line of sight, attacking with mutation power level. If the attack is successful, the mutant is in full control of the the target and unlimited by range—using the target's traits for physical actions but the mutant's own traits for all other types of actions. While controlling a target, the mutant's own body is vulnerable, able to perform only the most basic functions and speak slowly and deliberately. All other actions are performed at 1d trait levels, and the mutant is unable to use any other mutations or abilities until mental control of the target is released.

The target may attempt to regain control of his body once per hour or any time he suffers Wound damage, re-rolling the results of the initial attack.

Paired Trait: Defended by Discipline (Mental Resistance).

Manifestation: The mutant doesn't gain access to the victim's memories or knowledge, so it might be obvious to people who know her that she's being controlled. Anyone who contacts the victim telepathically will immediately know of the control.

Mental Defense Shield (1d – 4d)

The mutant possesses an internal resistance to mental attacks and psychic damage. The mutation power level adds to defense rolls against any mental mutations or mentally-based tech. A mental defense shield also acts as armor against psychic damage equal to the mutation power level (see Chapter Six).

Manifestation: An attacker with mental mutations will sense the presence of the defense shield, but it otherwise goes unnoticed and may be outside of the mutant's own knowledge.

Mental Invisibility (2d – 4d)

Not true invisibility, the mutant clouds the minds of observers and redirects their attention elsewhere. For 15 seconds (5 turns) per die of the mutation power level (4d indicating 1 minute, or 20 turns) the power allows the user to be undetectable to anyone not actively looking. If someone is actively searching the area (a guard or someone searching for the mutant), he may add the mutation power level to other stealth measures, and the difficulty is automatically Hard for those searching. This mutation affects artificial intelligence but not simple detection traps (motion control or a trip-wire with a bell attached). Mental means of detection ignore this power, but physical means (sonar, smell, etc.) are affected, as bodies receive the data but the minds ignore it.

Frequency: Once every 12 hours.

Manifestation: To anyone unaffected, the mutant is fully visible while those nearby look through, around, or otherwise ignore him.

Mental Paralysis (4d)

By overpowering the will of a living target, the mutant temporarily disconnects conscious motor functions to one target up to 50 feet away. If the attack is successful, the target may not move or take physical actions for 30 seconds (10 turns) per die of the mutation power level, after which the power may be maintained by a Discipline (Concentration) action each turn. If the target takes Wound damage, she may repeat the initial opposed roll to attempt to break free.

Paired Trait: Leadership (Command), defended by Discipline (Mental Resistance).

Manifestation: The mutation requires a small amount of focus and concentration; a keen observer might notice the mutant staring intently at the target.

Mental Reflection (1d – 4d)

Instead of defending against a mental attack normally, the mutant uses this ability to potentially deflect the power and use it against the attacker. Add the mutation power level to defense against the mental attack, and if succesfully defended the attack reflects back—forcing the attacker to suffer the attack as it had been rolled against him in the first place.

Manifestation: Any visible effect which accompanied the attack will likewise accompany the return volley.

Molecular Disruption (1d – 4d)

A truly terrifying power, this enables the mutant to disrupt the bonds holding matter together. Roughly one half-pound of dense matter is affected per die of the mutation power level. If the attack roll is successful, bonus damage is rolled using the mutation power level and is expressed in Wounds. Use of this power is highly taxing, and the mutant suffers an equal amount of Fatigue damage based on the roll for damage. The mutant may lower the dice rolled for damage if he chooses.

Paired Trait: Alertness (Observation), defended by Constitution (Fortitude).

Frequency: Once every 12 hours.

Manifestation: A destroyed object explodes in a cloud of dust; a living being dissolves into a wet mist. Larger objects and strong living creatures will exhibit obvious damage or horrible wounds, but there is no obvious connection to the mutant other than a brief, intense gaze.

Precognition (2d)

This ability offers a glimpse into a possible future. With difficulty based on how many variables might affect the outcome, the mutant concentrates for a full turn (no other actions), silently stating an intention, then rolls the mutation power level as an Easy action. Each additional achievement over the first indicates a clearer picture of what may lie ahead. The intention must be clearly defined ("I intend to enter that door" not "I intend to look around this area") in order to receive a vision. Going through a door might show a vision of an ursoid leaping from the shadows and attacking. The vision is based on what would happen if the power was not invoked, never includes any foreknowledge, and is only a possible future, not a certainty. The referee may simply describe the vision to the player, or it may be played out as if it were reality and require additional action rolls.

Frequency: Once every two hours.

Manifestation: The character gets small glimpses of a second or two ahead without being fully aware of it. She may reach for a cup an instant before it is knocked over, or she may answer a question before someone asks it.

Pyrokinesis (1d – 4d)

The mutant agitates molecules to the point of generating noticeable, even damaging heat. The target can be an object or creature within 50 feet or line of sight. On the first turn, the object is noticeably warmer than surrounding environmental temperature. After that point, the heat is increased each turn until it reaches a maximum level equal to the mutation power level—1d indicating uncomfortable heat, 2d scalding or blistering heat, 3d the heat of open flame, and 4d the white-hot of molten metal. Objects will react and suffer damage accordingly. Living creatures automatically defend against the attack, but they will take +1 Wounds bonus fire damage equivalent to the current "level" of the power each turn the attack is maintained if it's successful. The power can be maintained at maximum level as long as the mutant continues to make an action each turn and can still observe the target.

Frequency: Once every 6 hours.

Paired Trait: Alertness (Observation), defended by Constitution (Fortitude).

Manifestation: There is no outward sign of this power other than the mutant's concentration and the effects on the target. Any observation that detects heat signatures and temperature might notice a strange field that radiates from the mutant to the target, as well as the unexplained spike in temperature.

Psionic Healing (2d or 4d)

The mutant may use psionic energy to heal his body at a fantastically accelerated rate as well as to overcome pain and fatigue. After one hour of rest and meditation, the mutant heals as if he had rested a full day and heals additional Wound damage (a dice pool equal to half the mutation power level). He may use the ability to cleanse his body of a toxin with a full turn of concentration using the mutation power level as the dice pool of the action (difficulty determined by the referee based on the strength of the toxin). At the 4d level, the mutant may also heal 1d Wounds as a second wind action (see Chapter Seven, Restoring Fatigue and Trauma).

Frequency: Once every 8 hours.

Manifestation: The concentration of the mutant and results of his healing are visually obvious.

Repulsion Field Generation (4d)

Similar to force field generation, the mutant creates a bubble of transparent energy up to 10 feet in diameter that materializes around a target up to 50 feet away and within line of sight. The bubble both protects and traps the target inside, allowing the mutant to move the target with the bubble. The repulsion field lasts for 30 seconds (10 turns) and may be maintained afterward with a check each turn, with any failure ending the repulsion field. The field can be moved up to 15 feet per turn while active if the total weight is 100 pounds per die of the mutation power level or less. The repulsion field ignores Fatigue damage, can absorb up to 15 Wound damage per turn, and resets each turn it is active. If damage exceeds the protection, the mutant receives a backlash of 1d Fatigue electrical damage, and the repulsion field ends. The field does not block mental attacks.

Frequency: Once every 12 hours.

Paired Trait: Discipline (Concentration) to maintain.

Manifestation: The field is a transparent bubble flickering with energy, though it can be colored or more visible at the mutant's discretion. When the field absorbs damage or backlashes against the mutant, there is a loud crackling and a flash of energy.

Stunning Blast (2d – 4d)

The mutant releases a burst of mental energy in a 50-foot radius that affects all living beings (computers, robots, and other artificial intelligence are immune). Each target must succeed a check (Easy at the 2d mutation power level, Average at 3d, and Hard at 4d) or take 1d Fatigue psychic damage and are stunned for a number of turns equal to the mutation power level.

Paired Traits: Defended by a Discipline (Mental Resistance) check.

Frequency: Once every six hours.

Manifestation: The mutation may manifest as a psychic scream, psionic static, or a similar effect.

Symbiotic Control (4d)

By making physical contact a mutant might establish physical control of a living target—making it essentially a puppet. Once physical contact has been made, the mutant asserts dominance using a mental attack. If successful, the mutant may dictate the physical and combat actions of the target until physical contact is broken—something that must be voluntary on the part of the mutant or the result of a Hard action to separate the two. The mutant uses one action per turn to maintain control, but she cannot read the target's mind nor force it to use actions using other types of traits. The target may resist by repeating the original roll every 5 minutes or if ordered to take an obviously self-destructive action.

Paired Trait: Leadership (Command), defended by Discipline (Mental Resistance).

Manifestation: The mutant's extremities may contain partially-hidden organs which become probing nerve tendrils tipped with lamprey-like mouths or some similar physical trace of their power. It's also extremely obvious when the power is being used; attempting to disguise it and still maintain constant contact will require a successful Deception (Disguise) action.

Telekinesis (1d – 4d)

Sheer mental force allows the mutant to physically manipulate a single target (living or inert) from a distance. The mutant may not target himself. The manipulated mass is equivalent to 1d plus the mutation power level as if it were the Brawn trait but from up to 300 feet away and within line of sight. Only actions applicable to the Brawn trait can be used with telekinesis, as finer manipulation of objects (such as pulling the trigger on a gun) are not possible. Actions against unwilling targets are opposed and resolved accordingly. The power cannot be used to directly assault a target, though it could be smashed into a wall or another object to cause damage.

Frequency: At will, though if the mutant uses it more than once every two hours he becomes Weary (see Chapter Seven, Conditions) as if he had gone 24 hours without sleep.

Manifestation: There are sometimes visible lines of force which show telekinetic manipulation. The mutation may manifest as ghostly hands lifting and moving object or similar odd effects. Rarely does the mutation show no outward signs other than the results of the telekinesis itself.

Telekinetic Claw (2d)

The mutant may generate a telekinetic attack that is very similar to a claw or talon. It may be used on any target within 30 feet and line of sight. A successful attack has +1 Wounds bonus damage and leaves injuries as if a large claw had slashed at the target.

Frequency: Once per turn.

Paired Trait: Alertness (Awareness), defended as normal against physical attacks.

Manifestation: The mutant decides what form the claw takes. It may resemble an animal's talon, a small cutting weapon, a ball of sharp spikes, or anything else of similar size.

Telekinetic Flight (4d)

The mutant gains the power of flight through pure mental effort. She may move her normal speed in any direction (and may increase movement normally as if on the ground), with special maneuvers and complicated stunts resolved with Dexterity and appropriate specialties. If the character is Injured (more than half total wounds suffered), she must succeed a Discipline (Emotional Control) check or fall—which also happens if the mutant is stunned or knocked unconscious during flight.

Frequency: At will, though if the mutant uses it more than an hour every 8 hours she becomes Weary (see Chapter Seven, Conditions) as if she had gone 24 hours without sleep.

Manifestation: The flight is obvious. The mutant might radiate a glowing aura or manifest partially-transparent wings. Some mutants with this ability show no other sign than the flight itself.

Telekinetic Hand (1d)

The mutant creates a mentally-projected appendage within 50 feet that may be used to manipulate small objects. It may push buttons, carry small objects, pull triggers, etc. This projection uses the mutant's own traits as if he were using his own hand, but any Brawn-based actions use the mutation power level. The hand is destroyed if it suffers any Wound damage, and the mutant suffers 1d Fatigue psychic damage.

Frequency: At will, though if a telekinetic hand is destroyed, the mutant cannot create another for 24 hours.

Manifestation: The psychic hand appears as a translucent replica of the character's normal hand or appendage.

Telepathy (4d)

The mutant is able to both send and receive thoughts within a range of 100 feet. The mutant is automatically aware of any sentient living creature's presence within range, unless somehow concealed from psychic detection. The simplest active use of this power is to act as a relay, allowing willing allies (up to as many as the mutation power level) to communicate wordlessly between each other. The mutant may also detect the surface thoughts of a target, which can be done without a check unless the target is actively attempting to shield her thoughts, requiring a successful psychic attack. Probing for memories is a complex action with a 1 turn increment and is automatically resisted by the target. A botch when using telepathy results in 1d Fatigue of psychic damage for the mutant.

Paired Trait: Alertness (Awareness), defended by Discipline (Mental Resistance).

Manifestation: Telepathy rarely has a visible manifestation. Anyone who is aware of telepathic contact will feel a buzzing or other unwelcome sound or sensation in her mind.

Teleport Object (2d)

By focusing on an object within 100 feet and line of sight exclusively for one turn, the mutant may teleport an object with a mass less than 10 pounds per die of the mutation power level to any other open space within that range. If the object is being actively held by a living creature, a mental attack is necessary to successfully use the power.

Frequency: Once per hour.

Paired Trait: Alertness (Observation), defended by Discipline (Concentration).

Manifestation: The most common manifestation of this power is a brief colored flare which appears around the target object and mutant.

Teleportation (4d)

This mutation allows its user to physically vanish from one space and instantly reappear in another. He may teleport freely to any open space within line of sight, taking any gear he is wearing or carrying. The mutant may also teleport to any other location he can visualize very clearly—either a very familiar place or requiring a Discipline (Memory) check. Using the mutation correctly is taxing, causing 1d Fatigue psychic damage; a failed memory teleportation causes both Fatigue damage and 1d Wound damage, leaving the mutant stunned for 1d turns (see Chapter Seven, Conditions) and unable to use the mutation again for 24 hours.

Frequency: Once every 8 hours.

Manifestation: Teleporting may be a quick vanishing and rush of air, a fade-out and fade-in, or the creation of a portal through which the mutant may step.

Thought Imitation (1d – 4d)

The mutant is able to remember and duplicate a damage-causing mental mutation used against it. The mutant may copy the ability regardless of whether the attack was successful or not. The mutation must be copied within one minute of being attacked. The power is identical to what was used, although functioning at the mutation power level of the Thought Imitation, and is under the same limitations. The mutant may choose to forget one mutation in order to copy another.

Frequency: At will, though only one copy may be maintained at a time. The memory fades after 24 hours.

Manifestation: A copied mutation manifests identically as it was originally used.

Will Force (2d or 4d)

The mutant can channel her force of will into physical energy. She may voluntarily reduce Alertness or Discipline by 2 or 4 dice and increase one physical or combat trait (Athletics, Brawn, Constitution, Dexterity, Melee Weapons, Ranged Weapon, Unarmed Combat) by half the number of dice sacrificed. The mental trait may not be reduced below 1d, but the enhanced physical trait may go beyond the normal 5-dice limit.

Frequency: Once every six hours with each use of the mutation lasting no more than one hour or ended voluntarily before that time.

Manifestation: After a moment's concentration, the mutant becomes noticeably more powerful in the chosen area while seeming somehow distracted or otherwise less mentally acute.

MENTAL DEFECTS

Psychic energy and scrambled brains don't always result in beneficial abilities, and it should come as no surprise that there is often a serious downside. Some mental defects present in ways similar to brain damage or serious psychological problems, while others are psychic powers working against the mutant's best interests.

Boomerang (4d)

The mutant's psychic energy center has grown so strong that it pulls failed mental attacks back in a harmful fashion. If the mutant fails a mental attack, it will rebound, causing her to roll defense as if the attack had been made against her in the first place. The referee determines choice-based repercussions based on the attacker's intentions for the original target.

Manifestation: The mutant is likely to utter a short expletive when the target of her power resists or avoids the attack, followed by a short scream of pain.

Mental Block (2d)

The mutant exhibits a complete inability to perceive a single type of entity—category of animal, plant, or class of robot. (Examples: Wolfoid, mutant kudzu, maintenance robot.) The mental block is so pervasive that the mutant cannot even conceive of the notion of such a being, and he cannot detect one by any physical sense or psychic ability. Interactions and even damage from the blocked entity are rationalized away or come as total surprise. To the mentally-blocked mutant, companions interacting or fighting the listed entity seem to be hallucinating or otherwise acting bizarrely.

Manifestation: None other than the strange behavior caused by this defect.

Special: Humans and mutated humans are not normally included in this defect due to how common they are aboard the *Warden*, but if chosen, they represent a 4d-level mental defect.

Multiplied Damage (2d or 4d)

The mutant's mind is hypersensitive to pain and disruption, and it magnifies the impact of damage. Either mental or physical damage is chosen at random or by the referee when this defect is acquired. Each turn the multiplied damage type is suffered by the mutant, she rolls half the number of dice of the mutation power level to determine additional Fatigue damage. Additional damage suffered on the same turn does not cause multiplied damage.

Manifestation: The mutant appears to be a complete wimp to physical pain or otherwise prone to constant headaches with occasional nosebleeds. The mutant tends to shy away from the type of damage to which she is sensitive.

Phobia (1d – 2d)

An irrational, subconscious fear of something makes the mutant's life more difficult. The mutant must make a check anytime he encounters the object of his fear. Otherwise, he tries to get away from it by any means necessary or becomes unable to take any constructive action. The check covers one minute (20 turns) of time before it must be repeated, and even if successful, the mutant suffers a die penalty to actions equal to the mutation power level. The referee determines or approves the type of phobia, which can include creatures (spiders, wolfoids, robots), situations (crowds, rain), objects (blood, guns), or even abstractions (darkness, a particular color). A phobia shouldn't be something the mutant would encounter in his everyday

life, but also it is not so rare that he would never expect it to become an issue at all. Something more common might justify a higher die level.

Paired Trait: Discipline (Emotional Control).
Manifestation: Only the mutant's reactions reveal the existence of this defect.

Stress-Induced Amnesia (2d)

High-stress situations such as combat often cause the mutant to experience short-term amnesia. In these situations, the mutant must succeed a check or be stunned for one turn and lose all memory of the last 3d hours. The difficulty of the check is determined by the referee based on the amount of danger or stress the mutant is facing. The mutant's ability to identify locations, enemies, and even allies is forgotten, and she acts accordingly.

Paired Trait: Discipline (Emotional Control).
Manifestation: There are no obvious signs of this defect other than the mutant's strange reactions or admissions under pressure. The mutant might develop habits, such as writing in a journal, to help offset this condition.

Weakened Mental Defenses (1d – 4d)

The mutant's mental defenses do not function properly, causing him to suffer a die penalty to all mental defense rolls equal to the mutation power level—sometimes leaving the mutant completely vulnerable to such attacks.

Manifestation: Attackers will recognize the weakness, as will anyone with telepathic abilities.

PLANT MUTATIONS

The physiology of a plant is different enough from animal life that it lends itself to some unique mutations—just another perk for being able to metabolise light and water into energy.

Berries (1d – 4d)

Each day, the mutant plant grows 1d large berries, whose properties vary depending on the mutation power level. The plant can choose the next day's variety equivalent to the mutation power level or lower. The berries benefit any animal-based creature, human or otherwise, that consumes them and they take effect one minute (20 turns) after consumption. Only one berry of any kind can benefit a recipient per day.

☣ *Mental Enhancing* (1d): For one hour after taking effect, the beneficiary receives a +1d bonus to all actions making use of mental traits (Alertness, Discipline, Tech).

☣ *Physical Enhancing* (1d): For one hour after taking effect, the beneficiary receives a +1d bonus to all actions making use of physical traits (Brawn, Constitution, Athletics, and Stealth).

☣ *Battle Enhancing* (2d): For one hour after taking effect, the beneficiary receives a +1d bonus to all actions making use of combat traits (Melee Weapons, Ranged Weapons, Unarmed Combat).

☣ *Invigorating* (3d): The berries relieve exhaustion and heal bruises and scrapes. 1d Fatigue damage is healed.

☣ *Healing* (4d): The berries stop bleeding, close wounds, and repair internal injuries. 1d Wound damage is healed.

Frequency: Each day, any previous berries lose their potency and visibly shrivel, eventually falling off as a new cluster of berries grows in their place.

Manifestation: The berries grow in appropriate places on the mutant plant, sometimes invoking snickering and jokes among its companions that it will never understand.

Cones (2d or 4d)

Each day, the mutant plant grows 1d cones roughly the size of a human fist, whose properties vary depending on the mutation power level. The plant can choose the next day's variety equivalent to the mutation power level or lower. The cones can be detached by the mutant plant or by an ally. Cones can be unwillingly taken from a mutant plant, requiring an opposed Brawn check. A cone loses potency after one minute (20 turns) once it is detached. Each cone may be thrown up to 30 feet.

☣ *Stun Spores* (2d): The cone erupts with tiny spores in a radius of 10 feet from the point of impact. Every breathing creature within the area takes 1d Fatigue damage. If a potential victim knows to hold his breath, he can reduce the effects with an Alertness (Responsiveness) reaction, with each achievement lowering the damage by 1 (minimum 1 damage taken).

☣ *Explosive* (4d): The cone explodes in a ball of fire with a radius of 10 feet from the point of impact. Each creature within the area takes 1d Wound fire damage. If a potential victim knows to avoid the oncoming explosion, he may reduce the damage by making a Dexterity (Dodging) reaction, with each achievement lowering the damage by 1 (minimum 1 damage taken).

Frequency: Each day, any previous cones lose their potency and drop off as new cones grows in place of the old.

Manifestation: The cones grow randomly along the mutant plant's body, but never in such a way as to impede its senses or movement.

Hardened Bark (2d or 4d)

The exterior layer of the mutant plant is hardened to the point of offering increased protection. At the 2d mutation power level, the hardened bark is stiff and leathery, offering Armor 1 protection. At the 4d power level, the bark is as hard as metallic plating that provides Armor 2 protection. (See Chapter Six, Armor and Chapter Seven, Damage for more information on such protection.)

Manifestation: The protection grows out of the plant's body and looks natural.

Plantspeak (1d)

The mutant plant has developed a means of generating modulated sound approximating human speech. The mutant plant is able to verbally communicate.

Manifestation: The mutant plant may develop a crude mouth and approximate vocal cords, or it may generate the speech by grinding together bark in a specific way. To human ears, the speech will sound strange and possess an odd rhythm.

Thorns (1d, 3d, or 4d)

Sharp thorns protrude from the mutant plant's extremities, ensuring it is never unarmed. The thorns can be used in combat with a +1W bonus damage. At the 3d power level, up to 8 thorns per day may be hurled up to 15 feet. At the 4d level, the thorns also contain an injected neurotoxin, requiring any opponent who takes Wound damage on a thorn attack to succeed an Average Constitution (Fortitude) check to avoid its effects (see Chapter Seven, Specialized Damage, Toxins).

Paired Trait: Melee Weapons for personal combat. Ranged Weapons for hurled thorns.

Manifestation: The thorns are large, sharp, and easily visible. Venomous thorns are literally dripping with poison.

Vines (2d or 4d)

The mutant plant sports vines which grant a 10-foot reach and the ability to manipulate objects with natural strength and the precision of human hands. They aren't dense enough to make unarmed strike attacks, but they can be used to grapple an opponent at a distance. At the 4d level, the vines secrete a paralytic contact poison, requiring a successfully grappled target to succeed an Average Constitution (Fortitude) check to avoid its effects (see Chapter Seven, Specialized Damage, Toxins).

Paired Trait: Brawn (Grappling) when used to hold an opponent.

Manifestation: The vines generally match the structure and appearance of the plant to make it look like natural growth. Poisonous vines ooze a sticky sap-like substance.

PLANT DEFECTS

While some plant mutations can be highly beneficial—including the potential for throwing exploding pine cones—some demonstrate distinct disadvantages, often related to a normal plant's very means of survival.

Attraction Odor (2d – 4d)

The mutant plant emits a powerful pheromone that attracts creatures of lower intelligence. The reach of this defect is 250 feet per die of the mutation power (meaning 500 feet at the 2d level, for example). Depending on the psychology of those attracted, the character might smell like food, a mate, a rival, or a threat—but he is a target one way or another. Any group with such a mutant has an increased likelihood of being attacked by local wildlife. In combat situations, given a choice, animals and sentient plants will attack the mutant with this defect first. Intelligent creatures are not overwhelmed by this scent, but the mutant suffers a –1d penalty to all social traits. Artificial life is not affected by this defect.

Manifestation: The odor itself is the manifestation; the mutant plant might smell like well-done steak to a carnivore or lush flowers to a nectar-sucking insect.

Photodependent (4d)

A lack of light makes it difficult for the mutant plant to function. In dim light, the character suffers a –1d penalty on all actions using mental and physical traits. In total darkness, the character must succeed an Average Discipline check to make any actions (though reactions are unaffected). Others might have to drag the character through the darkness.

Manifestation: The mutant plant's reaction to any drop in ambient lighting is usually obvious (wilting, sluggish movement, etc.).

Water Dependent (2d)

The mutant plant has internal systems highly dependent on moisture, multiplying its water requirements. It must be exposed to a source of water at least once every 8 hours or become Starving (see Chapter Seven, Conditions), with additional penalties occurring every two hours thereafter.

Manifestation: The mutant plant is generally focused on meeting its water needs and easily distracted from other goals when a source of water is found.

Built to transport the future of an entire world, the *Warden* is filled with vast storage sheds and warehouses of equipment. Some was scattered, ruined, misused, or lost while much remains locked away, waiting for anyone smart or lucky enough to find it.

In Metamorphosis Alpha, equipment is crucial to survival. Finding out how to use a device can mean the difference between life and death for characters. Each new piece of gear represents a challenge, opportunity, or potential danger. Identifying tech and figuring out its proper use is the difference between recovering an enemy-crushing weapon and melting your face off.

This chapter deals with gear of all kinds—from the most mundane tool or weapon to a technological relic that must be understood before it can be safely used. The descriptions of items offered here not only describe the function of the equipment but offers the players and referee inspiration for more.

The tech aboard the *Warden* isn't just sitting around. There are facilities and robots capable of repairing, recharging, or even building items as needed by those capable of issuing proper instructions. The items listed in this chapter only scratch the surface of the possibilities that exist among the ship's many decks.

ECONOMY ON THE WARDEN

A holdover from a dimly-remembered time, there is a unit of currency known as the **domar**. Once it was used as a centerpiece for a simulated economy aboard the ship; values placed on goods and services established levels of scarcity and rewarded those aboard for hard work and needed expertise.

While the real value of domars is now questionable at any given moment, the cultural memory has lingered in these more savage and primitive times—bolstered by the fact that some computer and robotic systems still accept them as a means of exchange. Thus some individuals and tribes place high value on domars, while others ignore them entirely.

Physically, the domar is a small rectangular card made of nearly indestructible plastic, bearing the hologram of a human face identifying them as some past figure of importance, such as Arneson, Gygax, or Ward. The domars come in different colors, depending upon denomination.

6.1 - Currency

Denomination	Color
1 domar	Red
5 domars	Orange
10 domars	Yellow
20 domars	Green
50 domars	Blue
100 domars	Indigo
1,000 domars	Violet

The true value of hoarded domars comes to light when encountering artificial intelligence that is programmed to sell valuable resources or tech for the correct price. Suddenly, the bits of plastic left behind last week as so much junk could be worth a perfectly-functioning disruptor pistol or a near-unlimited supply of food. They could allow for the rental of a security robot for personal protection or a comfortable and safe place to sleep. Just hope that you aren't misidentified as a former colonist deeply in debt or your stash could be seized against bills that were never paid (and never will be, thanks to centuries of accumulated interest).

For most aboard the *Warden*, there is only a primitive economy at best, barter being the primary method of trade. Interactions become more sophisticated among some human and mutated human tribes that still use the domar system out of cultural habit and have enough currency for the system to work.

Being a savvy trader is a combination of having what the other party needs and excellent haggling skills. Almost anything can be traded, from the most mundane staples to the most unsavory forms of service. And in such a violent world, it pays to be able to protect your property with claw, fist, or laser rifle.

GEARING UP

Characters don't usually have more than the clothes on their backs when they begin a Metamorphosis Alpha campaign—with a reminder that clothes aren't always worn and mutants may not even have a back. While other games possess concrete and carefully balanced rules that allow starting characters to purchase equipment, adventuring on the *Warden* can start in so many varied ways that the following are only guidelines. The ultimate decisions are left to the referee.

Adventures aboard the *Warden* are often about scarcity punctuated by sudden windfalls of resources and opportunity, which in turn make the newly-wealthy characters targets for anyone with reason to covet the discovered treasure.

Characters who begin their career as primitives (be they human or mutants) generally have the following:

- ☣ **A basic weapon** (knife, club, or bow)
- ☣ **Rudimentary protection** (clothing or simple armor if they don't have a protective mutation)
- ☣ **Survival gear and tradable resources** (food, tools, a few domars)

Human characters usually start the game with one tech item, chosen by the referee or rolled.

6.2 - Human Starting Tech

1d	Gear
1	Doctor's Bag
2	Color Band (Red)
3	Yellow
4	Metasystem Goggles
5	Vibroblade (Knife)
6	Laser Pistol

Technology can easily lead to overconfidence, as powerful weapons or extremely potent items can make previously difficult challenges seem like a breeze. But nothing is more temporary than a piece of tech, as it can run out of energy, malfunction, break, or be taken away. The feast-or-famine cycle is all part of the fun!

Getting Weighed Down

You never know what you might need, so it's tempting to take everything and the kitchen sink (assuming you can find a kitchen and tear the sink out of the wall). The problem with such an approach is that it's exhausting to haul so much stuff around all day. You won't perform at your best, and you'll tire more quickly.

Characters may carry 20 pounds of gear for each of their Brawn dice without any problems, the totals reflected on Table 6.3 for easy reference.

Ignoring Encumbrance

The style of adventure aboard the *Warden* is fast-paced action filled with surprises, which doesn't always fit with tracking weight carried along with the math to figure out how much gear a character has slung over his mandibles. Some referees choose to not worry about carrying capacity, and instead just use a common-sense approach to determine how much a three-eyed human or shambling cactus might haul around. If this is the case in your game, enjoy one less thing to worry about but don't abuse the privilege. If you have a club, a knife, two swords, a pistol, two alternate armor types, and a portable kitchen set, you might get slapped with arbitrary penalties, and you'll deserve them.

Carrying capacity is not a reflection of the maximum weight possible, just what can be hauled around without impeding the character. When carrying beyond normal capacity up to twice that weight, the character is **burdened** and suffers a –1d penalty to all physical actions. If continued for more than an hour without rest, the character becomes **weary** and incurs an additional penalty (see Chapter Seven, Conditions). A character may carry up to three times the normal amount to be considered **encumbered**, with a –2d penalty to physical actions and becoming weary after only 15 minutes. A character may spend an action point to ignore those penalties for one hour, but carrying beyond three times the base weight is not allowed.

STYLE VS. SUBSTANCE

The descriptions in this chapter are relatively straightforward, offering the information about an object's function in the game and any necessary rules. It's up to the players and referee to provide the context and description to make the insane world of the *Warden* come to life.

6.3 - Carrying Capacity

Brawn	Normal	Burdened (−1d)	Encumbered (−2d)
1d	20 lb.	40 lb.	60 lb.
2d	40 lb.	80 lb.	120 lb.
3d	60 lb.	120 lb.	180 lb.
4d	80 lb.	160 lb.	240 lb.
5d	100 lb.	200 lb.	300 lb.
6d	120 lb.	240 lb.	360 lb.

Much of the "primitive" equipment used each day by tribal humans and mutants is actually repurposed objects that were once used quite differently. An axe used in combat may have been cobbled together from the handle of an airlock and a sharpened metal plate from a defunct robot—secured with a section of power transfer cable. A shield might be a directional sign ripped from its post.

It's highly encouraged that players give a moment to offer their most-used gear the kind of description that makes things fit the post-spaceship-apocalypse setting and give each character some memorable flair. A prized piece of jewelry might be a necklace strung with old computer chips. (Look carefully at the cover of this book!) A heavy club might be three baseball bats bound together with duct tape. A shaman's mantle of station might have once been a plaid terry cloth bathrobe. Even the most mundane details can be used to emphasize the style and personality of the setting.

UNDERSTANDING TECH

Discovering a potentially useful technological wonder is the first step. Figuring out how to use it without breaking it or leaving a smoking hole in the ground where your character once stood is the next step. The good news is that a character who has used or has been properly trained with a particular gadget will be good to go if she gets an identical piece of tech in the future.

Deciphering large or intricate technology—such as specialized computer systems, dormant robots, widget factories, or power rerouting stations—will involve complex actions or even minor adventures decided upon by the referee. But for tech that has been won on the battlefield or otherwise purchased or scavenged for the first time, there is a standard procedure for deciphering its function and use.

Tech items have a complexity level that reflects the number of achievements needed with a complex Tech trait action (see Chapter Two, Complex Actions) to successfully understand the item and use it normally. But there is danger along the road to using technology, and a difficulty based on the item's ease of use. (A straightforward weapon might be Easy to figure out, while a food synthesizer with touchscreen controls might be Hard.) The increment for figuring out tech is usually 1 minute per roll.

Once you get half the needed achievements … you get a basic understanding of the item's purpose. (For example, if it's a toaster you understand that this object makes use of heat.)

If you succeed … you understand the item without any hindrances!

If you roll three failures in a row … you've broken the item and it must be repaired by someone who has a clue what she's doing.

If you botch … not only do you break the item, but Something Bad Happens. It might melt, explode, shoot you in the face, or otherwise cause problems determined by the referee.

While an item is being examined, the referee may provide descriptions and the player may offer explanations for what she is doing to try and figure things out—possibly getting a bonus for a clever idea.

GEAR ENTRIES

Below is a template for gear entries in the game, though not every item will have the need for each category and different types vary. Note that the names listed here are those that might have once been used on the *Warden* by the trained and educated—and still might be learned by those with sufficient Tech. However, most would call a flashlight a "cold torch" or a "light stick" or some other descriptive nickname.

Item Name

Following the item's name is the main description, which includes any game information needed.

Inspection: This tells how many achievements are needed to properly understand the item's function, and how difficult the complex action is for each roll under normal circumstances. Next are a few ideas for the referee on what might go wrong if a botch is rolled during the process.

Power: If the device requires a replaceable or external power source, it's listed here along with how much use is granted by any finite power supplies.

Weight: Expressed in pounds.

Special: Any noteworthy information related to how the item might work and under what circumstances.

General Items

Miscellaneous is usually the largest category. This section is where you'll find items that aren't about protection or dealing damage. These include a large selection of tools and items both for everyday use and for specific, specialized purposes.

Note that there are hundreds (if not thousands) of items that may be found aboard the *Warden* that are not listed here. Mundane items such as backpacks or water bottles are around to be scavenged or even re-created by those with the necessary skills. Only items that require explanation or require game rules are listed here.

Acid

Once used for many operations aboard the ship, acid is stored in 18-inch tall bright red canisters marked with a yellow skull. While it can (and should!) be used for noncombat actions, it can be sprayed up to 5 feet away and up to a 10-foot wide arc for a single discharge. When spraying in a wide arc targets are generally Easy to hit, and the caustic acid inflicts bonus damage of 2d Wounds on metal targets, or 1d Wounds on all other types. Each canister holds 25 sprays, with no normal means to refill.

Inspection: 6 (Easy) Mishaps include accidental discharge on self or an ally, or causing the canister to detonate and spray acid in a 20-foot radius.

Weight: 8 lb.

A.I. Disabler

Designed to deactivate robotic units without damaging the hardware, this small handheld device can be used on any computer-based system within 10 feet. Robots take 2d Fatigue and are Stunned for 1d turns, while other artificial life suffers similar effects as determined by the referee.

Inspection: 4 (Average) Mishaps include local artificial intelligence going haywire or an electrical surge that inflicts 1d Fatigue damage to a nearby character.

Power: Small Hydrogen Power Cell (10 uses)

Weight: 0.5 lb.

Android Sticky Flesh

Designed as a non-violent method to subdue dangerous animals, this device is a 36-inch tall cylinder that is set on the ground or floor. It lasts for up three full days on a single charge. It ignores humans or plants, but activates at the presence of a mutated human or mutant animal up to 100 feet away—the canister launching a glob of white goop as a 5d attack on the target. If the material hits the target it adheres and absorbs moisture from the air and grows in the space of one turn and becomes a 200-pound coiling mass of grabbing, spongy flesh, which grapples the target at 5d until it is able to break free. The sticky flesh ignores Fatigue damage and may sustain 20 Wounds before dissolving into loose red gel.

Inspection: 8 (Hard) Mishaps include accidental discharge on self or an ally, or accidentally resetting it to activate in the presence of a different variety of life.

Power: Small Hydrogen Power Cell (72 hours of dormancy), cylinder is one-use only.

Weight: 5 lb.

Aquatic Breather

Designed to fit a human-shaped face, the device will attach snugly until the release-button is depressed. The breather allows for normal breathing underwater but is useless as a gas mask or filter, and only fits over the mouth and nose—offering no protection to eyes or ears. The mask interferes with speech.

Inspection: 4 (Easy) Mishaps include the mask strapping on without being able to remove without cutting, or functioning incorrectly and causing Fatigue damage due to inhaling an unsafe air mixture.

Power: Small Hydrogen Power Cell (12 hours)

Weight: 1.5 lb.

Atomic Torch

Capable of cutting through any material, the torch has an adjustable cutting point of up to 1 to 12 inches away from its business end. Though not designed as a weapon, if used as one it inflicts 1d Wounds as bonus damage (improvised weapon penalties apply, and the wielder must be within close reach of the target).

Inspection: 4 (Easy) Mishaps include accidental discharge on self or an ally, or causing a critical overheat that melts the device into slag.

Power: Small Chemical Power Cell (5 uses, up to 5 minutes each)

Weight: 2 lb.

Autosurgeon

An artificially-intelligent device created to treat injuries, the autosurgeon is a coffin-shaped container that can hold and will respond to the presence of one humanoid that lies inside and correctly activates the device. It will use a combination of integrated instruments and nano-technology to efficiently assess and treat the occupant. Nothing happens if the occupant does not have any Wound damage. Otherwise it heals 1d Wounds, at a rate of 1 per 10 minutes of time—though the process is exhausting, causing 1d of Fatigue. The autosurgeon ignores plant life.

Creating Tech Items

Science fiction can be great inspiration for creating new tech items. A referee need only decide on game effects and how easy or hard it will be for semi-primitive characters to figure out. One way to quickly come up with fun tech is to flip through the mutations in this book (see Chapter Five), as many such abilities could be accomplished with technology.

For example, need a syringe-delivered poison? Look no farther than Poison Bite. A jet pack works very similarly to Telekinetic Flight. Sonic Blast could easily be ported into a sonic weapon. These ideas also offer human characters tech-based options to compete more evenly on a giant spaceship filled with mutants.

Inspection: 10 (Average) Mishaps include changing its settings to use incorrect procedures that injure instead of heal, or accidentally resetting it to activate in the presence of a different variety of life.

Power: Must be physically connected to a power station to function.

Weight: 400 lb.

Chemical Defoliant

Contained in a canister with a handle on top and an attached hose with a nozzle, this is a terrible poison to all plant life. Contact with the defoliant is the equivalent of a neurotoxin (see Chapter Seven, Specialized Damage). It's toxic for animal life to injest this poison, and it will cause 1d Wounds within an hour of consumption if not immediately vomited up.

Inspection: 4 (Easy) Mishaps include accidentally ingesting the chemicals or puncturing the canister and causing a small, damaging explosion that also sprays the chemicals everywhere nearby.

Power: Each canister holds enough for 25 uses.

Weight: 8 lb.

Color Band

A colored bracelet coded to radiate at a unique frequency, color bands act much like a key or security card—permitting access to otherwise restricted areas on the *Warden* and allowing certain tech to be activated. The band's color denotes areas and levels of access: blue (command), green (horticultural), red (security), brown (general, for families), gray (engineering), white (medical). Any entrance requiring clearance has a small rectangle matching the color of the band, and simply placing the band within six inches will open the door or activate the locked device.

Each band also has a built in communicator activated by twisting an area near the clasp, allowing voice contact to all other bands of the same color within a one-mile radius on the same deck. The unique signature of each band allows it to be located by computer systems, artificial intelligence, and anyone possessing the right kind of tracking device.

Inspection: 4 (Easy) Note that a band's primary function or opening doors and activating technology can only be revealed through experiment—though there is enough knowledge and rumor that an Average Tech (Tech Lore) check can at least reveal a solid guess as to their function. Mishaps include accidentally activating the communicator or breaking the tiny power supply inside, rendering the color band inert.

Weight: 0.25 lb.

Command Ring

Only four of these rings exist—one for each captain of the *Warden*—and appear as a metallic red-and-blue ring sized to fit an average human finger. They function identically to a Color Band except they have universal access to any area and all technology on the ship. They glow in alternating pulses of red and blue if within 150 feet of another command ring and may communicate with others across the entire ship on any deck.

Inspection: 4 (Easy) Note that the ring's primary function of opening doors and activating technology can only be revealed through direct experiment. Knowledge of command rings is quite rare, requiring a Hard Tech (Tech Lore) check. Mishaps include accidentally activating the communicator or breaking the tiny power supply inside, rendering the ring inert.

Weight: Inconsequential

Cryo Chamber

These huge coffin-shaped containers are designed to hold one human in suspended animation. A control panel at the base monitors the occupant and can be used to activate either a normal revival procedure (an 8-hour process) or the emergency alternative (10 minutes, but a chance of permanent physical or mental damage to the occupant). The chamber is sealed shut unless a revival procedure has been completed, as abruptly opening the chamber will kill the occupant.

Inspection: 4 (Easy) to identify; 6 (Average) to understand the revival procedures. Mishaps include putting the chamber in lockdown for 24 hours (preventing all attempts at revival) or deactivating the chamber and killing anyone inside.

Power: Must be physically connected to a power station to function.

Weight: 1,500 lb.

Note: A former crew member or colonist suffering amnesia from an emergency revival procedure is a possible origin for a human character.

Doctor's Bag

This is a collection of simple tools, bandages, and medicine designed to assist a doctor or field nurse in treating injuries. It provides a +1d bonus to most uses of the Medicine trait. It also includes a broad-spectrum antitoxin (5 doses) that will neutralize almost any poison and a canister of liquid flesh that closes and sterilizes cuts and lacerations, for up to 20 Wounds of healing (requiring 1 turn per point healed).

Inspection: 4 (Easy) Mishaps include emptying either the antitoxin or liquid flesh unintentionally, injuries mishandling the tools, or breaking the equipment to the point of uselessness.

Power: Doses of medication must be re-stocked.

Weight: 4 lb.

Duralloy

The same ultra-lightweight metal the *Warden* is constructed from, duralloy can sometimes be found (especially in engineering sections) in four-foot triangular pieces that can be clamped or welded together—though it requires specialized equipment to do so. Duralloy is nearly indestructible, and aside from being used in construction some individual pieces are made into makeshift shields for melee combat.

Inspection: 2 (Easy) Mishaps are not catastrophic, though its lightness can cause some to not realize how hard the material is and hit themselves or someone else.
Weight: 0.5 lb.

Energy Flooring

Stored as a sphere with a three-foot diameter, energy flooring unspools to cover a flat area of 900 square feet that adapts to the shape of the area (circular if open, otherwise extending down a more narrow corridor or to fit the shape of a room). The flooring can be set to activate under a specific set of conditions and can recognize the difference between human, animal, and plant life, though not individuals. It takes 10 points of Wound damage to disable the flooring (Easy to hit, but it is equivalent to Armor 4).

When the flooring activates, it delivers a shock of 2d Fatigue electrical damage. Anything receiving any damage must roll an Average Constitution (Fortitude) check to avoid being paralyzed for 1d turns—otherwise the character is stunned for an equivalent time unless he gets at least 1 enhancement. A botch means the character is unconscious instead. (See Chapter 7, Conditions more information.)

Inspection: 6 (Average) Mishaps include damaging the spooling mechanism that allows the flooring to retract and expand, or interfering with the parts that allows the flooring to be selective when administering shocks, or even delivering a spontaneous shock to whoever is holding the sphere.
Power: 100 individual small hydrogen power cells, 2 of which are spent per discharge.
Weight: 30 lb.

Engineering Kit

This kit includes sophisticated diagnostic software and integrated tools to both identify and repair physical problems with most machinery and shipboard systems. If the user understands how to properly use the kit, use of Tech for repair purposes becomes one degree easier in difficulty—meaning Hard actions become Average, Average become Easy, and Easy repair tasks are automatically successful. Note that only items programmed into its database gain this benefit, so improvised items gain no benefit.

Inspection: 8 (Average) Mishaps include causing an energy surge and draining the power cells or corrupting the database and making the kit less useful (only +1d to repair tasks for its use).
Power: 2 medium chemical batteries for up to 72 hours of use.
Weight: 3 lb.

Gas Mask

Designed to fit a human-shaped face, the device will attach snugly until the release-button is depressed, while a hood protects the head and neck. The mask filters all types of contamination from the air and offers the wearer a normal oxygen-nitrogen ratio, but will no function underwater or in a vacuum. The filter is self-cleaning as long as there is available power. Speech is slightly muffled, but otherwise a wearer may communicate normally.

Inspection: 4 (Easy) Mishaps include the mask strapping on without being able to remove without cutting, or functioning incorrectly and causing Fatigue damage due to inhaling an unsafe air mixture.
Power: Small Hydrogen Power Cell (12 hours)
Weight: 2 lb.

Goggles, Metasystem

This eyewear offers alternate modes of assisted viewing, including infrared, night vision, radiation detection, telescopic magnification (x 50), and microscopic zoom (x 1,000). This might offer any number of advantages as determined by the referee.

Inspection: 4 (Average) Mishaps accidentally locking the brightness level to zero (making the image from the goggles nothing but black), pushing the brightness level so high a wearer sees only blinding light (blind for 1d turns), or causing a short that causes the goggles to cease functioning.
Power: Small hydrogen cell (24 hours).
Weight: 1.5 lb.

Goggles, Night Vision

As long as there is even the tiniest source of ambient light (and aboard the *Warden* there almost always is) these goggles allow you to effectively see in the dark—although the images are monochrome and it's not always easy to distinguish the details. A character suffers a –1d penalty to Alertness-based actions that require observing something using night vision.

Inspection: 6 (Easy) Mishaps include accidentally locking the brightness level to zero (making the image from the goggles nothing but black), pushing the brightness level so high a wearer sees only blinding light (blind for 1d turns), or causing a short that causes the goggles to cease functioning.
Power: Small Hydrogen Power Cell (48 hours)
Weight: 1 lb.
Special: Infrared goggles function in a similar way, but instead translates the infrared spectrum. This functions identically to the Infravision mutation.

Holographic Computer Necklace

A metallic torc of adjustable size that fits around the neck, this device creates a holographic computer interface directly in front of the wearer. It may be activated by either a vocal command or twisting a specific section. The unit is wirelessly connected to the ship's computer system, allowing access to general information and commands and requiring specialized access (by either worn color band or passkey) for more sensitive parts of the structure. Note the computer system on the *Warden* is damaged and it may not respond logically to commands or requests. The voice user interface of the device imprints on the first primary user, copying voice and speech patterns and leaving a distinct impression of talking to a "ghost."

Inspection: 4 (Easy) This is only to identify how to wear and activate the device. Interacting with the computer system beyond that involves roleplaying and additional actions determined by the referee. Mishaps include causing the size adjusting matrix to shrink around the neck, potentially choking the wearer, or sending a stream of gibberish to the computer that remotely disables access to the network until repaired.

Power: The device functions on broadcast power paired with data streaming, and will function normally anywhere inside the ship.

Weight: 0.25 lb.

Identifier Rod

This 8-inch metallic rod is a simple emergency beacon, calling to artificial intelligence for help. Local systems will attempt to aid, and a nearby robot will be dispatched to assist if one is close—prepared to offer defense, medical assistance, or transportation to a user identified as human. Otherwise the identifier rod will be confiscated and deactivated.

Inspection: 4 (Easy) Mishaps include causing the device to surge and inflict 1d Fatigue or prematurely activating the device without an actual emergency, causing a summoned robot to misunderstand the situation and react inappropriately.

Power: Small Hydrogen Power Cell (30 hours).

Weight: 1 lb.

Laser Fuser

This device is designed to bind two equivalent materials together, like a welder, automatically adjusting to conform to the needs of its target. Almost any material (including metal, plastic, flesh) can be fused, though the process is slow (30 seconds per foot of material). There is no heat involved and the fusing process does not cause damage, though a living creature that tears or cuts itself from another to which it is fused to will certainly cause injury (at least 1 Wound, depending on the points of fusion and the judgment of the referee).

Inspection: 6 (Average) Mishaps include accidentally fusing items or allies together or reversing the settings so it disrupts nonliving structures and cause things to unravel and fall apart.

Power: Small Hydrogen Cell (10 hours).

Weight: 2 lb.

Liquid Flesh

Contained in a spray canister that might once have held hairstyling product in a bygone era, liquid flesh can be used as a quick way to repair wounds on any human- or animal-derived character. The liquid sprays on like loose foam but quickly seals, anesthetizes, and repairs injuries. Within a few hours it looks just like an old scar. The downside is that it only works for cuts and other surface wounds and cannot repair broken bones or internal injuries. Each "dose" heals 1d Wounds in one turn, though only one dose can be used on a character within an hour to any beneficial effect.

Inspection: 2 (Average) Mishaps include mistaking it as an edible food source (which it is, but disgusting), accidentally spraying a dose in a random direction, or accidentally puncturing the can (1d Fatigue damage to the inspector, foamy flesh everywhere).

Power: 6 doses per cannister.

Weight: 0.5 lb.

Special: Liquid flesh has no effect on plants.

Medical Analyzer & Healing Kit

Intended as a portable field kit for trained medical personnel, this unit is programmed to assist even a novice to provide first-aid treatment and even on-site surgery. If the kit's functions are properly understood, use of Medicine for most purposes becomes one degree easier in difficulty—meaning Hard actions become Average, Average become Easy, and Easy medical tasks are automatically successful. Note that only human anatomy is programmed into its database (meaning animal and plant characters will not be helped unless a variant unit designed for veterinary medicine or botany is discovered). The kit also includes anti-radiation spray (5 doses, heals 5 points of Wounds from radiation damage at a rate of 1 per hour) and stimulants that reverse exhaustion and eases pain (5 doses, heals 5 points of Fatigue in moments). The included vibroscalpel suffers improvised weapon penalty if used in melee combat (and is attached/powered by a retractable cable from the kit only up to 5 feet away) but offers a +3 Wounds damage bonus.

Inspection: 6 (Average) Mishaps include accidental injury with the vibroscalpel, breaking the device, changing the language setting to something unintelligible, or incorrectly overloading the sonic scanner to deliver 1d Fatigue damage.

Power: Two small chemical power cells for up to 24 hours of use. Doses of medication must be re-stocked.

Weight: 6 lb.

Nano-Fix Gel

Contained in an unassuming tube that should not be mistaken for toothpaste, this green gel is teeming with nanites—microscopic robotic units that work in tandem to repair damaged circuitry. This will automatically repair minor damage to robot or computer systems or provide a +2d bonus to Tech actions for more difficult jobs. Each dose repairs up to 2 Wounds of damage to robotic life, otherwise the number of doses depends on the extent of the damage to be repaired.

Inspection: 4 (Easy) Mishaps include misidentifying the gel as something edible (1d Fatigue and nearly a full day of feeling horrible and suffering, –1d penalty on all actions) or inadvertently emptying the tube in a place it will have no useful effect.

Power: 10 doses
Weight: 0.25 lb.

Onalogic Force Field Generator

The generator is only the size of a human fist, but using a few simple buttons and voice commands, it is capable of generating a force field as either a sphere with a 5-foot radius centered around the generator, or as wall projected up to 20 feet away that stands 10 feet high and 20 feet long. The force field ignores Fatigue damage and can absorb up to 15 Wound damage per turn and resets each turn it is active. If damage exceeds the protection, there is a backlash that overloads the unit and it will not be able to generate a replacement force field for 1d turns.

Inspection: 6 (Average) Mishaps include spontaneously generating a field without understanding how to switch it off, causing an overload that electrocutes anyone touching the generator (1d Fatigue electrical damage), or causing a feedback cycle that could cause an explosion.

Power: Medium Hydrogen Cell (48 hours).
Weight: 1 lb.

Optic Bot

A small robot designed for scouting, it is incapable of independent thought or action. It is generally paired wirelessly with a pair of goggles for both commands and transmitting—though an optic bot may be configured to work with other control systems or even a more sophisticated robot. The optic bot is a one-foot wide cube mounted on a small set of tracks that can navigate on horizontal surfaces (25 feet per turn) and can climb almost anything (10 feet per turn). It can focus on even small details from one mile away can switch to low-light vision or infrared with the correct commands. If detected by an enemy it's not difficult to damage or destroy, with protective plating (Armor 4) and can sustain 10 Fatigue before temporarily deactivating and 10 Wounds before shutting down past the point of repair.

Inspection: 6 (Average) Mishaps include damaging the bot's movement tracks (causing it to travel in weird arcs until repaired), permanently locking its visual mode to infrared or night vision, or damaging its primary logic circuits to the point where it will never behave as intended.

Power: 2 Small Hydrogen Cells (48 hours).
Weight: 35 lb.

Pain Block

Each "dose" is a self-contained tiny self-injecting syringe that contains a cocktail of drugs that severely reduce feelings of pain in any human- or animal-derived character for a duration of 4 hours. This temporarily reverses 2d Fatigue damage and removes any action penalties for being Injured (see Chapter Seven, Consequences of Damage). Once the medication wears off, however, any Fatigue damage that has not since healed will immediately take effect—possibly knocking the character unconscious.

Inspection: 2 (Average) Mishaps include accidental injection (and potentially wasting the medicine), opening the seal and spilling the medication, or breaking off the spring-loaded needle held inside.

Power: Each dose is one-use only.
Weight: Inconsequential
Special: The medication has no effect on plants.

Portable Energy Lamp

The size of a small briefcase, a PEL can generate either an intense pinpoint beam of light or brightly illuminate an area in a 500 foot radius.

Inspection: 4 (Easy) Mishaps include temporarily blinding the user or overloading the unit and frying the power cells.

Power: 2 Medium Chemical Cells (24 hours).

Weight: 7 lb.

Power Cell, Atomic

Atomic power cells are portable self-contained cold-fusion reactors that produce a tremendous amount of energy. These are all designed to be rechargeable (by restoring the necessary nuclear material) and come in three sizes: small (blue cylinder about 6 inches in length), medium (a thick cylinder roughly a foot in length), and large (barrel-shaped and 3 feet in height).

Inspection: 6 (Hard) Mishaps include initiating a failsafe that permanently renders the power cell inert, triggering a radiation leak that can cause radiation damage (see Chapter 7, Specialized Damage), or triggering an intense explosion that can cause severe damage to anyone in the vicinity.

Power: Atomic power cells may be restored to full use at a power cell recharger requiring a varying amounts of time for small (2 hours), medium (8 hours), or large (1 day).

Weight: 2 lb. (small), 8 lb. (medium), or 50 lb. (large)

Power Cell, Chemical

These are the most primitive form of battery power available, but completely adequate for the power needs of many devices. These are all designed to be rechargeable, and come in three sizes: small (coin-like disk), medium (small cylinder barely over an inch in length), and large (human fist-sized and comparatively heavy).

Inspection: 6 (Easy) Mishaps include ruining the power cell or causing a leak that might cause small burns and irritation for minor Fatigue damage. Note these types of mishaps may also occur if the power cell is struck in combat or other dangerous situations.

Power: Chemical power cells may be restored to full use at a power cell recharger requiring a varying amount of time for small (15 minutes), medium (45 minutes), or large (90 minutes).

Weight: n/a (small, medium), or 2 lb. (large)

Power Cell, Hydrogen

Not strictly a battery, hydrogen power cells make use of an internal reaction to generate power. These are all designed to be rechargeable (by restoring the necessary "fuel") and come in three sizes: small (flat rectangle similar in size to a domar),

medium (cube shaped, small enough to be held in the palm of a human hand), and large (a thick cube about the size of a human head).

Inspection: 6 (Average) Mishaps include ruining the power cell or causing a small but damaging explosion that can cause minor Wound damage to those nearby. Note these types of mishaps may also occur if the power cell is violently struck.

Power: Hydrogen power cells may be restored to full use at a power cell recharge requiring a varying amounts of time for small (10 minutes), medium (30 minutes), or large (2 hours).

Weight: n/a (small), 1 lb. (medium), or 6 lb. (large)

Power Cell Recharger

These large charging stations can be found throughout the ship (though they are highly valued) and will recharge power cells of all types. In addition to a drained or empty power cell, the recharger requires a supply of nuclear material for atomic power cells or appropriate chemicals for chemical and hydrogen fuel cells . The amount of time necessary for a full recharge depends on the exact type (listed in those entries).

Inspection: 8 (Average) Mishaps include destroying gear that was placed in the recharger incorrectly or causing a radiation leak that might damage (or mutate!) anyone exposed. Note these types of mishaps may also occur if the power cell is struck in combat or other dangerous situation.

Power: Must be physically connected to a power station to function.

Weight: 300 lb.

Radiation Decontamination Gel

Contained in 18-inch tall canisters, this is a green goop that completely absorbs and neutralizes all radiation contained in a 100 square-foot area (10' x 10') per application. Within 30 seconds after the gel is applied the local radiation is negated and the gel crumbles away as a harmless red dust.

Inspection: 4 (Easy) Mishaps include mistaking the gel as edible (no damage but intense digestive discomfort, meaning a full day of –1d penalty to all actions) or otherwise completely misidentifying the gel's purpose.

Power: 25 applications.

Weight: 8 lb.

Smartpad

Appearing to be little more than a small rectangle of black glass, when activated it is revealed as a portable touchscreen computer (which can also perform many tasks using verbal commands) that is capable of many functions. Its original memory was wiped by the long-ago disaster as well as the links to the shipboard network, but its built-in functions work just fine. The device can record sound, take pictures, keep notes, perform calculations, set time-based alarms, and perform other simple tasks as a digital portable assistant. The smartpad is waterproof up to 20 feet but is otherwise somewhat fragile.

Inspection: 6 (Easy) Mishaps include accidentally wiping the unit's internal memory (rendering it useless), permanently locking the device into a "parrot mode" in which it repeats all phrases spoken nearby, or causing it to completely short out for 1 Fatigue electrical damage to whoever is holding it and "bricking" the unit forever.

Power: The device functions on broadcast power and will function normally anywhere inside the ship.

Weight: Inconsequential

Clothing & Armor

While some mutants are lucky enough to adapt to the environment or are born with protection from a hostile world, most require a little extra help in those departments. The items listed in this section include noteworthy clothing and other "worn" pieces of tech, as well as everything from primitive to sophisticated armor. Note that mundane clothing—whether tanned leather or machine-spun synthetic cotton scavenged from old crew quarters—is not listed here but absolutely exists aboard the *Warden*.

The weight and general notes about armor and clothing are made with humans in mind, and anything modified or built for larger or smaller individuals would vary (as determined by the referee). Note that armor has an additional notation about the specifics of the protection it offers, along with any penalties to movement or actions. See Chapter Seven, Armor.

Cloth Armor

Often made with tightly packed cloth, such protection could also be constructed of scavenged padding or soft hide. It only offers minimal protection, but it can be made quickly as needed and does not slower the wearer down.

Protection: 1
Weight: 8 lb.

Combat Gauntlet

Appearing as a loose metallic arm-length glove, a combat gauntlet adapts to almost any arm-like appendage of roughly human size. It offers both the ability to block melee attacks without injury (like a shield) and a +1d to any Athletics, Brawn, or Unarmed Combat actions that make use of the affected arm.

Some combat gauntlets include a mounted laser pistol that requires its own power source (see Weapons).

Protection: +2d to Melee Weapons (Weapon Defense) actions for active blocking.

Inspection: 6 (Easy) Mishaps include tightening around the arm uncomfortably (1 Fatigue damage per turn), powering on and swinging wildly in random directions and possibly striking the wearer or others nearby, or the gauntlets shorting out and unspooling into a random pile of metallic strips.

Power: 1 Medium Hydrogen Power Cells (10 days)
Weight: 4 lb.

Combat Leggings

A set of metallic combat leggings will adapt to legs of almost any size and shape, molding to the wearer. They provide a small amount of combat protection in the lower area, but are also prized for enhancing movement (adding 5 feet to base speed) and offer a +1d to any Athletics, Brawn, or Unarmed Combat actions that make use of legs and feet.

Protection: 1 (unless attack specifically targets upper half of the body)

Inspection: 6 (Easy) Mishaps include tightening around the legs uncomfortably (1 Fatigue damage per turn), powering on and running the wearer in a random direction (Hard Brawn check to resist), or the leggings shorting out and unspooling into a random pile of metallic strips.

Power: 2 Medium Hydrogen Power Cells (10 days)
Weight: 10 lb.

Energy Absorption Suit

These lightweight suits were built for working in dangerous areas, not offering any protection from physical damage but able to negate up to 10 damage of all energy (electricity, fire, radiation—Wounds negated first, then Fatigue) per turn while powered on. It can also allow the user to pass through weaker force fields as if they were not even there. The suit is self-repairing under most circumstances, but if the wearer takes enough Wounds to risk dying the suit is ruined beyond the point of repair.

Protection: See Above

Inspection: 4 (Average) Mishaps include causing the suit to glow in bizarre colors and patterns while active, turning on its normally disabled audible geiger counter (which means at the very least a constant annoying hissing sound aboard the *Warden*), or causing the suit to leak radiation to the wearer (1 Wounds radiation damage each minute worn).

Power: 3 Small Hydrogen Power Cells (10 hours)
Weight: 8 lb.

Invisibility Suit

Designed for camouflage, the suit was build to adapt to human shapes from small and slender to tall and thick by stretching or retracting its fibers. The web-like filaments that comprise the suit bend light and heat around the wearer when activated, making her effectively invisible to both normal vision and infrared. The suit is self-repairing under most circumstances, but if the wearer takes enough Wounds to risk dying the suit is ruined beyond the point of repair. The suit has a secondary benefit of offering a +1d bonus to radiation resistance (see Chapter Seven, Specialized Damage), because of the shielding built in to protect the user from its own ambient energy.

Protection: 1

Inspection: 4 (Average) Mishaps include causing the suit to shrink while worn (1 Fatigue every turn until it's corrected or cut off), causing the suit to flash with white-hot light (blinding those nearby), or causing the fibers to unweave into a useless pile of multicolored thread.

Power: 2 Medium Hydrogen Power Cells (3 hours)
Weight: 10 lb.

Leather Armor

Made with strictly primitive methods, hardened leather armor can easily be manufactured with the correct materials and tools. It protects vital areas without impairing movement, but unfortunately offers little protection.

Protection: 2
Weight: 10 lb.

Personal Force Field

This small cube can be strapped to a belt or anywhere else within easy reach. Once properly set up for the size and shape of its wearer, a forcefield can be activated with the touch of a button. The force field ignores Fatigue damage and can absorb up to 10 Wounds per turn and resets each turn it is active. If damage exceeds the protection, the field goes down and takes 1d turns to reset. Each use of the device lasts for ten minutes before requiring a reset, and if the field is knocked out that counts as a use as well.

Inspection: 6 (Average) Mishaps include spontaneously generating a field without understanding how to switch it off, causing an overload that electrocutes anyone touching the device (1d Fatigue electrical damage), or causing a feedback cycle that could cause a small explosion.

Power: Small Hydrogen Power Cell (6 uses)
Weight: 4 lb.

Powered Armor, Heavy

Combining duralloy construction with servos and motors for movement and activity along with enhanced combat functionality, this armor is designed for survival and intense combat situations. The suit can be fitted to most human-like shapes and allows for thruster-based flight (movement 25 feet, no ability to go any faster). It offers a complete seal and an internal environment that can function anywhere (even a vacuum). By switching visual modes, the wearer may activate low-light vision, infrared, or to detect radiation. Powered armor also enhances base ground movement by 5 feet per turn, offers +1d to Brawn-based actions, and provides +2d bonus to radiation resistance (see Chapter Seven, Specialized Damage).

Some suits of heavy powered armor include a personal force field generator or an arm-mounted laser pistol that all work with the same power supply.

Protection (Penalties): 6 (–1d to Athletics, Dexterity, and Stealth actions).

Inspection: 8 (Average) Mishaps include causing the armor to heat to uncomfortable levels (1 Fatigue every turn until shut off or removed), causing it to seal without activating environmental filters (risking suffocation), or causing an overload that delivers a potentially fatal electric shock.

Power: Medium Atomic Power Cell (100 days)
Weight: 150 lb.

Powered Armor, Light

Constructed from flexible bands of duralloy and other advanced materials, light powered armor can be fitted to most human-like shapes. The suit offers thruster-based flight (movement 25 feet, no ability to go any faster). It offers a complete seal against the outside environment, can filter air and has a built-in underwater adaption—but does not offer the ability to breathe in a vacuum. By switching visual modes, the wearer may activate low-light vision, infrared, or to detect radiation. Light powered armor also provides +2d bonus to radiation resistance (see Chapter Seven, Specialized Damage).

Some suits of light powered armor include a personal force field generator or an arm-mounted laser pistol that all work with the same power supply.

Protection (Penalties): 4 (–1d to Athletics, Dexterity, and Stealth actions).

Inspection: 8 (Average) Mishaps include causing the armor to heat to uncomfortable levels (1 Fatigue every turn until shut off or removed), causing it to seal without activating environmental filters (risking suffocation), or causing an overload that delivers a potentially fatal electric shock.

Power: Medium Atomic Power Cell (200 days)

Weight: 100 lb.

Radiation Suit

Lightweight suits designed for humans, these offer complete protection from radiation. Internal monitors track the levels with a readout on the the left arm. If the wearer takes enough Wounds damage to become Injured (see Chapter Seven, Consequences of Damage) the suit's protection is compromised—causing an alarm to sound and only 5 turns before any radiation-based effects or damage will be suffered normally; if the wearer takes enough Wounds to risk dying the suit is ruined beyond repair. Lesser damage can be repaired quickly with patches that adhere to the legs of the suit (3 per leg).

Protection: See above.

Inspection: 4 (Easy) Mishaps include causing an accidental small tear, triggering the alarm, or removing all of the repair patches and sticking them in inappropriate places.

Power: 3 Small Hydrogen Power Cells (10 hours)

Weight: 5 lb.

Shield, Duralloy

Repurposed from special spare plating intended to patch the hull of the *Warden*, duralloy shields are prized because they are incredibly lightweight while being nearly indestructible and deceptively hard. Duralloy is clearly a metal but cannot be reproduced, only repurposed. Simply carrying a duralloy shield in a way that partially blocks the body offers light cover against ranged attacks, and by crouching behind it (preventing other actions on the same turn) the shield may be used as heavy cover against ranged attacks.

Protection: +2d to Melee Weapons (Weapon Defense) actions for actively blocking attacks.

Weight: 2 lb.

Shield, Large

Offering greater protection than its smaller counterpart, a large shield can sometimes slow down a combatant. Shield may be constructed from many different materials or repurposed from items of the right size and shape. Just carrying a large shield offers light cover against ranged attacks, and by crouching behind it (preventing other actions on the same turn) the shield may be used as heavy cover against ranged attacks.

Protection: +2d to Melee Weapons (Weapon Defense) actions for actively blocking attacks / –1d to Athletics, Dexterity, and Stealth actions.

Weight: 10 lb.

Shield, Small

Whether built specifically for protection in mind or cobbled together from scrap, a small shield is lightweight and gives the user an advantage in blocking attacks in hand-to-hand combat. In addition to its normal use, by crouching behind the shield (preventing other actions on the same turn) a shield can be used as light cover against ranged attacks.

Protection: +1d to Melee Weapons (Weapon Defense) actions for actively blocking attacks.

Weight: 5 lb.

Space Suit

Pressurized to allow safe activity in a vacuum, the suit allows survival in outer space, under water, and in other hostile environments. It offers minimal combat protection, though getting into a fight in such an environment is extremely dangerous as the suit might become compromised to fatal effect. Maneuvering thrusters assist the wearer in orienting and other actions that might otherwise be difficult in zero-gravity, but are not intended for truly independent motion (and are useless in ship-normal gravity). If the wearer takes enough Wounds damage to become Injured (see Chapter Seven, Consequences of Damage) the suit's protection is compromised—causing an alarm to sound and only 3 turns before its protection is gone and the wearer suffers whatever consequences are a result of his environment; if the wearer takes enough Wounds to risk dying the suit is ruined beyond repair. Lesser damage can be repaired quickly with adhesive patches on the legs (3 per leg).

Protection (Penalties): 1 Wounds (–1d to Athletics, Dexterity, and Stealth actions).

Inspection: 8 (Average) Mishaps include causing the suit to over-pressurize (1 Fatigue damage per turn worn), activating the thrusters randomly—causing the suit to skitter about until it is caught, or causing explosive decompression of the air supply that destroys the suit and might damage those nearby.

Power: 3 Small Hydrogen Power Cells (24 hours) power thrusters, small tank air supply (8 hours)

Weight: 15 lb.

Weapons

The best defense is leaving your enemies in a ruined heap. Protecting yourself from damage is great, but even the most powerful suit of powered armor augmented with a personal force field can only hold out for so long. Even the most primitive denizens of the *Warden* will scrounge up some basic weaponry, whether it's a misshapen club or an old steel strut sharpened into a crude sword. Ranged weapons—especially tech—are particularly prized since you can riddle your enemies with smoking holes without getting in harm's way yourself. Hokey mutations and ancient weapons are no match for a good plasma pistol at your side.

Note that the items below include a Damage Bonus entry to show how much extra damage is inflicted as long as at least minimal success is rolled on the attack. If the damage has a specific type (fire for laser, for example) than all damage dealt by an attack from that weapon is considered of that type, not just the bonus damage. The Special entry notes of any unique properties a weapon might possess.

Melee Weapons

Melee is an ancient term meaning "confused fight," and nothing is more confusing than standing your ground with a naked blade as a cougaroid is leaping for your throat. The weapons below make use of the wielder's strength and skill to face opponents who are close enough to fight back.

Using Shields

While some are comfortable either dodging attacks, relying on armor or mutation protection, or even blocking with a trusty weapon, a shield offers a few distinct advantages while admittedly suffering from a few drawbacks—primarily because it's most effective when it's used actively. A shield just hanging on your arm is never as effective as one you put in harm's way.

Blocking: Handheld shields are used for active defense in combat, meaning they don't do a whole lot of good in a fight if they are just strapped to your arm. They are used for blocking an incoming attack, and because they are specifically designed for the job they offer a bonus to those actions—enhancing the Melee Weapons trait (Weapon Defense specialty).

Cover: If you're being shot at in an open area the shield might be the best protection you've got. By getting as much of your body behind the shield it will offer at least light cover (more if it's a larger shield).

Shield Bashing: Just as a blade can parry, a shield can be used to smash someone in the face. It can be used as an attack action using Melee Weapons (Weapon Attack), with a damage bonus of +1F (small shield) / +2F (large shield) / +3F (duralloy shield).

Breaking: Depending on the materials the shield is made out of, it might wear out over time without replacement or maintenance, or break to uselessness if an enemy rolls enhancements in combat or the defender botches. The exception to breaking is the duralloy shields, which last forever without so much as a scratch from anything other than powerful energy weapons.

Axe, Large

Meant either to fell huge trees or equally dangerous enemies, these axes are generally used with two hands and require strength to properly wield.

Damage Bonus: 2W (+2W if at least one enhancement is rolled, but requires an action to pull the axe free).

Weight: 10 - 12 lb.

Special: Cannot be wielded by those with a Weak (1d) Brawn trait.

Axe, Small

While some of these items have been custom-created for battle, others are just scavenged hatchets or small woodcutting tools.

Damage Bonus: 1W (+1W if at least one enhancement is rolled, but requires an action to pull the axe free).

Weight: 4 - 6 lb.

Chainsaw

While not designed to be a weapon used in combat, its fearsome sound and the horrific rending it inflicts make it an object of fear.

Damage Bonus: 3W, +1d Wounds if at least one enhancement is rolled.

Inspection: 4 (Average) Mishaps include disconnecting the chain and rendering it useless until reattached, jamming the motor and causing the tool to be inert except for a strange hum, or causing a short-circuit that fries the batteries.

Power: 2 Small Hydrogen Power Cells (100 days of occasional use)

Weight: 10 lb.

Special: Incurs improvised weapon penalty.

Club / Staff

Whether fashioned from a thick tree branch or is simply an old, repurposed broom handle, this type of weapon is often wielded with two hands and used as a bludgeon.

Damage Bonus: 1F

Weight: 3 - 4 lb.

Special: Two-handed staves inflict +1F if at least one enhancement is rolled.

Knife

Any small blade is treated the same way so the individual characteristics of a knife are highly varied. Whether it was originally a kitchen tool, old-fashioned shaving instrument, sharp piece of a portable toolkit, or sharpened from materials

Improvised Weapons

Plenty of the weapons used on the *Warden* are cobbled-together from bits and pieces that were pulled from corpses, raided from rooms, or scavenged from trash piles—yet have been customized to be fully functional. Many situations, however, might find a mutant grabbing anything from a rusty old wrench to a nearby rock. These are Improvised Weapons.

The referee determines the properties of an improvised weapon, usually by finding a near equivalent among the official weapons in this chapter. But using an old letter-opener as a knife or a jagged metal strut as an axe is not ideal, so use of Improvised Weapons comes with a penalty.

Most of the time the Improvised Weapon penalty is −1d for the action; extremely cumbersome or exceptionally unwieldy objects incur a −2d to the action. Some items will simply prove useless in combat except to distract or amuse otherwise deadly enemies.

lying around, you're still holding a knife. Weaker materials mean there is more of a chance the knife will wear down to uselessness or break suddenly.

Damage Bonus: +1W if at least one enhancement is rolled.

Weight: 0.5 - 1 lb.

Special: Knives made for throwing have the same damage bonus with a range increment of 10 feet. Other knives can also be thrown but suffer the improvised weapon penalty.

Long Blade

Comprising long swords that can still be swung with one hand to huge blades that require two, a long blade delivers more damage but requires strength and room to wield.

Damage Bonus: 2W

Weight: 5 - 10 lb.

Special: Cannot be wielded by those with a Weak (1d) Brawn trait. Two-handed blades inflict +1W if at least one enhancement is rolled.

Sap / Brass Knuckles

Either a small bludgeon held in one hand or a hardened shell to add impact to an otherwise unarmed attack, such weapons are small and easily concealed.

Damage Bonus: +1F if at least one enhancement is rolled.

Weight: 0.5 - 1 lb.

Special: Brass Knuckles (or equivalent item) still make use of the Unarmed Combat (Striking) trait. A sap is still a Melee Weapons (Weapon Attack) action.

Short Blade

Including long knives and short swords, or perhaps machetes that double as weapon and brush-clearing tool, short blades are held in one hand and light enough for quick, decisive strokes. Their size allows fighting in confined spaces.

Damage Bonus: 1W

Weight: 2 - 3 lb.

Spear, Short

While some of these weapons might be sharpened and fire-blackened pointy sticks, others are carefully fashioned and meant for battle.

Damage Bonus: 1W

Weight: 3 - 5 lb.

Special: +2W if at least one enhancement is rolled, but requires an action to pull the spear free. Can be thrown with a range increment of 15 feet.

Spear, Long

These spears are not useful in close combat, but with someone offering protection they can allow for stabbing opponents that would normally be out of reach.

Damage Bonus: 1W

Weight: 8 - 10 lb.

Special: +2W if at least one enhancement is rolled, but requires an action to pull the spear free. Reach of 10 feet; attacks against adjacent opponents suffer a –1d penalty.

Vibroblade

Unpowered it appears only as a simple handle, but when activated with a tight grip and button press a glowing blue blade-shaped force field with a mathematically perfect edge appears—its size based on type. A vibroblade is capable of truly gruesome wounds and cuts through most armor like it wasn't even there.

Any "blade" weapon (knife, short blade, long blade) has a vibroblade version—though their lethal potential makes each one highly prized and valuable. If used unpowered, they useless as a weapon.

Damage Bonus: Equal to the blade type +1W, +1d Wounds if at least one enhancement is rolled. Vibroblades ignore armor, but not force fields.

Inspection: 4 (Average) Mishaps include shorting out the power cells (creating a cloud of foul smoke), misaligning the vibration causing the blade to swing wildly and potentially cutting those nearby, or causing an overload that warps and ruins the blade permanently.

Power: 2 Small Hydrogen Power Cells (50 days of occasional use)

Weight: Same as blade type.

Ranged Weapons

There is a school of thought (some call it "sensible") that says the best way to take an enemy down is from a safe distance. The only problem is that the safer the distance, the more difficult the shot. It takes a skilled marksman or a bit of luck to hit a target from long range. Whether slinging a rock, loosing an arrow, or firing a rifle, the weapons listed here are all about dealing damage without getting uncomfortably close.

Bow, Long

Tall enough and with enough tensile strength to offer an arrow more range and damage potential than a shortbow, it can nonetheless be crafted from a variety of materials. Arrows much be either replaced or retrieved from the target—assuming they are not damaged.

Damage Bonus: 2W

Range Increment: 50 feet

Weight: 3 - 5 lb.

Bow, Short

Whether built from wood and cord or other materials, the short bow is light and portable and can fire arrows—which must be replaced or retrieved—at an unlucky target.

Damage Bonus: 1W

Range Increment: 25 feet

Weight: 2 - 3 lb.

Pistol

While simple and easy to understand, these weapons still deal impressive damage from a distance with a loud crack and some recoil. An individual pistol might hold 6-14 bullets before requiring an action to reload assuming more ammunition is available.

Damage Bonus: 2W (+1 Wounds per enhancement)
Range Increment: 30 feet
Inspection: 4 (Easy) Mishaps include accidentally firing the weapon in a random direction, causing it to jam, or causing a misfire that destroys the weapon and injures the one holding it.
Power: 1 bullet per shot (revolvers or clips hold 6, 8, 10, 12, or 14, depending on type)
Weight: 2 - 3 lb.

Pistol, Laser

As a handheld energy weapon that's lighter than a projectile pistol and deals more damage at greater range, these weapons are prized and shots are saved for when needed unless a ready supply of power cells are available.

Damage Bonus: 3W fire (+1 Wounds fire damage per enhancement)
Range Increment: 40 feet
Inspection: 4 (Average) Mishaps include accidentally firing the weapon in a random direction, firing a lower-intensity beam that sets something nearby on fire, or causing an overload that burns anyone holding it (1W fire) and melts the pistol into slag.
Power: Small Hydrogen Cell (12 shots)
Weight: 2 lb.

Pistol, Plasma

The plasma pistol looks like a comically oversized toy weapon, but it's no joke. The pistol converts locally-condensed moisture into superheated gas contained in a miniature decaying force field that is propelled toward a target at terrific speed. The weapon delivers terrifying wounds that resemble scorched holes. The need for a rare atomic power cell makes this deadly weapon coveted and highly prized.

Damage Bonus: 4W fire, +1d Wounds if at least one enhancement is rolled.
Range Increment: 50 feet
Inspection: 4 (Hard) Mishaps include damaging the condensers (forcing the small water chamber to be refilled manually after every other shot until repaired), generating a localized force field around the weapon that will quickly drain the power cell, or activated a plasma overload that overwhelms the safeguards and causes a 4d Wounds fire explosion (10 feet increment).
Power: Small Atomic Cell (20 shots)
Weight: 3 lb.

Pistol, Protein Disruptor

Causing flesh and muscle to break down animal protein structures into a semi-liquid state, a protein disruptor is not only a lethal weapon but one that often strikes terror into anyone who's seen the results. It resembles a fat-bodied laser pistol with a strange lens array affixed to the firing end. Such weapons are rare and make those who carry them both hated and feared—except by sentient plants who understand they are immune to disruptor energy. Just witnessing the weapon used is sickening to most humans.

Damage Bonus: 2d Wounds
Range Increment: 20 feet

Inspection: 4 (Hard) Mishaps include accidental firing at self or ally, locking the safety mechanism in place and locking the weapon semi-permanently, or triggering an overload with a 10 second beeping warning before a 2d Wounds flesh-melting explosion (increment 10 feet) occurs.

Power: Small Atomic Cell (5 shots), power cell is destroyed if fully drained.

Weight: 2.5 lb.

Special: Protein disruption only affects humans, animals, and related mutants. It has no effect on plants, artificial life, or other objects.

Pistol, Stun

Using a concentrated sonic pulse capable of scrambling the nervous system, the stun pistol was designed to primarily subdue targets rather than kill. Unfortunately sonic weapons generally do not have the range of other energy weapons.

Damage Bonus: 3F sonic, if at least one enhancement is rolled the target must succeed a Hard Constitution (Fortitude) check or be stunned for 1d turns. Ignores armor but not force fields.

Range Increment: 25 feet

Inspection: 4 (Average) Mishaps include misaligning the sonic projector (causing a −1d penalty to firing it until fixed), activating a high-frequency shriek that deafens any nearby for 1d minutes, or causing a sonic explosion that stuns those in a 25-foot radius (equivalent to the enhancement effect).

Power: Small Hydrogen Cell (15 shots)

Weight: 2 lb.

Rifle

Designed to fire a devastating projectile at long range with accuracy, the rifle makes use of pre-made bullets and has sights on the barrel to assist with aim.

Damage Bonus: 3W (+1 Wounds per enhancement)

Range Increment: 60 feet

Inspection: 4 (Easy) Mishaps include accidentally firing the weapon in a random direction, causing it to jam, or causing a misfire that destroys the weapon.

Power: 1 bullet per shot (clips hold 10, 20, or 30 depending on type)

Weight: 10 - 15 lb.

Rifle, Laser

With no recoil and excellent range, the laser rifle is an excellent alternative to the projectile version. It fires a searing beam of intense heat.

Damage Bonus: 4W fire (+1 Wounds fire per enhancement)

Range Increment: 80 feet

Inspection: 6 (Average) Mishaps include accidentally firing the weapon in a random direction, firing a lower-intensity beam that sets something nearby on fire, or causing an overload that burns anyone holding it (1W fire) and melts the rifle into slag.

Power: Medium Hydrogen Cell (20 shots)

Weight: 10 lb.

Rifle, Plasma

Resembling a heavy plastic novelty squirt gun but but betrayed by a surprisingly heavy weight, a plasma rifle is deadly serious business. It functions much like the pistol version—sending superheated gas in a concentrated burst toward an unlucky target—but with superior punch and range. A plasma rifle can reduce an enemy to a smoldering ruin from a safe vantage point.

Damage Bonus: 5W fire, +1d Wounds if at least one enhancement is rolled

Range Increment: 100 feet

Inspection: 4 (Hard) Mishaps include damaging the condensers (forcing the small water chamber to be refilled manually after every other shot until repaired), generating a localized force field around the weapon that will quickly drain the power cells, or activating a plasma overload that overwhelms the safeguards and causes a 5d Wounds fire explosion (10 feet increment).

Power: 2 Small Atomic Cells (35 shots)

Weight: 15 lb.

Rifle, Protein Disruptor

Appearing to be a fat-bodied laser rifle with cascading clear lenses attached to the firing end, a protein disruptor rifle melts human and animal flesh and can often reduce either to a sticky pile of disgusting goo. The differences between the animal and plant kingdoms protect the latter from gooification. They are power-hungry weapons that destroy the batteries that make them function, but they inspire such fear that even the threat of firing one can intimidate an enemy into unconditional surrender.

Damage Bonus: 4d Wounds

Range Increment: 35 feet

Inspection: 6 (Hard) Mishaps include accidental firing at self or ally, locking the safety mechanism in place and locking the weapon semi-permanently, or triggering an overload with a 10 second beeping warning before a 4d Wounds flesh-melting explosion (increment 10 feet) occurs.

Power: 2 Small Atomic Cells (10 shots), power cells are destroyed if fully drained.
Weight: 18 lb.
Special: Protein disruption only affects humans, animals, and related mutants. It has no effect on plants, artificial life, or other objects.

Rifle, Stun

Firing a long-distance punch of sonic energy, this weapon can effectively knock a target unconscious without having to get close. The weapon hums but makes no obvious sound until the shockwave hits.
Damage Bonus: 4F sonic, if at least one enhancement is rolled target must succeed a Hard Constitution (Fortitude) check or be stunned for 1d turns. Ignores armor but not force fields.
Range Increment: 50 feet
Inspection: 4 (Average) Mishaps include misaligning the sonic projector (causing a –1d penalty to firing it until fixed), activating a deafening shriek that deafens any nearby for 1d minutes, or causing a sonic explosion that stuns those in a 50-foot radius (equivalent to the enhancement effect).
Power: Medium Hydrogen Cell (30 shots)
Weight: 10 lb.

Shotgun

Pre-manufactured shells blast a target with rending force, making the shotgun a devastating weapon at short range. They come in either a single or double-barrel variety, allowing an attacker to fire one or both.
Damage Bonus: 3W (per barrel), (+1 Wounds per enhancement)
Range Increment: 20 feet
Inspection: 4 (Easy) Mishaps include accidentally firing the weapon in a random direction, causing it to jam, or causing a misfire that destroys the weapon and injures the one holding it.
Power: 1 shell per shot
Weight: 8 - 10 lb.
Special: If both barrels are fired the damage bonus is doubled to 6W but the weapon is emptied. An action is required to reload each barrel individually.

Sling

While a basic sling can be thrown together in a pinch (and would be considered an improvised weapon), one intended for regular use is crafted with rope or tightly wound cloth and makes use of smooth stones or specialized "bullets" (clay, stone, metal spheres, dense plastic, etc.) to hurl at an enemy.

Damage Bonus: +1F if at least one enhancement is rolled
Range Increment: 20 feet
Weight: Inconsequential

Slug Thrower

The term "slug thrower" is a catch-all for variants of any of the traditional bullet-flinging firearms (pistol, rifle) but use special rubber bullets designed to subdue a target rather than kill.
Damage Bonus & Range Increment: Equivalent to weapon type, substitute all Wounds with Fatigue.

Explosives

Some warriors prefer precision, choosing the exact place for damage to be dealt. Others enjoy a ball of fiery death that incinerates everything in a huge area without discrimination. Explosives can be used as a tool, a trap, or in the heat of battle.

Grenade, Frag

Easily held and thrown, once the pin is pulled there are three seconds before detonation and flings shrapnel in every direction to potentially rip enemies to shreds.
Damage: 4d Wounds
Explosion Increment: 10 ft.
Throwing Range: 30 ft. increment
Inspection: 4 (Average) Because grenades are such simple devices, the primary mishap is accidentally detonating it at close range. If the casing is dismantled during inspection, a more mild mishap is simply rendering the weapon a dud.
Weight: 1 lb.

Grenade, Plasma

This horrifying weapon explodes in white hot flames and lays waste to a large area—which is why it's generally thrown as far away as possible, since accuracy isn't always the point.
Damage: 6d Wounds fire
Explosion Increment: 10 ft.
Throwing Range: 25 feet increment
Inspection: 4 (Average) Because grenades are such simple devices, the primary mishap is accidentally detonating it at close range. If the casing is dismantled during inspection, a more mild mishap is simply rendering the weapon a dud.
Weight: 1.5 lb.

Grenade, Smoke

Unlike most other grenades, this one doesn't injure. It emits a large cloud of colored smoke (indicated by the color of the grenade). Upon detonation the smoke spreads to a radius of 10 feet and grows by an additional 10 each turn until it obscures in a 40-foot radius from the grenade. The smoke lasts for 2d minutes.

Throwing Range: 30 ft. increment

Inspection: 4 (Average) Because grenades are such simple devices, the primary mishap is accidentally detonating it at close range. If the casing is dismantled during inspection, a more mild mishap is simply rendering the weapon a dud.

Weight: 1 lb.

Special: One variant is a tear-gas grenade, in which the smoke not only obscures but causes 1d Fatigue and blinds any exposed character with eyes for 1d minutes or until they receive helpful treatment.

Grenade, Stun

This small explosive is meant to leave foes unconscious but without causing serious injury. It unleashes a burst of electrical energy in all directions.

Damage: 4d Fatigue electric

Explosion Increment: 10 ft.

Throwing Range: 30 ft. increment

Inspection: 4 (Average) Because grenades are such simple devices, the primary mishap is accidentally detonating it at close range. If the casing is dismantled during inspection, a more mild mishap is simply rendering the weapon a dud.

Weight: 1 lb.

Special: There is a variant stun grenade that uses high-frequency sound to generate the same effect, but the damage is sonic rather than electric.

Multipurpose Explosive

Looking like thick, gray clay wrapped in a specialized multi-layered "paper" it generally comes with a timer-detonator that is inserted before use. The timer can be set for up to a full 24 hours in the future, or if properly set can be triggered remotely by radio. A full "charge" detonated is a huge explosion—though it can be cut into smaller pieces.

Damage: 1d Wounds fire per charge, 6 charges per kit

Explosion Increment: 10 feet

Inspection: 6 (Average) Mishaps include ruining the explosive compound entirely, misidentifying it as edible, prematurely detonating the bomb.

Power: One-use detonator

Weight: 0.5 lb.

Ammunition

While energy weapons make use of the same power cell types as other devices aboard the *Warden*, projectile weapons require good old-fashioned bullets. And while tracking specific calibers is beyond the scope of this game, it is generally assumed that pistols and rifles use ammunition specific for those types.

The referee might decide to simplify things and declare that, on the *Warden* at least, a bullet is a bullet and any you find will work with any gun. But you'll still need to find shells for that shotgun, though!

Lobbing Grenades

While it would be priceless to bean someone you're meaning to kill right in the face with the grenade that will then explode right next to him—with grenades and other hurled objects that create zones of effect you just need to know how close you got to your intended spot.

Grenades can be thrown using Athletics (Throwing) for as many range increments as the one hurling has dice in Brawn. Hitting your mark is Easy within the first increment, Average on the next, and Hard for anything beyond that. If you score at least 3 achievements—congrats! Your hurled object landed where you wanted. Otherwise roll 1d, double the result, and use it to determine the direction of the miss as it were a clock face centered around the intended target area. The object landed 10 feet away if you only scored 1 achievement, 5 feet if you scored 2.

If you miss, you still need to determine where the grenade landed. Use the same 1d doubled "clock" method, but begin with 10 feet distance and a die roll of 1d and add an additional 5 feet per number on the die rolled. A little luck and the intended target will still be in the zone of effect. If you botch, there is a chance you dropped the grenade, forgot to pull the pin, or it turns out to be a dud.

SCKETRE
human, distrustful warrior

movement	15 ft.
initiative	3d
dodge	2d
radiation resistance	5d

TRAITS

amazing (+3D)	Constitution
good (+2D)	Discipline, Melee Combat
competent (+1D)	Alertness, Brawn
weak (-1D)	Influence, Crafting, Survival
hopeless (-2D)	Artistry, Performance

WOUND CAPACITY

18

FATIGUE CAPACITY

15

UNIQUE FEATURES

mutations	n/a
qualities	Brutal (1d), Talented at Tech Lore & Melee Weapon Attack (1d); Unhelpful (1d)
gear	Long Blade (2W), Vibroblade (1W*)

NOTES

He lost his family as a young child, and the man who raised him taught him caution and not to trust, which was reinforced with brutal discipline. Scketre's harsh upbringing has made him physically gifted, cautious, and tough. But years of isolation have left him lacking in social skills. He prefers interaction with others to be brief and pragmatic, but he's grown to realize he may need information and allies in order to get what he truly wants. More than anything, Scketre wants to find and kill the man who raised him, the man who murdered his entire family.

SCARFACE

mutant animal (musteloid/badger), explosives enthusiast

movement	15 ft., Burrow 1ft.
initiative	1d
dodge	1d
radiation resistance	3d

TRAITS

amazing (+3D)	Athletics
good (+2D)	Brawn, Crafting
competent (+1D)	Constitution, Tech
weak (-1D)	Alertness, Dexterity, Medicine
hopeless (-2D)	Discipline, Stealth

WOUND CAPACITY
17

FATIGUE CAPACITY
15

UNIQUE FEATURES

mutations	Biped (1d), Larger (*), New Body Parts (claws 2d, teeth 1d), Rapid Recovery (2d)
qualities	Burrower (1d), Speech (1d), Talented at Fortitude (2d); Inept at Emotional Control (2d)
gear	Knives (3, 1W*), Frag Grenades (2, 4dW Explosion)

NOTES

As a bipedal honey badger who stands taller than most humans, Scarface would be intimidating enough without his obsessive love of knives and shredding explosives. (His name was given to him for the scars he enjoys giving to others, not for his own sleek-furred face.) The huge badger is a creature of excess, who loves the company of others and eating until his belly aches. He's always looking for a bigger experience—be it a hellacious battle, a gigantic stash of loot, or a celebration that lasts for days.

WAHT-AM

mutant animal (musteloid/otter), inquisitive explorer

movement	15 ft., Burrow 1ft.
initiative	4d
dodge	2d
radiation resistance	2d

TRAITS

amazing (+3D)	Survival
good (+2D)	Alertness, Athletics
competent (+1D)	Ranged Weapons, Unarmed Combat
weak (-1D)	Influence, Leadership, Tech
hopeless (-2D)	Brawn, Deception

WOUND CAPACITY

12

FATIGUE CAPACITY

16

UNIQUE FEATURES

mutations	Dual Brain (1d), Force Field Generation (2d), Larger (*), Levitation (2d), New Body Parts (teeth 1d)
qualities	Burrower, Literate (1d), Lucky (2d), Speech (1d), Talented at Swimming (2d); Inept at Jumping (2d), Unfocused (2d)
gear	Knife (1W*), Sling (10 stones, 1F*); Shoulder bag (rations)

NOTES

Huge for an otter but small for a human, Waht-ahm has somewhat adopted a humanoid look at dignity and "nudity," so he scrounges for clothes that will fit his small frame. He is always curious about what's around the next corner, over the holographic horizon, or why that robot is firing lasers at him. While Waht finds most tech beyond his understanding, he has knack for repurposing items for more primitive use. The toaster he once used as a flail lasted a whole week before it was eaten!

SPIKE
mutated human, curious mechanic

movement	15 ft.
initiative	3d
dodge	4d
radiation resistance	2d

TRAITS

amazing (+3D)	Alertness
good (+2D)	Melee Weapons, Tech
competent (+1D)	Crafting, Medicine
weak (-1D)	Influence, Performance, Unarmed Combat
hopeless (-2D)	Deception, Leadership

WOUND CAPACITY

14

FATIGUE CAPACITY

14

UNIQUE FEATURES

mutations	Infravision (2d), Intuition (2d), New Body Parts–Quills (1d), Telekinetic Hand (1d)
qualities	Knowledgeable (1d), Literate (1d), Talented at Fixing (1d); Far Sighted (1d)
gear	Sword (2W), Wrench (tool, -1d to attack, 1F), Nano-Fix Gel (6 doses), Scavenged mechanic tools & clothes

NOTES

Always curious past the point of caution, Spike enjoys figuring out how things work and has a knack for fixing broken tech. Having barely survived a childhood encounter with a wolfoid pack she is initially distrustful any canine mutants, but once a companion gets past her prickly nature she is a loyal friend. Spike has heard legends about the "tomb of the sleepers" and will chase even vague rumors to find this mythical place.

EXTERNAL CAMERA 07

●ACTIVE

CAMERA 07 POWER

The badgeroid has already taken several hits from the maintenance bot's cutting laser, and he's steeling himself to rush it. The human used the keycard recovered from the Tomb of the Sleepers on the hatchway, but it requires an additional code! If things weren't bad enough, howls and the sound of claws on metal mean the wolfoid pack is drawing close. If the pair doesn't escape through the hatch, they'll have to make a stand with their backs to it.

The action is often intense in METAMORPHOSIS ALPHA, but the rules bring order to the chaos. Chapter Two covers everything a new player needs to get started, including understanding the information on a character sheet, rolling actions, and figuring out just what the dice mean.

If you want to be a referee, or if you are a player who wants a more in-depth understanding of the game, this chapter provides the full rules for handling pretty much anything. Just always remember that the rules are here to facilitate fun, not get in its way. If the group can't figure out how to resolve an action or situation using the guidelines here, the referee should improvise and move on.

You'll find some information repeated from Chapter Two, but this is a complete rules reference, with the previous chapter intended for new players.

RULES & ACTION

The rules are the structure which provide fairness and allow everyone at the table to know what's going on. At their best, the rules will fade comfortably in to the background, and the scenes will be remembered as if they were from a page-turner novel or an intense action movie. The players are the focus and hold the key decision-making points in the story, as the actions, reactions, abilities, and luck of the player characters are most important. Most scenes in the game are some combination of the following elements:

Problem Solving: Whether it's figuring out the difference between a toaster and a three-dimensional object replicator, solving a riddle, or deciphering a coded message, there are plenty of times the player characters are trying to figure things out. Solving problems within the game is often a combination of the players coming up with a solution as well as relying on the traits and other abilities of their characters.

Roleplaying: Sometimes it's about negotiation, talking your way out of an unwinnable fight, or turning an enemy into a friend. Whether it's hard-edge diplomacy or trying to coax secrets out of a mutant wombat over a shared mug of foul-tasting hooch, roleplaying actions are another element of game play that combine the player's performance and the game information written on a character sheet.

Combat: In the real world, it's almost always best when punches aren't thrown and guns aren't drawn. However, on the *Warden*, violence is a regular part of life and one of the elements that make it a great place to find adventure. In a combat scene, the players make quick decisions, and the dice do the talking depending on just how talented the characters are with tooth, fist, gun, and blade. Sound tactics and clever ideas can make a big difference, as a combat that boils down to a series of traded dice rolls would be as much fun as watching static on a damaged vidscreen. Fair fights rarely happen on the *Warden*, as those who entertained romantic notions were ripped to bloody ribbons long ago.

While many scenes played out in the game focus on one element almost exclusively, the best adventures alternate between them and a single scene can include all three. Imagine trying to convince a former enemy to assist you as your friends fend off attackers, while another ally attempts to activate a weapon that could turn the tide of the battle.

One important idea to remember that a player should never be punished for not having a talent when his character does, while a character should always benefit from a player coming up with a clever idea or engaging in some great roleplaying. If a player can't solve a puzzle, a smart character should be allowed to roll for it, while a character with pathetic social skills should receive a bonus if the player impressed the whole group with some great roleplaying. When in doubt, it's best for the situation to favor the players and their characters. They're the stars of the show, after all.

TRAITS & ACTIONS

Anytime a character is trying to accomplish something, it is called an action, and those actions are governed by traits. Characters are defined by how they vary in relationship to the baseline of a typical human with no particular strengths or weaknesses.

If there is no reason a character can't try something (such as an action that requires special training or tools the character doesn't possess), the roll automatically defaults to the average: **2d**.

Traits modify that baseline by telling us the actions at which the character is truly awful or amazing, as well as those that fall in-between. Everything is listed as a modifier to the basic roll (2d), so traits listed as Good (+2d) mean that a 4d dice pool is rolled for that particular action. Traits in a character's Weak (–1d) areas leave him with only one die to roll, while any Hopeless (–2d) are automatic failures most of the time.

Difficulty for an action defines which numbers on the dice score achievements. Easy actions score achievements for a result of 3 or higher. Average actions score achievements on a 4 or higher. Hard actions score achievements only on a 5 or 6.

Success for an action depends on the number of achievements rolled, with one achievement meaning the action wasn't a failure or a setback but barely qualifies as a success. Two achievements indicate modest success. Three achievements show that the action was a success by anyone's standards.

Enhancements are earned beyond three achievements, and the more earned by a character for an action mean spectacular success and additional opportunities for things to happen in his favor as a result.

If all dice in the pool come up as ones, the character has botched, which leads to embarrassing failure and some form of setback as determined by the referee.

These concepts are explained in greater detail in Chapter Two.

Requirement-Based Actions

Characters may try whatever they want, but the referee might determine that some actions are doomed to fail without needing a roll. If an attempted action defies the laws of physics—stepping over a chasm with the hope of floating—without the benefit of a mutation or necessary tech … well, the most perfect roll isn't going to help the situation.

Some actions can be attempted only with the appropriate background or training. Anyone can perform battlefield first aid, but open heart surgery requires specialized training as well as equipment and minimum conditions. Anyone can fire a blaster once they figure out its basic workings, but reprogramming environmental controls can only be attempted by someone who's learned how to code. Anyone can try to kick down a door, but picking a lock requires at least an improvised tool for the job.

Whether it's a lack of training, gear, or proper conditions, the referee enforces which actions are inappropriate under the circumstances and discusses possibilities with the player. Special training usually doesn't change a character's traits, but it will allow certain kinds of actions and should be noted on the character sheet.

Unspecified Difficulties

You may see certain actions, checks, or other required rolls with no listed difficulty. In these cases, assume the difficulty is Average unless otherwise determined by circumstance and the referee.

Bonuses & Penalties

The difficulty for a particular action covers a lot and is pretty easy to wrap your head around. If something is Easy, you'll rarely fail. If something is Hard, it's tough to succeed. Average actions fall right in the middle. If the situation changes for the character making an action, the referee adjusts the difficulty accordingly.

If there is a situational advantage, the active character receives a +1d or +2d bonus to her dice pool (to a maximum of 5 dice under most circumstances). These can be the result of an enhancement from a previous action or a situational edge (firing a ranged weapon point-blank or attacking melee from higher ground). Of course, if things are not quite in a character's favor (using an improvised weapon, acting while temporarily shaken), it's a –1d or –2d penalty, and anything that reduces the dice pool to zero results in an action's automatic failure.

Group Efforts & Assistance

Characters don't always have to go it alone; sometimes you have a little help from your friends. Assistance makes certain kinds of actions easier, though there are two different kinds.

Group Effort: All characters are making a direct contribution toward getting the job done, such as several characters surrounding a heavy object and lifting it together. Simply add together all scored achievements to determine success.

Assistance: If another character is offering advice or some other kind of indirect aid, such as one character trying to talk another through how to remove a power cell from a device without breaking it, an assisting character offers a bonus die to the pool for every 2 dice in his own trait for the action to a maximum of 5 dice for the character attempting the action.

Complex Actions

For actions that cannot be resolved in a short period of time or require more than one step, complex actions determine how successful an elaborate action turns out to be, and just as importantly, how long it takes to complete.

The **threshold** is the number of achievements necessary to complete a complex action. Once the threshold has been reached, the action succeeds—assuming you made it in time.

An **increment** is determined by the referee and represents how much time is taken up by each roll. It could be a turn (3 seconds), a minute, an hour, or even longer for something truly involved. Difficulty and the dice pool are determined in the same manner as simple actions, but achievements accumulate with each roll.

A botch during a complex action ruins the entire attempt. The referee determines the consequences and declares if starting over is even an option. An action point can transform it into ordinary, boring failure for that increment only.

While some complex actions might be successive rolls of the same trait, others might involve an unordered collection or predetermined path of different traits necessary to solve the problem. Such situations can involve a single character or might involve teamwork with different characters contributing.

Examples of Complex Actions

Water supply to an entire area has been mysteriously shut off, and a tech-savvy character has decided to tackle the problem. This involves dealing with a complicated maze of plumbing and electronics, even as a group of sentient but immobile mutant trees are in danger of dying from lack of moisture. The referee determines that each increment is a 4-hour block of time, and the problem requires 2 achievements to diagnose and 4 to repair. Diagnosing the problem allows for one use of Alertness as well as Tech, while repairing it allows for one use of Discipline as well as Tech. The referee also decides that one of the sentient trees will die every 8 hours until the water system is repaired.

The group has taken a wolfoid hostage, hoping to learn about the mysterious object they are guarding. However, if the questioning goes on too long, the pack might track them down and crash the party. The referee says that each increment is five minutes of game-time and allows the players to decide on interrogation approach (and relevant trait is involved). Secretly, it's determined that the pack will arrive in 30 minutes, and the threshold to get the information is 4 achievements. The questioning can make use of Deception (lying to the prisoner), Influence (to gain his trust), or Leadership (to intimidate) as opposed rolls against the wolfoid's own traits. A combination of roleplaying the interrogation and rolls involved will determine if the players succeed in time.

ACTION POINTS

Life is brutal on the *Warden*, and characters have another resource to help them survive and succeed. **Action points** offer a character another chance when an action might otherwise have failed, can be used to add achievements to make an action even more successful, and also be used to cancel out damage that would otherwise knock a character straight out of the fight. The points represent inner strength, resolve, and force of will to overcome the odds.

Re-roll: The character may re-roll the entire dice pool for the cost of 1 Action Point, but he must accept the results of the second roll and may not spend additional points to re-roll again. More points may be spent to add achievements, however.

Achievements: A character may add achievements to the results of an action at a cost of 1 Action Point per achievement.

Damage Reduction: A character may roll 1d per Action Point spent to reduce damage, using the total rolled to determine the amount of damage negated.

Wounds are reduced first, followed by Fatigue, with any excess points lost if the total roll exceeds the damage. Damage may only be reduced with Action Points immediately after it is taken, before other characters take actions, and represents extraordinary effort upon part of the character to avoid (or at least survive) the injury. They do not indicate healing.

Action Point Awards

The referee awards action points during the course of play as rewards for good roleplaying, completing a challenge, or achieving important goals. One or two points are the standard awards, with specifics at the discretion of the referee.

REWARDS OF SUCCESS

If a character rolls even a single achievement in the dice pool, she has managed at least to not fail. The degree of success depends on how many achievements are scored, leaving the possibility for amazing results or spectacular and embarrassing failure. Whether you fall straight on your backside or catapult to glory depends on the size of your dice pool and how much the odds are in your favor.

Levels of Success

No matter how hard an action may be, the level of success depends on just how many achievements you roll.

1 Achievement: Minimum Success

You've barely scraped by and are amazed that you didn't fail. You graze your target; you barely make it to the other side of the pit you're leaping over; you manage to find a decent handhold in the wall you're climbing. This action may not make your parents proud, but it sure beats the alternative. For some actions, the referee may require an action with minimum success to be attempted again or followed up with some other kind of action to get the real result you were hoping to reach.

2 Achievements: Modest Success

You managed to demonstrate basic competence. It's a solid hit but not a bullseye; you safely clear the pit over which you've jumped; you manage to scale a section of the wall. Whatever you were doing, this is solid enough work that no one should make fun of you, even if no one's going to be talking about how great you are at dinner. The referee will interpret the exact results of your action, but the important thing is you got the job done.

3 Achievements: Good Success

Well played! Your action was executed with style. Your shot gets near the bullseye even if it's not perfect; you vault to the other side of the pit with room to spare; you speed up the wall like a spider monkey. Your action is the kind that makes your allies grateful that you're on their side. The referee will explain exactly why your action was awesome.

Enhancements

It's one thing to do something well. It's another thing to kick ass, take names, and write the names down with your off-hand at the same time. Enhancements are ways in which you can produce really spectacular results—or some grisly deaths if you're in more of a killing mood. With enhancements, an action can have intended or even unintended consequences in a character's favor, so sometimes the effects will be caused by unadulterated skill or pure, dumb luck. Some enhancements might be specific to the area or circumstances in which the action took place or a result of other factors. These are always up to the final determination of the referee, but at minimum, there should always be something positive in the rolling character's favor. Here are a few examples of enhancements in different situations:

1 Enhancement …

Combat: Your enemy is startled or distracted by your attack and suffers a –1d penalty on its next action; you may take a quick non-attack action, such as half-movement, reload a weapon, or use a non-offensive mutation or piece of tech.

Exploration: You quickly find a sought-after item or notice a hidden detail instead of taking the normal time involved; you pick up a detail that grants you +1d to the next time you attempt a similar action.

Roleplaying: You impress, anger, or intimidate the object of your action, giving you the temporary upper hand, which is represented either by the referee's roleplaying or a –1d on the next opposing roll.

2 Enhancements …

Combat: You knock your enemy prone, disarm it, or drive it to a location of your choosing (within half of your movement); you attack with such swift fury you may take an additional attack action with no penalty (using the same dice pool you just rolled) or make a standard move.

Exploration: You not only immediately find what you were looking for or notice the hidden detail, but also you gain +2d to a relate action for either searching or following up on what you have discovered.

Roleplaying: You've made an impression that lasts through the short-term, both to your target and any nearby witnesses. The difficulty of opposed rolls is reduced by one level (from Hard to Average, Average to Easy) for the remainder of the encounter.

3 Enhancements …

Combat: Your enemy is grievously wounded (no additional wounds but something permanent); your enemy gains a debilitating condition (dazed, blinded); your attack strikes a secondary target.

Exploration: You are on a roll and gain a +1d bonus to similar actions for the remainder of the game session; you gain automatic surprise on a hidden foe or an extra chance to overcome a trap or obstacle.

Roleplaying: Relationships are permanently defined or changed by your words or actions (enemy, friend, or even an amorous relationship); you sway a large group to your side; you enrage a potential enemy, so he attacks in a blind fury.

FAILURE

While few are fond of failure, it certainly keeps life interesting. If at first you don't succeed … you might get your skull smashed. The results of a failed action might be more interesting than success.

Mundane Failure

If you don't score a single achievement when an action is rolled, the result is failure. Whatever action the character attempted didn't succeed. The opportunity is lost, at least for the moment. The character might get another chance if circumstances permit but must endure the consequences. While sometimes not succeeding is bad enough (for example, if you're trying to stop a bomb on the verge of detonation), there aren't any direct negative consequences for simply failing an action.

Epic Failure

Sometimes every die in your pool comes up as a one. This unfortunate run of bad luck is called a **botch**, and it means your character really screwed up. You tripped, dropped your knife, your gun misfired, or you just broke something you were trying to handle carefully. In other words: Oops.

The exact results of a botch depend on the circumstances and the determination of the referee. The penalty for a character should never be severe but indicates a temporary setback. Here are a few possibilities a referee may use as guidelines:

Combat: You lose your footing and are driven up to a half-movement in the direction of your enemy's choosing; your ranged weapon misfires and may require an action to restore it to functionality; you drop a melee weapon and will require an action to pick it up; you are momentarily disoriented and suffer a –1d penalty to your next action.

Exploration: You not only fail to notice something, but you accidentally distract others, causing them to suffer a –1d penalty to their actions; you are oblivious to an enemy or other hazard, causing a –1d penalty to initiative or some other reaction.

Roleplaying: You insult, offend, frighten, or anger the object of your action. You suffer a –1d penalty to future opposed rolls until the mistake is corrected.

If you don't want to suffer the consequences of a botch, an action point may be spent to make things less bad. One point transforms a botch to an ordinary failure. In pure game terms, a botch is –1 achievement, which can be modified by other factors.

TIME ON THE WARDEN

The ship came from Earth of long ago, and it operates on cycles of time based on the days, months, and years of old that ultimately mean little in the void of space. But with computer-operated calendar cycles, many of the simulated environments still have artificial day and night with the hours and minutes in between.

In the game, the tracking of time can shift between vague and fluid to extremely specific, depending on the needs of the current scene. If a group is resting, healing, or puzzling over the latest tech artifacts, a day might go by with only a few minutes of discussion at the game table. When the tension and action ramp up, it suddenly becomes extremely important to know exactly what's going on and when everything happens. It may not be important to know who finished their dinner first at camp, but it's awfully important to know whether or not the mutant melts your face with radiation before you rip out his throat with your claws. So while the referee keeps track of time on the larger scale with simple description, the game makes use of **turns** when things get hairy.

Initiative

When combat or some other tense sequence begins, the referee determines who takes the first actions. It's usually going to be whoever started the trouble, so if there are tense negotiations and one party decides to end the talks by unexpectedly belching poisonous gas, he would get to take the first action. Characters with special qualities or mutations might get to act or react immediately in these situations.

Once initial actions are resolved, the referee establishes an order of action using the **initiative** scores of those involved going from highest scores to lowest. Initiative is based on Alertness and the Responsiveness specialty. By counting down from 6 to 1 each character or group gets the chance to act, with anyone on the same initiative acting at roughly the same instant.

Sometimes it's crucial to know who acted a split-second before another. In those cases roll Dexterity as an opposed reaction, with the winner beating out the other. A tie in this case means complete simultaneous action with whatever that might imply.

The order is repeated each turn. New characters introduced to the scene act on their initiative the turn after their arrival and are added to the order. A character can voluntarily delay action later in the turn, with initiative restored to normal once the turn is over.

Turns

A turn represents roughly 3 seconds of time in the game, enough for a character to accomplish one simple action with any degree of focus or up to 3 that are rushed and sloppy. A character who is highly gifted in the action they're attempting (a crack shot firing a gun, for instance) might not mind the penalty for rushed actions, while one of limited talents may not be able to rush an action without automatically failing. The penalties apply to all actions that require a roll.

3 Seconds, 3 Actions

With only 3 seconds to accomplish things with tension and danger present, each character has limited options. Do one thing well or multiple things badly (or at least less well). Multiple actions carry a die penalty that applies to all actions within a turn. One action is no problem, but each additional action attempted incurs a –1d cumulative reduction.

7.1 - Rushed Actions

No. of Actions Per Turn	Penalty
1	n/a
2	–1d
3	–2d

When the fur and bullets are flying, it's not easy to walk and chew gum. There are many types of actions a character may attempt on a given turn.

Response

There are many times when a character is reacting rather than making a wholly independent action. Whether it's diving away from a volley of quills fired by a rage-filled mutant or resisting an enemy's psychic mind control, these sorts of things are known as a **response**. Defending against an attack is by far the most common, but there are many others that occur in play. Some responses are nonactions (for example, checking to see if you are affected by a toxin), while others (blocking or dodging) are considered actions which will count against total actions taken on the next turn.

The referee may use poker chips, gaming stones, or some other marker for an easy note on how many "extra" actions will go into a character's following turn.

MOVEMENT

Movement is always considered one action within a turn, though moving with greater speed brings on increasing penalties that affect all other actions taken during a turn. A walk is base movement (15 feet for humans) and brings no penalty; a hustle (double base movement) incurs a –1d action penalty; a run (triple base movement) incurs a –2d action penalty; a sprint (quadruple base movement) incurs a –3d action penalty.

7.2 - Movement

Movement	Speed	Penalty
Walk	Base Movement	None
Hustle	x2	–1d
Run	x3	–2d
Sprint	x4	–3d

A mutant character might have access to other modes of movement (flying, swimming, even burrowing) that are described by their mutation. Climbing and jumping are usually determined by appropriate rolled actions as determined by the referee.

Chases

It's not all walking around and fights to the death on chosen killing grounds. Sometimes the person, beast, or shrub you seek is running away; other times you've encountered a problem you're not prepared to handle, and discretion is the better part of getting the hell out of there alive. That's when chases come into play.

Variant Iniative

If the group prefers to mix things up with a bit more randomness, the referee may choose to roll the dice for determining initiative instead.

Every character must roll initiative at the start of conflict to establish the order of actions. This is a special roll and one of the rare times you roll dice to obtain a total instead of scoring achievements. Every character rolls Alertness (with Responsiveness as the relevant specialty) and carries a total result. Characters act in order of initiative from highest to lowest. Ties are resolved by favoring characters with the highest Dexterity and re-rolling only between those characters if those attributes are the same as well.

The following rules cover one individual chasing another. For groups that are running together, they must go at the speed of the slowest member or break apart and be handled separately.

For every 5 feet of movement one side has over the other, apply a –1d cumulative penalty to rolls involved in the chase to the group with lower movement.

There are three abstract distances within the chase:

Close → Near → Far

The referee determines the starting distance and the difficulty of the action depending upon the terrain, and the chase is on. Both sides make opposed actions to gauge their relative distance to each other, often Athletics but could be others depending on the terrain and described actions within the chase.

If both sides of the chase succeed or fail equally, the status quo is maintained for that turn. If one succeeds and other other fails, one side advances (the pursuer getting one step closer, or the one fleeing getting farther away). A botch causes an additional advance, depending on which side rolled it. Enhancements on either side can be used to create opportunities in favor of the side that rolled them at the discretion of the referee, such as hazards or obstacles to slow down the opposing side.

When the two sides are Close, one can attempt an action to end the chase—usually by beginning combat or doing something to stop the other's movement. If the two sides are Far and the pursuer loses the opposed action, the chase ends as the one fleeing has gotten away for now. Of course, there might be a trail or other way to keep up the pursuit, just not in a direct chase!

ATTACK

Whether it's slashing with a blade, blasting with a laser, or swiping with claws, an attack action is resolved using the appropriate trait determined by the referee—Brawn , Melee Weapons, Ranged Weapons, and Unarmed Combat being most often employed. (Note that fighting with Brawn to smash opponents with brute strength incurs a –2d penalty to defensive actions. See Chapter Four, Brawn.) However, shooting at a tree isn't the same as an ursoid that's lunging out of the line of fire, just as slicing your blade at a control panel isn't the same as an enemy who's blocking with a jagged length of pipe. Most of the time, an attack is going to be opposed with a defense action that makes it trickier to land a hit.

The base difficulty needed to score achievements for an attack action is based on circumstance.

There's nothing quite like taking a cheap shot at an unmoving target. Not only is it an Easy action, the poor sap doesn't even know enough to dodge or block, so there's a fair chance your sucker punch will score some damage.

Sometimes you're toe-to-toe with an enemy who is trying to tear your face off with no thought to its own safety. If you are attacking an enemy who's standing still, he's still Easy in terms of difficulty, but you must contend with whatever defenses he is putting in your way. Then it's an opposed action (see Defense, below).

If you're attacking a moving enemy or one that's consciously trying to avoid your blows without making an active defense, the situation gets a bit trickier, and it ramps up to being an Average action. If the enemy is actively dodging or blocking, those actions will oppose your attacks. Alternately, if you're attacking an enemy behind light cover (less than half), the same applies.

It shouldn't come as a surprise, but sometimes fighting is Hard—the difficulty of attack actions against a target that's difficult to see (near-invisibility or from cloaking darkness), moving quickly (a Run or Sprint, see Movement), or has most of its body is behind cover.

The referee is always the final judge of action difficulty, and simultaneous circumstance may make an action easier or harder than it might be otherwise. An enemy walking behind a chest-high wall would be Hard, since he's moving and behind light cover.

Range

Distance attacks add a small level of complication to matters, whether you are firing a gun or shooting poisonous quills from your barbed tail. Base difficulty is determined using the factors listed above, but the dice pool is modified based on distance. It's generally easier to hit a target that's closer than one far away, and it's also true that a more skilled marksman has a chance at actually tagging the enemy disappearing into the distance. That's where range increments come into play.

7.3 - Attack Difficulty

Target is …	Difficulty
… unmoving, unaware, or prone	Easy
… moving, avoiding, or behind light cover	Average
… difficult to see, moving at high speed, or behind heavy cover	Hard
Attacker is …	**Modifier**
… injured (more than half of Wounds capacity)	–1d
… fighting with off-hand	–1d

Any target within the range increment of the weapon uses the attacker's full available dice pool (not including any other modifiers). For each additional increment, the attacker's dice pool receives a cumulative –1d penalty. As usual, if the action reaches zero dice, it will automatically fail. A target that's within 5 feet is "point blank" and earns the attacker a +1d bonus—though firing a ranged weapon so close also earns the target an opportunity to attack with any melee options available as a response (see above).

Reach

Some creatures have greater reach than others. They can attack in hand-to-hand without being within the normal five foot distance required for close combat. Whether it's because of exceptional size, long appendages (such as tentacles, vines, etc.), mutations, or technology, reach simply extends the distance from which a combatant can launch melee attacks. It is noted in terms of five feet increments (10', 15', and so on).

Size

Many of the creatures and objects that come into play aboard the *Warden* are Medium in game terms (see Chapter Three, Size), from a short human adult to a grizzly bear. When creatures and objects that exist on a different scale interact, it's all about just how much bigger or smaller one is than the other. The size categories are:

Tiny → Small → Medium → Large → Huge

It is more difficult to hit a smaller target if it's moving or dodging, increasing the difficulty by one (from Easy to Average, Average to Hard as a maximum difficulty) for each "degree" smaller the defender is from the attacker. However, any successful attack receives +1 achievement toward determining damage for each degree of difference.

The inverse is true as well. It's easier for something small to hit something larger, with each degree of difference making it progressively easier but when determining damage a penalty of –1 achievement per degree of difference makes it extremely challenging for a mouse to damage an elephant.

DEFENSE

Sometimes you're the one getting shot at or your face slashed with wicked claws. Whoever said that the best defense is a good offense likely was not in the sights of a blaster rifle. Cover and movement make life more difficult for the enemy trying to rip out your insides, but you might want to leap out of the way or block a deadly swing with your own blade—actions collectively known as **active defense**.

The good news? You don't have to declare your defense in advance if you so choose. The bad? Active defenses are still actions and still count against you in terms of multiple actions. Consolation: A chosen active defense counts as only one action until your next turn unless you make a change before your turn begins. (For example, if you declare a dodge and decide later to switch to blocking, that would count as two actions.) Essentially, you enter your turn with an action deficit, having already taken your first action in the coming turn and incurring multiple action penalties.

While an active defense only counts as one action, it is rolled independently against each attack.

Blocking

Be it a fancy parry delivered with flourish and style or simply placing a sturdy plank between you and the enemy's swing, blocking is an active defense to deflect an enemy attack. Roll the appropriate trait and it becomes the opposing action the enemy must overcome to deliver damage.

Blocking unarmed is better than nothing, but if you win the opposed action, you still suffer any bonus weapon damage.

Distance attacks cannot be blocked under normal circumstances, though mutation, tech, etc. can break this rule. Cover and distance are generally the best way to avoid getting shot.

Dodging

While sturdier combatants may enjoy trading blows with a worthy adversary, others prefer being quick to getting dead. A dodging action means you're weaving around using movement to avoid the attacks

7.4 - Damage

Achievements Over Defense	Damage
1	1 F
2	2 F
3	3 F
4	4 F + 1 W
5	5 F + 2 W
6	6 F + 3 W
7+	Etc.

of enemies. You cannot actively dodge attacks from unknown enemies, so run really fast to make it harder for the enemies you cannot see.

Like blocking, dodging is a character's opposed action against attacks. If the dodge wins against an attack, no damage occurs.

DAMAGE

The whole point of fighting is to put the enemy down. Whether they're dead or simply out for the count, you'll leave them bleeding, bruised, burned, crushed, mangled, or disintegrated. The attack is the means; damage is the ends. The downside is that sometimes the one left in a crumpled heap to feed a colony of sentient mushrooms is you.

Fatigue and Wounds are explained in Chapter Three, but here they are once again in brief:

Fatigue is the result of pushing oneself in action or combat, exhaustion and strain, along with any minor number of bumps, bruises, cuts, and scrapes. When a character's accumulated Fatigue approaches maximum capacity, the closer she is to falling over on the spot. Additional Fatigue damage suffered by a character already at maximum accumulates as **Trauma**, which could leave a character out of the action for quite some time. Fatigue recovers relatively quickly through rest and other means.

Wounds are the kind of injuries not taken lightly. This type of damage indicates serious business—deep cuts that bleed, bones fractured or broken, internal injuries that won't heal quickly without intervention. When a character reaches maximum Wounds capacity, he could easily die. Injured characters perform poorly.

Since attacks are opposed actions, the amount of base damage is a function of how many achievements the attack succeeded over any defense. Success always indicates Fatigue damage, with each enhancement indicating 1 additional Wound. Finally, apply any bonus damage from the weapon itself.

A well-struck blow with a high-damage weapon can ruin the target's entire week or leave another broken corpse on the decks of the *Warden*. Of course, the right protection can make even a powerful attack completely survivable.

Damage Type

In game terms, damage is no more than additional flavor to describe what's happening. A mutant chicken doesn't care of it's decapitated, roasted, or beaten to death. However, there are times when armor, mutation, or tech might interact with specific types of damage. Whether it's reduction of the given damage type or an amplification of it, the damage type is a keyword that lets everyone know whether special circumstance applies to the damage dealt.

Resistance & Vulnerability

With the right mutation or handy piece of tech, you might have resistance to a particular category of damage: cold, electricity, fire, radiation, or sonic. Your resistance score reduces the number of achievements rolled by the opponent before any other factors are applied. Of course, if you're unlucky, you might be vulnerable to a particular energy type, meaning the attack gains one or more achievements with those attacks, and it sucks to be you. Flat numbers not determined by achievements are either reduced (for resistance) or increased (for vulnerability) by 1 for each "level."

Armor

A giant mutant lobster might be a tempting target, but he wears an extremely tough shell around his delicious innards. Even a squishy human might be savvy enough to cobble together some protection against the many things on the ship that might do her harm.

Armor reduces damage based on its armor rating—eliminating some or all damage from a given hit. Wounds are reduced first, followed by Fatigue, with any excess points lost if the armor rating exceeds the damage. Worn armor (not a result of natural biology or mutation) might slow a character down and reduce mobility (see Chapter Six) but could still be worth it in the long run. Some types of armor may offer additional protection to a particular type of damage (see below).

Armor cannot usually be specifically bypassed by an attack, as it's assumed that any attacker is trying to get around his opponent's protection. However, enhancements used to make called shots against an unarmored area (a head or appendage, for example) ignores the listed protection.

Consequences of Damage

Getting hurt is never a good thing—though certain mutations might channel the pain and fear into something useful. Like any other rules, the following are subject to modifications and exceptions for mutations, qualities, and tech.

Fatigue Damage: Unconsciousness

A character is on the verge of passing out when Fatigue damage reaches the character's capacity, the combination of sheer exhaustion and any minor injuries overwhelming the character's will to stay awake. When a character reaches maximum Fatigue, he must make an immediate Easy Discipline roll to stay conscious. At the beginning of every subsequent turn, he must make the check again, the difficulty raising to Average and then Hard (where it will remain until the character either falls unconscious or reduces Fatigue).

Breaking Stuff

Suppose you're a hulking brute and want to smash something that's not technically alive. How is that resolved? Most of the time the referee simply assigns the action a difficulty and appropriate trait (Brawn, Crafting, depending on the nature of the breaking that you're trying to accomplish.) Other times it might take a while to break something down, and the referee will rule it a complex action (see above) to be resolved appropriately.

Note that some materials (like duralloy) aboard the *Warden* are beyond the abilities of most characters to have much of an effect on—so lacking a specific mutation or tech, smashing such objects will have about the same effect as yelling at them.

All actions performed at maximum Fatigue damage are Hard. Any additional Fatigue damage is counted separately as Trauma (see below).

Wound Damage: Death

Wounds are serious business, and a character whose total Wounds equals her full capacity is in immediate danger of dying. The character instantly falls unconscious. For every 30 seconds of game time (ten combat turns) the character must succeed a Constitution (Fortitude) check to stay alive, the first check being Easy, the next Average, and all the rest Hard. A dying character can be kept alive with an Average Medicine (First Aid) action (see Medical Assistance, below), which will stabilize him enough where the survival check is only necessary every 30 minutes of game time. Further intervention is required for a character on death's door to recover any more (see Recovery & Healing, below).

Sometimes a character is killed in a particularly overwhelming and grisly manner and nothing can be done. If a character receives twice his total possible Wounds in damage, he is completely dead and probably little more than a greasy smear or a pile of charred bones.

Injured Actions

Slogging on after you've left half your blood on the floor is no walk in the park. A character is considered **injured** if she has taken half or more possible Wounds, and suffers a –1d penalty to all actions until she has recovered. Special drugs or mutations that eliminate pain might remove this penalty.

Specialized Damage

Most of the time you're being ripped apart with tooth and claw or bludgeoned by clubs—the mundane stuff. But some types of injuries are extra-special and require further game rules to cover the many reasons your character needs to be clever, fast, or tough to survive.

Burns

Whether from being shoved into a tribal bonfire or seared with the laser of a rampaging robot, a burn is a particularly nasty injury that doesn't heal as quickly. Any fire damage suffered heals at half the normal rate of recovery (see Recovery & Healing, below).

Disease

The unforgiving conditions and constant struggle aboard the *Warden* have bred hardy creatures that shrug off most germs and minor illnesses. But there are horrible viruses and flesh-eating bacteria that give even the mightiest cause for concern. Most disease is resisted by a Constitution (Fortitude) response, with difficulty and consequences varying depending on the variety. Some viruses are just inconvenient, resulting in action penalties, while others may genuinely attack the body and cause increasing damage until fought off or cured.

Falling

Gravity is a harsh mistress. Birds, bats, and flying squirrels are less worried, but for everyone else that sudden stop at the end leads to injury. Falling is treated literally as if the ground is attacking you, with Dexterity used as a defense. Every 10 feet of the fall is considered an achievement to be overcome, with the "weapon damage" of a fall generally being 1d Fatigue (or worse depending on what's waiting at the end of the fall).

Explosions

An explosion is a terrifying and unique event that is always worse the closer you are. Each explosion has damage that is expressed in dice and type (4dW) and an Explosion Increment as a unit of distance (10 feet).

First the damage dice are rolled, then damage is assessed based on the location of anything within the first increment (distance from the center of the explosion). For each increment after the first, remove one die from the damage dealt—from highest-value dice to lowest. This continues until all the damage dice have been removed and anything in the radius of the explosion has been effected.

Light cover reduces the damage by 1d, Heavy by 2d, the same as distance. Armor and damage resistance apply normally.

Inhospitable Environment

Uncomfortable environmental conditions pose long-term dangers for creatures exposed to them. Everything being relative, it could be anything from a normal human exposed to excessive heat or cold to an amphibian not having access to adequate water at least once a day. The referee must determine the exact effects, but as a guideline for "unusual conditions" for a human character, every half-day exposed to such conditions causes 1d Fatigue damage. Adequate protection or innovative methods (which might involve related traits such as Survival) to endure the environment might eliminate the damage entirely. Extremely incompatible conditions (penguin in a desert) might make the frequency of the damage based on an hour or minute.

Extreme Environment: There is a difference between "uncomfortable" and "deadly." If exposed to the vacuum of space or some other condition that poses instant harm to a character, he suffers 1d Wounds for every turn exposed. Specialized gear or other methods might mitigate some or all of this damage.

Radiation

The invisible but potentially lethal energy known as radiation is a dual-edged threat aboard the *Warden*. Reactor leaks, areas unshielded against the naturally-occurring radiation in space, and some biologically generated by mutations all expose characters to damaging or life-changing doses. Characters have a resistance to radiation as explained in Chapter 3, Derived Stats.

Exposure to radiation is an "attack," the intensity and timing specific to the situation. Minor background radiation may accumulate 1 achievement per half-hour of exposure against the character (making it harder to avoid damage the longer exposure occurs), while a concentrated blast of radiation might result in an immediate 1d achievement attack against the character. Damage is determined normally plus 1 Wound, healing at half-rate (equivalent to a burn, see above).

Human characters are only harmed by radiation, though they've generally developed a higher resistance against it. If a mutant character receives radiation damage that's more than Wounds capacity, a special check is required to see if they instead develop a new mutation. See Chapter Five, Radiation Exposure, to determine if mutation occurs. If a character is instead mutated by the radiation, continued exposure to the same source does no further harm. That does not make them immune to the same radiation, however. If they encounter it again after a one day lapse they will be subject to potential damage normally.

Suffocation

Every living creature requires a source of oxygen (or carbon dioxide for plants), whether it's air or water (for fish and amphibians). When denied the chance to breathe, life becomes uncomfortable very quickly. The first 30 seconds without air (or water) is not a problem, but after that it becomes an "attack" against the character of 1 achievement cumulative per turn, defended by Constitution check. Damage is determined normally until the character is unconscious—after which the damage is +1 W until the character is freed of the situation or dies. Plants need air as well, but they check every 5 minutes instead of 30 seconds.

Toxins

Some substances aren't particularly healthy to ingest, inject, breathe, or even touch. Whether it's strong-smelling hooch distilled by a mutant tribe and swallowed on purpose or the potentially lethal bite of a viper, you may need to find out exactly how you fared against a foreign substance in your body. The difficulty and effects of a given toxin are specific to the situation, but the following are a few examples. Unless otherwise determined by the referee, all toxins are resisted by Constitution (Fortitude).

Alcohol: For each drink consumed, the character must succeed a Hard check. Each failure results in a –1d cumulative penalty to all actions, and three failures indicates the character falls unconscious for 1d hours.

Paralytic: Depending on the strength of the toxin, the character suffers 1d Fatigue and must succeed a check of varying difficulty. Failure means the character suffers 2d Trauma and cannot move until it has been recovered.

Neurotoxin: These deadly poisons attack the body from within. The character suffers 1d Fatigue immediately and must succeed a Hard check or take 1d Wounds as well. For every minute of game time, the character must make another check or continue to suffer equal damage each time until he has succeeded three concurrent times or the toxin has been somehow neutralized.

Conditions

If all the ways you might get shot, stabbed, mangled, burned, or jettisoned into the vacuum of space weren't quite enough, there are other ways your character might suffer. But if you've been knocked to the ground and are leaking some vital fluid, at least you're alive.

Bleeding

Lots of wounds will leave you bloody, but this condition refers to a major blood vessel severed and you are bleeding out. A bleeding character loses 1 Fatigue each turn (3 seconds), and then 1 Wound each turn when Fatigue reaches zero. Applying pressure to an external bleeding injury can slow it down (every 10 turns, or 30 seconds), while an Average Medicine (First Aid) action is required to stop the bleeding (see Medical Assistance, below). Internal bleeding requires different actions, mutations, or tech.

Plants and artificial life cannot suffer this condition.

Blind

Not being able to see means you are an Easy target in close combat and –2d for physical actions that normally require sight. Ranged attacks automatically miss unless circumstances and the referee dictate you may attempt with the penalty.

Paralyzed

If you can't move, you're an Easy target in close combat and can't move or take other physical actions.

Prone

Laying on the ground makes you more difficult to hit at a distance (–1d to anything out of reach) but it makes you an Easy target for close combat and makes your own attacks Hard.

Starving

A character's basic needs are determined by its stock (see Chapter 3), though these might vary depending on mutations and qualities. If a character's food needs are not met, he suffers the same penalties and damage as being Weary (below), except these cannot be reversed except by getting sufficient nourishment. Lack of water is more serious, with the penalties beginning after 24 hours and getting worse every 6 hours after that.

Stunned

Your bell has been rung and you are dizzy, fuzzy-headed, or otherwise disoriented. A stunned character's base movement is reduced to 5 feet and may only

attempt one action per turn, suffering a –1d penalty on all actions until the condition is removed.

Unconscious

If you're snoozing in a dangerous situation, it's the game equivalent of being prone and paralyzed at the same time. If you're merely sleeping you can wake up and act normally after a one-turn period of being stunned (see above). If you are unconscious for some other reason then you might be in serious trouble.

Weary

If a character has been pushed beyond normal limits without rest or has been through exertion or trauma that leaves him exhausted, he is considered **weary**. For most human and animal characters this means staying up for more than 24 hours. For every 12 hours after that he suffers 1 point of Fatigue that cannot be recovered without rest. Base movement is slowed by 5 feet and all actions suffer a –1d penalty, and these penalties accrue for each 24-hour period without rest. Extreme exertion can be counted as equal to a 12-hour period for terms of determining just how weary a character may be.

RECOVERY & HEALING

If you're one of the lucky ones you'll get to crawl away from combat with a chance to lick your wounds and patch yourself up. That which does not kill you may come back and try to kill you again—so get whatever rest and healing you can, while you can. While resting up is the slow-but-sure method of recovery, field medicine, mutations, and tech can speed up the process and get you back in the fight.

Restoring Fatigue & Trauma

Fatigue recovers quickly. Six hours of uninterrupted rest removes all Fatigue damage. Otherwise it recovers at a rate of 1 point per hour of light activity. A character who has accumulated Trauma must succeed an Easy Constitution check at the end of each hour spent unconscious to remove a trauma point.

A character who is Injured (see Damage, above) recovers Fatigue at half the normal rate.

Second Wind: Once per a day a character may take a moment to shake off some of the exhaustion and push harder. Second wind is the only action that may be taken during a turn, and restores 1d Fatigue.

Recovering From Wounds

When you've got Wound damage, you've been more seriously messed up. Your body needs to knit bone, mend organs, or at least recover sap and grow more bark (if, for example, you happen to be a tree). It's a much bigger deal.

As long as you're not Injured (see Damage, above) you'll recover on your own at a slow but steady pace: 1 per day.

If you are Injured, your body has to fight hard (or requires help) to begin a true healing process. After a full day of rest you must succeed an Average Constitution check to begin healing at the above-listed rate. If the check fails, you need another full day of rest to try again. If you botch the check, your body is losing the fight and you take 1 Wound damage per day until you succeed the check to just to stabilize the situation (then must rest to attempt actual recovery once more).

Medical Assistance

It sure would be nice to face-crawl to safety after a battle and simply rest until you're all better. But chances are you'll be in your next fight before you could heal up from the last one—at least without a bit of extra help. The "natural" way to heal up is usually a last resort rather than the first choice.

First Aid: Most now living aboard the *Warden* don't have sophisticated medical expertise, and the diversity created by mutation makes it truly difficult to have an advanced understanding of anatomy and biology of all intelligent life. That's the bad news, but the good is that keeping someone alive and doing some basic patching up isn't all that difficult. Stop the flow of blood (or sometimes sap), set breaks, keep conscious, etc.

If a character is bleeding, they can be stabilized with an Average Medicine (First Aid) action that takes 1d turns to complete. (Sometimes it's as simple as tying a tourniquet to stop one point of bleeding, sometimes it's more involved.) Success means the patient is no longer bleeding. The exact same type of action can be used on someone who is dying, but it's a Hard action instead. Someone who's all-the-way dead cannot be revived without extraordinary intervention. Once a character is stabilized, they can begin healing on their own.

A first aid action can be made simpler (+1d) by possessing the right supplies or conditions, whereas battlefield chaos or makeshift tools might make the job more involved (−1d).

Medical Tech: Speaking of extraordinary intervention, there is advanced healing technology about the *Warden* if one knows how to find it and decipher its use. Everything from spray-on bandages to limb regeneration and full-on cloning could be found, though such artifacts are prized and often guarded jealously if they are understood at all. The more prevalent medical tech is listed in Chapter Six, while the rare and truly unusual must be encountered during the course of adventure.

Mutations: Some creatures from nature possess remarkable abilities to heal from damage and even to regrow severed limbs. Fortunate mutants exhibit these traits or even more rapid regeneration, and might be able to recover in hours what would take weeks for others. Such abilities are discussed in Chapter Five.

WHERE TO NEXT

If you arrived here after reading **Chapter Two: Basic Gameplay** to get the full rundown on the game system, we recommend **Chapter Three: Mutants & Mankind** to learn character creation. If you'd like to learn about the *Warden* or want to become a referee, jump to **Chapter Eight: Storyteller & Referee**.

The **referee**—sometimes titled Game Master, Judge, Storyteller, Director, or even more fanciful names in other roleplaying games—has a highly rewarding role at the game table. It's a role that may seem complex, even overwhelming at first, but it's not as hard as it looks. If you're new to roleplaying games in general, this section will give you the basics of how to be a referee. If you've run games before, or have been a player in other games and want to try your hand at running one, this section also goes into detail on the specific features of METAMORPHOSIS ALPHA that a referee, experienced or otherwise, needs to understand. Adventures aboard the *Warden* borrow from other genres to create a unique blend that you'll want to have in mind so your game sessions are fun and memorable.

That said, this book and the rules themselves are just tools for you and the players to have fun. You are encouraged to customize the setting, the style, and even the rules to fit the kind of game you enjoy running and that keeps your players coming back for more.

ROLE OF THE REFEREE

As a combination of host, rules judge, narrator, and actor, the referee is a vital ingredient to a successful METAMORPHOSIS ALPHA game session or campaign. A good referee is a conduit to the world of the game, in our case the decks of the *Warden*, acting as the eyes and ears of the characters (along with any other senses and information gleaned from mutations and technology). The players make decisions for their characters, and it's the referee's job to say what happens next, relying on both the rules and personal judgement to figure it out as the game progresses. The situation keeps changing, and the referee continues to narrate, resolve actions, and keep the excitement going, whether it's exploration, diplomacy, or desperate battle.

In between game sessions, the referee crafts new adventure ideas, designs new allies and opponents, and creates new sections of the *Warden* ripe for exploration. Even published material needs be studied so it's familiar for play, and at best is customized for an individual group's needs.

It's up the referee to set the stage but then allow the stars, the characters as guided by their players, to make decisions that drive the action forward. It's good to have an idea of where things are going, but possess flexibility

and fallback ideas if events take an unexpected twist. Players make surprising decisions and dice will occasionally yank the rug out from under the best-made plans.

A referee should hold fairness and objectivity as two of the most important traits to keep in mind. Decisions should be based on the rules and the overall fun of the game but without favoritism or emotional attachment to a player or non-player character. Judgment calls should be consistent and reasoned to keep things moving and the entire table enjoying the game.

RUNNING A GAME

It's a job that balances out the most power at the gaming table with the most responsibility. The referee must juggle several jobs seamlessly, and aside from the one implied by the title (judging the rules impartially), the storytelling aspects can generally be divided into two areas.

Narrator

Without the referee giving effective description of areas, events, people, creatures, or things encountered along the way, the humans and mutants portrayed by the players would be blind and deaf. Whether it's detailed descriptions of a new room or a quick summation of a long stretch of uneventful time, the referee gives tone, detail, and emphasis to spur the players toward their next set of actions.

For example:

Referee: *"The small room you entered has finally ceased vibrating madly. The doors slide open again, but instead of the steaming jungles you've known all your life as home, you see a blinding field of bright light reflecting off something crystalline, and you feel a rush of cold such as you have never known before. Still blinking from the sudden flare, you notice that the glowing lights that formerly lined the room have gone dull and grey."* (In this case, the players entered an elevator which took them from a jungle level to an arctic level and also drained the elevator of power.)

The referee should describe all features which are immediately obvious to a quick inspection: visibility, ambient sounds and odors, anything moving. Items that are likely to arouse interest should be highlighted: *"There are some rocks that are an unusual color,"* or *"There are glints of something reflective in the woods."* Players may ask lots of questions in response to the initial description (though you should keep your descriptions as brief as possible). If the answers are self-evident (*"What color are the leaves?" "How warm is it?"*), just tell them. If the answers may be hidden or obscure (*"Is anyone hiding in the woods?" "How old is that burned-out campfire?"*), you may call for a the appropriate trait to be rolled—Alertness (Observation) in this case—or you may decide another action is required, such as moving closer.

Actor

While each player usually only has one character to portray and keep track of, the referee literally takes on the role everyone and everything else. How you go about these portrayals is a matter of personal style. Some referees prefer to handle things in the third person. (*"The wolfoid snarls some threats at you and demands you leave his lands."*) Others prefer direct first-person roleplaying. (*"You dare to trespass on my hunting grounds, hairless weaklings? Flee now, or I shall make toys for my cubs from your bones!"*) And of course, it's fine to switch styles as appropriate for the situation. Trivial or mundane interactions can be glossed over if desired. (*"You spend an hour negotiating and reach a deal with the merchant."*)

When running allies and opponents with which the players must interact, the referee should always consider their motivations, abilities, and knowledge. Some will fight to the death; some will surrender or try to negotiate; some will flee. Some will be natural allies against a common foe. Some may be treacherous.

The most important thing to remember is that the player characters are the stars. Non-player characters should never be run as the referee's personal character. Having useful allies is fine, but the game should always center on the decisions and actions of the players' characters.

A SHIP TO EXPLORE

Even more than most other roleplaying games, METAMORPHOSIS ALPHA is a game of exploration. A typical game session or campaign begins with characters who do not even understand that their "world" is actually a ship. The contained yet varying areas of the *Warden* are natural environments for exploration and discovery. The nature of the *Warden* allows for an amazing variety of places to find within short distances of each other. There are oceans and deserts, tropical jungles and fertile plains, vast automated industrial complexes and abandoned high-tech cities, dense under-corridors and maintenance hatchways, and even areas open to the black void of outer space.

Exactly how easy or difficult it might be to get from one area to another is very much up to the referee. There may be many still-functioning transit tubes and lifts, or it may be an arduous struggle through the ship's engineering and interdeck areas to move around.

The referee should feel free to create any setting that is even vaguely plausible for the *Warden*—remembering it was intended to serve as a safe home for a large number of people for hundreds of years. Entertainment areas inspired by the "Holodeck" or *Westworld*, laboratories where genetic experiments took place, industrial or residential areas shrouded in overgrown hydroponics, areas where the artificial gravity has been turned off (or was never turned on), cryogenic chambers with frozen colonists who are unaware of the disaster—the possibilities are limitless. This is how to make the ship yours.

Genre & Concept

METAMORPHOSIS ALPHA defies genre pigeonholing, but you might think of the game as science-fantasy. That doesn't mean robots and wizards, but that absolute scientific accuracy is simply less important than ideas that are simply cool and given enough pseudoscientific gobbledygook to fit. Bizarre mutations, nanotechnology that ignores issues of heat dissipation and energy sources, sentient plants—it's all good.

This is also a game of high adventure, exploration, and excitement. While you certainly can focus on personal relationships, the meaning of life, and other other deep issues, METAMORPHOSIS ALPHA is often at its best when the focus is on discovering the wonders of the setting. METAMORPHOSIS ALPHA is not about the human heart in conflict with itself. METAMORPHOSIS ALPHA is about the mutant with two hearts in conflict with a laser-eyed, flying grizzly bear.

That said, many of the novels and other media that inspired METAMORPHOSIS ALPHA did focus on a higher level of conflict—that of knowledge vs. ignorance, with the main characters discovering the truth of their world and its history and having to deal with the cultures that denied it, cloaking the past in myth and superstition. This is a theme that often emerges organically in METAMORPHOSIS ALPHA games, as the characters try to tell others what they've found and are met with doubt or outright violence.

Tone & Mood

The exact tone of a campaign is ultimately up to the referee and the players, but there are a couple of general defaults that fit the history and mechanics of the game. Each of these can be adjusted and ignored as the gaming group sees fit:

- **Gonzo** (but not wacky): METAMORPHOSIS ALPHA features lots of "high weirdness," bizarre characters, and gruesomely slapstick deaths from misapplied technology—but it's not a fully comedic or satirical game. A flying rhino generating clouds of sleep gas is gonzo. A flying rhino dressed as a Japanese schoolgirl is wacky. Stick to gonzo.
- **Deadly:** There's no plot immunity, no story to be told that requires the heroes survive. Life is cheap and short, and there's plenty of ways to die instantly on the *Warden*. This doesn't mean the referee should go out of her way to rack up a body count, but she shouldn't be overly concerned with precisely balanced encounters and ways for the player characters to always come out alive. Players should be given a lot of choices as to what to do, and if they choose a high-risk path, so be it.
- **Free-Roaming:** While there's lots of options for a game setting in a single level or region of the *Warden*, the traditional METAMORPHOSIS ALPHA game is one of travel and exploration. There are few long-term relationships and recurring villains. Moving on means leaving the old behind and having the new just around the next corner.
- **Discovery & Wonder:** "Big Dumb Object" is an affectionate term in science fiction fandom for the kinds of stories that involve people exploring some immense artifact, such as *Ringworld* or *Rendezvous with*

Rama. METAMORPHOSIS ALPHA is very much this sort of setting. There should always be something cool, creative, fun, or inexplicable to stumble across. The size and scale of the *Warden* should be emphasized: Engineering sections packed with quarter-mile-high machines, warehouses that store supplies for the colonization of a world, wilderness zones which take days to cross by foot. Manhattan Island (13 miles long and 3 miles wide), along with its tallest buildings, could easily fit into one of the *Warden*'s larger decks with plenty of wilderness or parkland surrounding it.
- **Technology Is Mysterious:** The technology of the *Warden* is centuries ahead of our own, and it is as likely to resemble modern devices about as much as a tablet computer resembles a 1950's movie depiction of a futuristic computer. The natives of the *Warden* have even less of a grasp on what strange artifacts may do, and many of the things they find will be malfunctioning or used for purposes other than those intended. Every encounter with a machine can lead to surprising discoveries and the chance of serious injury or even death.

Humans & Mutants

The world of the *Warden* is one where life has changed in countless ways and the rules of heredity are more like polite suggestions (which life forms are free to ignore). In some ways, pure humans seem to have the worst of it, with no special powers or abilities. However, they have some advantages to keep in mind. The systems of the ship are designed for them to use, both in terms of physical access to controls and the system's security protocols recognizing them. Robots, in particular, will generally have strong (though not absolute) built-in protections against harming something they recognize as being human. And by having resisted mutating energies, humans have become tougher than their ancestors and adaptable enough to survive in such a chaotic environment.

The referee must decide how "humanocentric" his *Warden* is going to be or if it varies from one area to another. It may be that most of the inhabitants are human, and mutated humans and sapient mutant animals or plants are rare freaks. It may be that some regions of the ship were exposed to higher levels of mutating energy than others, and those areas are considered mutant territory. Another option is to have villages or settlements where humans, mutated humans, and mutant animals work together.

Tech & Powers

Technology and mutant powers provide multiple ways to solve problems or overcome obstacles. Balancing these in a game can be complex. While METAMORPHOSIS ALPHA is not as obsessed with balance as some other games, trusting the referee's judgment and the luck of the dice to balance things in the long haul, it is still the case that a game where all problems are trivially solved by the right machines or mutations is not going to be fun for long.

Technology is the greatest resource on the *Warden*, and it's particularly helpful for humans who lack any mutant powers to gain an edge. The referee needs to provide enough tech to keep the game fun and exciting, while not letting the characters turn into walking storage cabinets, bedecked with devices that can handle any challenge. Machines break, attract thieves, or simply run out of juice. Sometimes an item which seemed trivial or cosmetic turns out to have an unexpectedly clever application. Reward players for being smart, but don't let such discoveries take over the game.

The above philosophy applies to mutant powers. Many of them are flexible and can be applied in ways not explicitly mentioned in the description but which seem logical and plausible. Again, the referee should reward intelligence and creativity, but not permit a great idea to turn into a rote solution. The best way is to discuss this with the player—explain that this particular tactic is boring and he should try something new. If the player doesn't care, the myriad radiation fields, medical droids, and unusual diseases of the *Warden* can have all sort of unexpected interactions with a mutant, altering his powers in various ways.

SLINGING DICE

The SYSTEM 26 rules were designed to be quick to learn and easy to understand. The game only uses one type of dice (six-siders), only three degrees of difficulty (Easy, Average, Hard), and a fairly intuitive system to interpret the results. Chapters 2 and 7 go over the rules in terms of playing, but there are a few things worth noting when running games.

To Roll or Not

Even more important than how the dice mechanics work is understanding when they're needed at all. Rolling dice is fun, and the sound of hard-plastic clattering around on a tabletop becomes the background sounds for tensions, success, failure, laughter, cheers, and wails of disbelief … which is why you shouldn't waste them on dull moments.

As a referee you should remember one rule: **Dice should only be rolled when something interesting is going on.**

There should be tension, uncertainty, or a chance of unpleasant failure to warrant the musical dice-sound. An action roll should never be required for walking across the room—unless instead of walking the character is sprinting away from a bloodthirsty cheetoid or gingerly avoiding hidden mines. Many character actions should just simply happen, such as flipping the lights on, cooking a simple campfire meal, conversing with a friendly guard, or sharpening a sword. Don't cheapen how awesome dice-rolling can be by pairing it with snore-worthy actions.

Problems of Probability

While the dice mechanics that form the backbone of the game were intended to be straightforward, they are also the secret weapon for a referee to get a rough idea of how likely a player might succeed or fail on a given roll. A player with one measly die for an action has better than even odds, while one who's sitting pretty with five dice has only a tiny chance at screwing things up. A character must be at least Good at something to even have a shot at scoring an enhancement. That said, the dice are fickle; if they behave like you expect, they are just lulling you into a false sense of security. You never know what might happen when the plastic bounces around, and that's part of the fun. Here are things to keep in mind when assigning difficulty to actions.

Easy Actions

Easy doesn't mean automatic; it means that for most this kind of action won't present much of a challenge. If real life were a SYSTEM 26 game, most of our daily tasks would be Easy. If there's no tension or real consequences for failure (as discussed above), there is no reason to roll the dice. But when there are real stakes, dice should be rolled even when the action is on the easy side.

Average Actions

Remember that average for us in the mundane, real world would be Easy on the scale we use in our game. When we say an action is Average, we're talking middle-of-the-road for an action hero who leads a life of danger and adventure. The *Warden* is filled with hazards and dangers, so when a challenge is neither a walk in the park nor a sprint across a moving iceberg, it's likely Average. To keep up the analogy, an Average action is jogging across loose gravel without falling down. Note that the chance to botch is exactly the same as Easy actions.

Hard Actions

If you've seen those action movie moments where a skilled badass accomplishes something ridiculously difficult—be it leap over a huge chasm, put an arrow through a distant bullseye, or drive a fast-moving vehicle through an obstacle course with fiery boulders crashing down from above—then you've got a handle on Hard actions. Even characters who know what they're doing and have the backup of mutations or tech will still only attempt a Hard action if they're feeling cocky or (usually) have little choice. Botching chances are always the same and suck just as bad no matter how difficult the attempted action.

When Not To Roll At All

While the dice should not be rolled when the action is boring, it's because success is assumed. The opposite end of that scale is when there is no rolling because failure is assured. There are generally two reasons for this:

● **0d:** If the dice pool is modified by unfortunate circumstance down to a big, sad zero, it's game over—for that action anyway. The action really can't even be attempted, and if the player insists on giving it a shot anyway, there is one recourse for that (see sidebar) or you can just describe the embarrassing failure in a manner that amuses you.

● **Requirement-Based Actions:** The majority of actions a player wants the character to perform will be covered under traits and can be rolled, though sometimes with a dice pool modified by how well the attempted action matches up to the character. But some actions are simply impossible without some requirement, such as extensive training (delicate surgery on a major organ) or specialized gear (tools for mechanical repair). This was covered in Chapter Seven, Requirement-Based Actions, so don't let the players whine too much.

DESCRIPTION & RULES

Which sounds more exciting? *"Your action point eliminates 4 of the Wounds you would have taken; your 3 achievements and bonus damage max out the mutant animal's wounds, dropping him."* Or, *"Scar-lock bats the hyenoid's axe aside and drives the blade straight into his throat! He dies choking and thrashing."* For most of us, it's the second. The game mechanics and dice-rolling serve to flesh out the scenes the referee and players create together, but in the best cases the rules fade to the background—leaving only exciting action set to a kick-ass soundtrack in our memories.

A great way to keep the game engaging is to let the rules guide your descriptions of success and failure, victory and defeat. The dice-rolling mechanics at the very heart of the game are already your baseline. Actions are either easy, hard, or in-between. Success is either minimal, standard, or solid—even perhaps amazing! Failure is either unremarkable or an awful setback.

We've tried to work descriptions in to other elements of the game throughout the book. Traits are written to suggest the type of characteristics that go along with them (high Brawn indicates muscle and physical power, low Discipline could mean someone with a short attention span). Both mutations and tech are written not just to say how they work, but how they might look and function beyond the rules. Next are a few suggestions on describing other elements of the game.

Qualities

While written to be short and sweet, it's worth remembering that some qualities can guide roleplaying for a player (with helpful suggestions from the Referee, of course) and also serve as hooks for how those characters interact with the world and are perceived by others. While Light Sleeper is advantageous in the game, it still might indicate restlessness or someone who is never able to relax and let her guard down. A Knowledgeable character could be a curious know-it-all. Someone who is Hesitant might be prone to panic and indecision, while a character with Combat Rage might have a legendary temper that leads others to watch their words carefully.

Action Points

Serving as the oxymoronic way to legally cheat the normal rules of the game, Action Points are there to let characters succeed more spectacularly, soften failure, and dodge death a little longer. They alter the results and don't truly represent anything concrete in the game world—though one could say they are a combination of grit and luck. The best way to handle them descriptively is to just roll with the changes. Avoided damage could be narrowly dodged or just shrugged off with sheer toughness; dodged failure could mean an unexpected reversal, while added success could bring a lucky break into play.

Enhancements

Achievements are about getting the job done. Enhancements are when awesome happens. Chapter Seven offers guidelines as to what might happen in general terms when enhancements are rolled (including possible game effects). But as enhancements aren't the norm, you should make sure to embellish and turn them into cool and memorable moments. Delivered wounds should be devastating and leave permanent scars (if the enemy survives at all), activating technology might reveal a previously unknown and limited function, or a mutation flares up with terrifying power. While you should stay in the ballpark of the listed

Doing the Impossible

Every once in a while a player is going to want to try something no matter how crazy, no matter how unlikely it is. You are under no obligation to do more than smile at their moans of protest, but if you're feeling especially generous, you can give them that snowflake-in-the-reactor-core chance of pulling off the impossible.

Allow the player to roll a 6d dice pool. They can succeed if they get all sixes, and it will be considered that many achievements! But if they roll even a single one, it's a botch. Don't let this happen often—once per game session is the recommended limit—but it will at least give them that tiny chance of doing something amazing. And if the statistically impossible happens (and it sometimes does!), make that player buy drinks later, as she is probably winning the lottery at some point.

examples, don't just say "opponent disarmed"—say how the barbarian speared the mutant's club with his sword and sent it flying away.

It's also important to remember the scenery when coming up with possible enhancements. Exposed power cables, open maintenance hatches, slippery floors, and more can provide inspiration for how enhancements play out. When designing areas and scenarios, it might be worth making notes of some possibilities ahead of time; when the scenery, story, and game rules interact, it keeps things fun and interesting. Plus it's always a good laugh for a character to scream "THIS … IS … ENGINEERING!" before kicking an enemy down an elevator shaft.

Specialized Damage

Not all damage is created equal, and the type that has to be noted separately is worth giving some extra descriptive attention. Burns are awful and usually leave nasty scars long after they heal. Disease can cause mewling and helplessness in the most powerful warrior. Environmental dangers might leave characters gasping or disoriented. Poisons might manifest as mysterious effects from an unknown source, or they might be a devastating secondary consequence of an enemy. The cultural memory of the long-ago disaster leaves most residents of the *Warden* fearful of radiation, so even the rumor or possibility of a flooded zone will keep humans and mutants away until it has somehow been confirmed as safe.

DESIGNING ADVENTURES

Part of the referee's job involves coming up with exciting and challenging scenarios in which the players can test their mettle and characters amid the strangely logical chaos of the starship *Warden*. While we provide a starting adventure in this book and more planned for the future, eventually you'll need to take off the training wheels and create one of your own.

This may seem like a daunting task, but the good news is that it doesn't have to be! While published adventures have fully written descriptions and game statistics and a bit of polish, a good adventure only truly lives in the experience of the group that's playing through it. If the players have a blast and come away with memories of laughing, rolling dice, palm-sweating excitement, and stories of epic moments, your job was well done even if you showed up with a half-sheet of badly scribbled notes and just decided to wing it.

The important thing to start with as the referee preparing an adventure for the next game session is understanding your own strengths and limitations. At least try to imagine how your game group might react to what you're throwing at them. Make sure your level of prep matches what you can handle—so if you're highly organized and perform your best when there is lots of written material to fall back on, go with a more thorough approach, while if you're comfortable with improvisation, just come up with a plot, some locations, and a few challenges and make things up as you go along.

What follows are some guidelines in creating adventures for METAMORPHOSIS ALPHA. Experienced gamers who've done this sort of thing before might be fine just skimming this section and focusing on the unique elements of the game, while those new

to adventure creation might benefit from giving the upcoming material some serious thought when putting a scenario together for the first time.

Adventure Concepts

Writers of any stripe are often asked, "Where do you get your ideas?" An excellent response might be a diner, hardware store, or Dimension X. Inspiration might come from anywhere, and the seeds of a METAMORPHOSIS ALPHA adventure could come from books, television, or movies—be they sci-fi, adventure, action, or horror. Ideas often develop with the players themselves. ("*I wonder if those mutant salamanders by the lake are guarding something interesting!*" Or, "*It would be really cool if we ever found that someone had bioengineered dinosaurs on the ship!*") The evolving story of an ongoing campaign might create natural springboards for a new scenario, whether it's success (someone coveting a powerful tech relic hard-won by the group) or failure (by not shutting off an AI production facility, a swarm of dangerous robots flood onto a deck and threaten everyone there). By looking around inside the game and the real world, the only trouble might be deciding which fun idea to explore first!

Some adventures may be written specifically for the characters in the group, while others are about interesting ideas or locations to explore on a giant half-ruined spaceship. Either approach is just fine, and some of the best adventures make at least some use of both. A location or concept-based adventure can benefit from a personal touch directly related to one of the characters. A more personal story, be it revenge or redemption, can be amplified by a unique location or element that explores the core ideas that build METAMORPHOSIS ALPHA.

The "elevator pitch" approach can help narrow down a basic adventure concept. Come up with a one-sentence summary that gives you a starting point. A few examples:

☀ A tribe of mutant amphibians jealously guard a small lake in a semi-tropical deck habitat, but instead of their eggs, it's actually an aquatic source of strange energy that allows their offspring to mature at rapid pace with stronger mutations.

✺ As the group hunts the thief who stole their artifact, they learn his motivations may have been more pure than their own—as his parents are hostage to a strange android that demands technological tribute that it keeps grafting to its body.

Adventure Structure

As creativity explores boundless imagination, the importance of structure may seem counterintuitive. But once you let your mind wander and come up with your great ideas, a solid structure will set you free to explore them in constructive ways, a skeleton upon which you can flesh out your ideas—mutations and all!

Any type of story needs to have a beginning, a middle, and an end. While it's completely unnecessary to follow a rigid Hollywood-style three act structure, it's useful to define these points when writing your scenario.

Establishment

What's going on that gets the characters involved? It could be as straightforward as them being attacked by a previously unknown enemy. A new area of the ship might represent the beginning of a new situation that the player characters will have to confront. Or they could follow a trail, riddle, or other clues to lead them on a journey. Either way, you want to define the nature of the problem to be solved or the goal to be achieved. If necessary to draw the characters in, you might need to come up with a few enticements—different introductory possibilities that will set things in motion.

Example: The characters are ambushed by amphibious mutants who attempt to subdue rather than kill and are able to heal incredible injuries with the use of strange blue-glowing orbs that dissolve into so much smoke when used. It's impossible to know whether or not this is a result of some strange mutation or if the healing orbs are created by powerful technology. Perhaps by following the trail of an escaped survivor of the battle, the characters will be able to learn the truth and obtain this ability for themselves.

Action

The meat of the adventure lies in the middle, where the characters attempt to solve the problem or confront the challenge. While the individual encounters will hold the specific details, you'll want to sketch out the major ways in which events can unfold, noting important antagonists, potential allies, perils, and opportunities for refuge and additional information. There should be opportunities for the three main elements of a good roleplaying game—combat, problem solving, and roleplaying.

Identifying the action beats in a well-defined adventure means understanding who (or what) opposes the player characters, the general terrain and specific important locations, and often what will happen over time independent or in reaction to the characters. It's okay to jot down ideas and loose notes. Some referees can run a solid adventure just off a few barely-legible words scratched onto paper. But preparation can often be your friend, so it's not a terrible idea to already have the major ideas for encounters when defining the middle of your adventure structure.

Example: The amphibians maintain a strange village in concentric rings that seem to radiate out from and protect a perfectly circular pond with disgusting, sludge-ridden water and a huge mound of shapeless flesh that could be plant, fungus, or some kind of animal mutated to the point it is unrecognizable. There are too many potential enemies to confront, but they encounter a potential ally in the form of a female amphibian who is unhappy with her tribe's way of life. There are two elements needed for the creation of the healing orbs. The first is a steady supply of animal life that is sacrificed to their "god" in order to supply the life-essence needed. The second are living eggs from the amphibians themselves. Unfortunately, the orbs are specific to the biology of the amphibians and would be useless to anyone else. But the blobby "god" is growing at a rapid pace and its hunger only increases. What happens when it spills out from its birthing pool? Encounters include combat with sentries, stealth infiltration deeper into the village, roleplaying with the unhappy female, and observing clues as to the true nature of the situation. If the characters get close enough to the pond, they observe hideous, slimy tentacles of multi-colored flesh covered with ears and eyes and mouths and fingers, writhing and pulsating in pain and hunger, ready to snatch anyone who steps too close. If they linger too long or are not careful, they will be captured and will be the next sacrifice to the shapeless god.

Resolution

The characters either run out of time or run out of options. Events come to a head and will resolve one way or another. Many METAMORPHOSIS ALPHA adventures might finish with a climactic battle or intense action scene, though that's not always the case. Sometimes the story ends when the characters escape from danger by the hairs of their chinny-chin-chins (perfectly possible with mutations). Negotiation or creative problem solving may eliminate the potential danger, a desired goal may be obtained, or the clock may strike midnight—the end of a time-specific situation that may have fantastic or horrific consequences for everyone involved.

It's not unusual for resolution to come with potential setup for whatever is next. Did a vindictive foe escape? Does a potentially amazing tech artifact require a missing piece? Are there unanswered questions just waiting to be explored? These adventure seeds can grow into entirely new and exciting stories to explore in the depths of the *Warden*.

Example: The characters may decide the shapeless god is not their problem and attempt to get out of town—though an abandoned ally may turn on them and make escape problematic. They could realize that others may be unhappy turning their offspring to medicine in the belly of a hideous beast and quietly raise a revolution. The characters could be captured and must use cunning and opportunity to escape becoming the next sacrifices. Or they could disrupt a nearby oil pipe to literally set the water on fire and destroy the shapeless god once and for all.

Encounters

Like scenes in a play, an adventure is broken down into bite-sized chunks we call encounters—separating individual significant pieces. These establish the important moments and action that build toward the overall story, while each has its framework with beginning and end points.

What this means is that constructing an encounter has the same skeletal framework as an adventure but with a more narrow scope and smaller scale. You'll need to figure out what establishes the encounter, what action might occur in the midst of it, and the ways it might be resolved—and where things will go from there into other encounters. And while there are no hard rules on how an encounter might be defined, here are a few commonly used in adventure design.

Location

A location-based encounter can be confined to a small room or sprawled across a large (simulated) outdoor area, as long as what occurs in the encounter is linked together to make it one related event in the course of the ongoing adventure. Whether there are enemies in wait, shelter to be found, important clues to be revealed, treasure to be discovered, or hazards to be overcome, these encounters don't take place until the characters reach a specific place.

Examples: Guards wait outside a treasure hut, but the artifacts inside are decoys smeared with contact poison to trick the greedy. An open area simulates blue skies and bright sunlight, a field covered in strange-colored flowers that give off hallucinogenic spores. A sealed passage in the bowels of the ship is flooded with radiation, risking death or mutation to those who venture inside—but incredible tech might wait where no one has dared venture.

Timed

Even as the player characters explore and fight, retreat and rest, regroup and carry on, the rest of the *Warden* goes on—generally not giving a twisted power coupling about the struggles of humans and mutants. Some events happen on their own timetable, with their effects or consequences spilling over onto the events of the adventure. A timed encounter might play out quite differently depending on the location and circumstances of the characters when it occurs. An explosion may be only a strange noise in the distance or it may be the last sound one ever hears.

Examples: A jackaloid pack finally catches the party and alerts them with the sound of incessant laughing, the alpha's son determined to earn his bones by slaying the most dangerous character alone. A malfunctioning communications relay goes critical, broadcasting conflicting, overriding signals that cause all artificial intelligence to go haywire until the unit is destroyed or its power supply is cut. Artificial night falls on the deck, allowing a dangerous albino mutant to resume stalking the characters who wounded it long ago.

Triggered

While timed events happen independently of character actions, triggered events are a direct response to them. Sometimes nothing bad happens until someone pushes the big red button that should never be pushed. (But someone always, always pushes the big red button.) Triggered encounters are about consequences—good, bad, or indifferent. The most interesting ones are usually bad.

Examples: The death of the green-eyed armadillo frees the human from its mind control, and her knowledge of the robot's override commands may save the village from destruction. The party believed it was being stealthy, but the simple tripwire alerts a grotesque group of spear-wielding guards. The group couldn't understand why the large hatch had so many layers of protection to prevent it from opening, but as they finally coax the ancient doorway open, a rushing wind threatens to blow them into an empty, dark void full of stars.

Random

Not every adventure needs or should have random encounters, but sometimes they add a bit of fun uncertainty to the game and allow even the referee to be surprised. They might relate to the events of the overall adventure, while some represent the chaotic nature of life and death about the *Warden*.

The referee decides whether random encounters occur based on a length of time elapsed or area reached and the odds of one occurring. A random encounter might be only 1 in 6 chance or an even 3 in 6. The possible encounters are often written out on a table with enough notes to play out the results. The encounter may be significant or just an oddity hinting at larger events.

Example: 2 in 6 chance, rolled once per hour of game time.

☥ 1-2: A tiny, wounded wolfoid cub who is clearly starving and injured but shows only aggression to any who approach.

✹ 3-4: A robot is smashed to pieces on the floor, hammered by something immensely strong, wires still sparking and smoking.

✹ 5-6: A small sub-pack of 4 wolfoids stalks the area, sniffing and searching for something that's more important to them than prey.

One-Offs & Series

Sometimes your group just wants to play for a few hours unrelated to anything else, or perhaps just one self-contained adventure. Gamers lucky enough to have a dedicated game night might enjoy the continuity that comes with a long-term campaign. There is no wrong way to play if it means everyone is having fun, but it's nice to consider your options.

Event

An event doesn't even qualify as a full adventure. It might be one large encounter or a short string of them—a few hours of action-packed gaming. It's best used for a group that can rarely get together but wants a memorable experience that takes full advantage of the fast pace of the SYSTEM 26 rules.

Pros: Events are easy to put together. Pre-generated characters (such as the ones included in this book) can be used since they will only be used once. And since there is no intention to pick up the action later, it can be intense and brutal. Character death is no big deal, and failure might be just as entertaining as success.

Cons: An event can only give a taste of what METAMORPHOSIS ALPHA has to offer, usually by showing off action and combat sprinkled with mutations and technology. There isn't a chance to tell a real story or get a feel for the characters and their personalities.

Adventure

A proper adventure follows the structure and grouped encounters as described above. A short adventure might contain 4-8 encounters and be squeezed in to a 4-hour time block (as is often the case at conventions or those played in hobby game stores), but most adventures take several linked gaming sessions to reach the conclusion. The group decides on a stopping point then resumes

the adventure right where things left off next time, unless the referee decides down time for the characters happened in between sessions.

Pros: A full adventure tells a (potentially) satisfying story with a beginning, middle, and end. It allows for an agreeable mix of encounter styles to allow for roleplaying, problem solving, and frantic combat with the possibility for each character to shine.

Cons: A standalone adventure can only reveal an isolated piece of the larger puzzle that is the starship *Warden*. The sense of discovery, unraveling larger mysteries, and seeing a character succeed and achieve over time is something that only happens through serialized play.

Campaign

A METAMORPHOSIS ALPHA campaign is a series of linked adventures making use of the same characters—though some will undoubtedly need to be replaced if individual characters or even entire groups are left as ruined corpses. (The *Warden* is and should be a dangerous place!) This allows for a sense of continuity, the chance for a larger story to be revealed over time, long-term enemies to be faced and eventually defeated, large questions to be answered, and a real sense of attachment to characters. A group of players who experience a long-term campaign will have shared experiences and stories that they'll discuss to the confusion of others for years to come!

The referee running a campaign can decide if there is one larger story playing out with its own overriding themes and structure (much like a trilogy of novels) or if it's just a serialized group of unrelated adventures strung together. Either approach can be equally fun!

Pros: Characters can evolve over time, acquiring additional mutations and more powerful technology. There is a real sense of achievement for long-term goals met and discoveries made. Campaigns allow for the different aspects of METAMORPHOSIS ALPHA to be fully explored.

Cons: It can be difficult to get a game group together on a regular basis with hectic schedules and real life interfering. Some players may want to try different kinds of characters or get the itch to experience different kinds of games entirely. The defeat of a group or the death of a favorite character might be extremely frustrating after months or even years of investment.

PLAYING THE PARTS

It's not only the referee's job to describe places and interpret the rules into descriptive action, there is also the role of an improv actor to consider. A referee takes on the role of everyone and everything in the game that's not a player character. That means that in the course of an evening the referee might portray the croaking leader of a hoard of burbling frog-men, a sultry mutated human attempting to trick the party, and a malfunctioning maintenance robot only able to answer questions with five pre-programmed responses. It's one of the most vital and challenging parts of the job, taking a handful of notes and numbers and creating memorable characters that take on life in the players' imaginations.

A first piece of advice for new referees is don't be self-conscious when portraying non-player characters. Be expressive, take on a different voice, adopt alternate posture and body language! When prepping an adventure it's worth taking a moment to think how a given character might sound or act. With experience the acting duties of the referee will become second-nature.

Stock Characters

The majority of beings encountered aboard the starship *Warden* are very much background players in any given adventure. If it was a television series, they would be extras or those with only one line. While it's important to give them description and a hint of personality, there is no need to work on unique characteristics (or define detailed game stats if they are not expected to be combat threats). They are there to support the overall theme and feel you are trying to create in this portion of the adventure. Village warriors might be stoic and disciplined in one instance, or grubby and hostile in another.

You should be ready, however, to add additional details and a sense of personality if the players unexpectedly focus on an otherwise unimportant character. If necessary, have a few names and random details jotted down and ready to use if the need arises.

To the players it should feel like the *Warden* is a living place and that every character encountered has a detailed backstory just waiting to be explored.

Important Characters

Contrasting the stock characters are those who are important to a particular adventure or possibly relevant to the course of an entire campaign. These are significant allies, dangerous enemies, love interests, quirky recurring characters, and others who stand out from the crowd as the player characters explore and adventure across the ship. Using the television analogy above, important characters would be the guest stars—either for one episode (adventure) or might recur many times over. Long established non-player characters will become significant to the group, and the death of one might become a significant event almost to the level of a player character's loss.

These characters should be well-defined, with a backstory that explains their motivations and helps you as the referee to decide their plans, reactions, and dialogue. Their personalities should be well-defined, and ideally the players can identify them by your adopted voice and gestures if they've encountered this individual before.

For roleplaying, it's best to come up with just a few "hooks" on which to hang a character: An accent or style of speech, a repeated gesture, or a catchphrase. This becomes the acting shorthand by which the players will recognize the character and you will be able to get into character quickly.

A villain is a specialized and fun important character—one who acts as antagonist to the player group. It could be a brutish wolfoid alpha male determined to acquire a powerful weapon, it could be a scheming mutant human manipulating the party into her dirty work, or might even be an artificial intelligence system that is fulfilling its programming with an imperfect understanding of the situation that causes it to thwart and endanger the group. Villains should be memorable and fun to hate. Over time a recurring villain's defeat will become a personal mission more than just an obstacle to overcome, and success will be a cause of celebration at the table.

Monsters & Robots

While there are many personalities aboard the *Warden* with complicated agendas and interesting things to say, there are also some who are delightfully simple. "Monster" is an old roleplaying game term that applies here to mutants with simple goals and limited vocabularies. It could be a predator hunting for food, a beast guarding its young in a lair, or a roving gang of mutants who want nothing more than to dominate a territory and acquire useful tech. Monsters are memorable for the threat they pose more than a nuanced personality or developed backstory. Put your energy into physical descriptions and the excitement of the inevitable combat.

Robots are an interesting case because they might range from being metal monsters themselves—simple, single-minded individuals who are a challenge to overcome—to complex beings with real personality. When portraying a robot it's important to remember that even the most complex is not truly alive and will revert to its primary functions and goals within the boundaries of the rules that have been set for it. Robots tend to be very task-oriented, plowing ahead with their short-term goals and only vary in actions in response to things that interfere with them.

For example, a robot may be tasked with maintaining and guarding a backup power generator that long since ceased functioning. It will tirelessly prevent anyone from entering the area and will not use lethal force against a pure human character, but might indiscriminately murder a mutant animal who is holding a piece of tech that might be useful toward the generator's repair.

Androids are a special case for artificial life. They are designed to be complex and even humanlike in their responses. With more exposure to social interaction they will become increasingly unique in personality and adept in picking up social cues, able to alter their own goals and missions based on the situation … but it's best to remember that there may be secret missions or pre-programmed reactions buried beneath the surface. An android might be helpful and subservient for months, but it might react to a certain threat with terrifying and deadly force.

Breaking the Mold

One way the referee can keep an ongoing campaign interesting is to break up the regular sessions with another type of adventure or different game! This might allow for the referee to take a break and let another player assume the duties for a session or two, and the figurative change in scenery can keep the appreciation for the regular campaign strong.

TIPS OF THE TRADE

The two best ways to learn the art of the referee are observation and practice. Take the opportunity to be a player in someone else's game and pay attention to how the referee or game master handles her table. And even more importantly—just dive in! Like most learning, on-the-job training is the best kind. You'll get a feel for running a game quickly and your table will ultimately be unique and memorable. Don't worry about getting every detail or rule right or handling every situation perfectly. We're all here to have fun, and if you keep a smile on your face everyone else will likely follow suit.

Pacing

There is so much going on aboard the *Warden* it's very important to remember to focus the attention when needed and to gloss over when detailed descriptions aren't necessary. If its unimportant to the adventure's story and otherwise boring, sum it up and move on. We don't need to follow each agonizing step of an archer crafting a new bow and fletching each arrow. Downtime between adventures need not be described in more than a few sentences. Don't obsess over minutiae or waste everyone's time with descriptions of the unimportant. Skip ahead to the fun and interesting stuff!

When there is a challenge to be overcome, a puzzle to be solved, danger to be faced, or enemies to battle, these are the times when you want to get the details right. This is why a month of village life might be covered in five minutes of game time at the table but a battle with ursoids might take half an hour.

It's important to note that even though dangerous and interesting situations need more detail, you don't want the game to grind to a halt. You always want to keep the action moving forward and in dangerous situations you want a feeling of limited time and forward momentum. The characters don't have ten minutes to think on an immediate threat, so neither do the players. Push the action forward—even if you judge that an indecisive player means the character is paralyzed with indecision for a turn. (Such an event usually happens only once, as players do not enjoy losing out on their characters' chance to act.) Make sure you always have a handle on what each player's immediate plans are for a character and move back and forth so that everyone is engaged.

Develop Your Own Style

Some referees focus more on the narrative and have a signature flow to the way things unfold in their games. Others keep their own descriptions brief and encourage the players to hold the spotlight. A referee might be bare-bones with dice and paper and words, another might like to use miniatures and background music and special props. And all of them could be excellent games.

Don't be afraid to try new things as you get your sea legs underneath you as referee. Find those elements that feel natural, the ones you most enjoy, and those to which the players respond strongly. Everyone needs to be having fun at the game table—and this absolutely starts with the referee. If the person running the game isn't having any fun, it's unlikely anyone else will.

As referee you will eventually become comfortable with doing things a certain unique way—and that's absolutely fine. It's why it's your game, not ours.

Learn From Your Players, But Run Your Game

As referee you hold godlike power over the starship *Warden* and everything inside of it. The lives and fate of the player characters can be changed with a brief decision or simple judgment of the rules. But with great power comes a great ability to lose all your players. Your job is to provide a fair and entertaining table for adventure, where it's always challenging but there is always a fighting chance for survival and victory.

In addition to the balancing act of keeping the tension high while not wiping out the party with one robotic juggernaut, you should listen to your players. Don't be afraid to explicitly ask what their favorite parts of the game might be. Make note of which rules they disagree with, or in which situations the fun seemed to dry up for a while. And if you can read people with the skill of a decent poker player, keep tabs on how things are going in the middle of the action. All of these things will not only teach you how to run a better game in general terms, but will help you specifically tailor a great experience for your group. Some groups favor subterfuge, diplomacy, and stealth, while others want guns and explosions and spectacular mutant powers. We say all of these are fantastic, so run with whatever keeps the game fun at the table!

All of the above said, the balance of power tips to the referee for a reason. While you should absolutely listen to your players, listening doesn't equate to bowing to every whim and wish. Be fair but firm and keep the game moving. The players need to respect you as well as like you. Some players may push a bit to gain the advantage, but remember who's in charge.

Act Versus Tell

METAMORPHOSIS ALPHA is a tabletop roleplaying game, which means everyone is sitting down and rolling dice and talking. This makes the concept of action even more important than a live-action roleplaying game (of which many involve folks mostly standing around and talking). Even if the players are passive, the events in the game and the interaction at the table should be lively and engaging.

If the largest percentage of game time is spent with the referee reciting long paragraphs of text with a little dice-rolling in the middle, the chances of everyone having as much fun as possible are on the low side. Absolutely be descriptive, but use words for impact and make them count.

Character action should be the center of gravity when it comes to description. So it should setting the stage to find out what the characters are going to do, seeing how those actions immediately play out, and what the other consequences of those actions might be. This is good advice for many roleplaying games in general, but especially so in METAMORPHOSIS ALPHA—a game with a fine tradition celebrating fast-paced action and adventure.

Disruptive Players

While we can't promise you won't ever experience a total jerk at your table, most of the time a disruptive player is a temporary situation. Sometimes it's a player who's had one too many, or one who's become bored and just trying to stir things up. Others won't let their objections go over a final call about the rules ("*I shouldn't have died from fire since I have that mega-awesome mutation of fire immunity!*"). Every once in a while a player won't separate his knowledge as a player ("*It's a toaster!*") from that of a character ("*It's a strange metal box with two slots and a sliding button.*") Or perhaps an out-of-game grudge ("*You drank the last root beer!*") gets brought to the table.

The first strategy is usually to keep the focus on what's going on inside the game. If you can get everyone—including the bozo causing trouble—back to paying attention to the ticking bomb and the endless hordes of sentient mushrooms surrounding them the problem may just solve itself. If a player seems bored or otherwise distracted, make a point to make sure there is something interesting for her character to deal with. Someone who is engaged is less likely to be a troublemaker.

If the former tactic isn't going to work, a general announcement that out-of-game issues or conversations about anything except what's happening at the table right now should be shelved until later might help. The players who are trying to keep their attention on the game and enjoy themselves will likely back you up. And if the problem goes beyond that, it's probably worth it to take five and ask for a private chat with the problem-player. You're hosting a game, remember, so try to keep things positive and focus on how you can make sure the player is having a good time. But if someone isn't having fun and only emphasizing how misery loves company, that player might need to take the rest of the session off.

Rules Debates & Arguments

The SYSTEM 26 rules were meant to be relatively straightforward and intuitive. We've done our best to organize the rules so it's easy to find things. And it's also a delightfully easy game to run on the fly and just wing it when necessary. But every roleplaying game out there has to deal with the rules lawyer—the player who obsesses about the letter of the law and tries to game the system to his advantage.

The most important rule is that the referee runs her table and is in charge. Her judgment calls supersede the written word of this book. Any rules discussion shouldn't take more than a few minutes at most. If the players are unhappy with a ruling or you just aren't sure it's the best way to handle it, declare that's how you're doing things for this session and you'll review and discuss it in between games to finalize that particular point.

Keeping Everyone Alive

It's okay to kill people. And mutant aardvarks. The *Warden* is a deadly place and encounters aren't designed with a detailed point-system to make sure things seems challenging but predictable. There is no guarantee that they won't walk into a room filled with deadly radiation and a rampaging guardian robot perfectly capable of reducing the entire party to ash. Adventuring is rough business. Players who get into the game should understand their characters could run into things that are incredibly dangerous, and that running and hiding are sometimes prudent and wise tactics.

The above said, a game in which everyone creates a bunch of exciting new characters and they get mauled by giant beavers and killed in the first encounter may be good for a chuckle, but makes for a lousy roleplaying game session. Like other forms of storytelling, there should be rising stakes and tension that progresses. Some encounters should be written so the players feel like badasses and trounce the opposition, others fair fights that can be won through clever ideas and teamwork, while a rare few should be deadly but survivable—even if only by finding a way to retreat. It's always better to look for ways to keep characters alive rather than kill them, and sometimes offer subtle (or sledgehammer-obvious) suggestions on how the players can take advantage of such opportunities.

Long-time referees and game masters know the initialism **TPK** (Total Party Kill), but it should be the rare exception rather than the rule. When designing encounters you should think not only of the character's abilities that help their odds of victory and survival, but offer refuge, healing, or escape if things go bad. Also remind players that one of the great uses of action points is to turn a deadly injury into something survivable, and that keeping one or two in the bank for that purpose isn't a terrible idea.

Character Death

Everyone dies. Humans take dirt-naps, frogs croak, and mutant daisies push themselves up eventually. In METAMORPHOSIS ALPHA characters might be killed unexpectedly and brutally, after a long struggle, or even after some heroic act of self-sacrifice. Death sucks, though. Players can get attached to certain characters, especially after many adventures and a successful career.

Most of the time it's best just to deal with the consequences of character death in-game and move on. Encourage the player to create a new character, perhaps with some interesting ties to the ongoing action that will be fun to play. This sort of carrot will help the player get into the spirit of things with a new character.

The *Warden* is a crazy science-fiction setting with a touch of comic-book sensibility, however, and if there's a good reason to bring a character back there is zero reason why it can't happen. Cellular regeneration technology could restore the recently-deceased to life, or a tissue sample might make it possible to create an identical-copy clone. You can get weirder, of course, and reveal that the dead character was actually an enemy mutant disguised as a member of the party. A shapeshifting blank-slate android might stumble on the corpse and decide to mimic the old character's appearance and mind-map his memories. Perhaps the character is from a near-identical family in which the oldest member holds responsibilities that must be assumed by the next in line.

One thing to keep in mind is that resurrection should have a cost, in storytelling terms. If the group decides they want to bring their friend back from the dead, that goal should be a difficult quest all on its own. If you want to use another method to bring a character back, make sure there are long-term consequences and fallout. Death should always remain a big deal.

THE STARSHIP WARDEN

For all intents and purposes, the *Warden* is the entire world for the characters, their enemies, their allies, and everything that lies in their future. It's a vast ship filled with simulated environments and habitations and factories, wrecked and rebuilt and repurposed, swarming with mutated and simulated life. For a referee it's a playground in which you can throw almost any idea from books, film, television, or comics and find a place for it. Despite being physically smaller than a planet-sized campaign world in other roleplaying games, the *Warden* offers more variety than most settings and has shorter travel-times between the characters and the adventure.

This book throws certain assumptions about the ship, its environment, and current state of affairs at you, but whether you run with them or not the incarnation of the *Warden* you create through play will be unique and different than anyone else's. It's your ship, so customize it and have fun!

History

There is plenty of mystery in the standard METAMORPHOSIS ALPHA campaign. Most characters are relatively primitive and their understanding of the "world" and its history is through the lens of misunderstood oral traditions, legend, folklore, and rumor. And like the saying goes, those who do not learn from history are doomed to walk into a radiation-flooded zone and grow prehensile tails.

Standard Knowledge

There is no "standard" knowledge of the past aboard the *Warden*. Each group or tribe usually has garbled, confused legends of their origins that generally involve them being a superior or chosen people. Some are so desperate in their daily struggle that they give no thought to the past at all, looking instead to their next

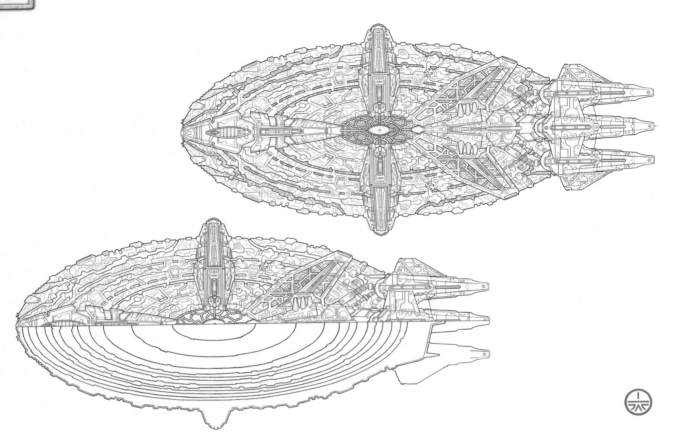

meal or a place of refuge. But there are bits and pieces of truth that often fall into the small pockets of culture aboard the ship.

Our ancestors journeyed from their home (Human, Mutated Human): There is often some vague cultural memory that during a glorious, golden age of peace and prosperity—everything's relative— brave ancestors left their homes in order to journey to a promised land or tame a wild frontier. Some attach specific names of leaders or heroes that might belong to members of the original crew or important colonists.

Our ancestors were prisoners or slaves (Mutant Animals): Those descended from the animal life being transported aboard the *Warden* carry a cultural memory (and resentment) of being kept in confinement. Whether in contained sanctuaries or literal cages, the animals raised with these stories have an inborn dislike of being contained.

Our ancestors woke from an ancient sleep (Mutant Plants): The biology of plants was and is so different, that they don't have an understanding of the past that quite relates to members of the animal kingdom. They know that some among them became different than their cousins, able to move and think and communicate. Plants tend to be creatures of the present moment and do not dwell on the past, and their beliefs on their origin tend to be highly personal, incomprehensible to animal life, or nonexistent.

A disaster, cataclysm, or calamity nearly killed us all: Whatever cultural traditions exist aboard the *Warden*, most include references to a terrible event that nearly wiped out all life. Much how the tradition of a great flood is reflected in many western cultures in the real world, the basic idea of a great disaster are common while the specifics and details are quite different. Sometimes it's a horrible plague, other times it's described as an evil army or the nameless wrath of a cruel god. People and animals died, plants withered, and most of those who survived were forever changed or even cursed. This is the event that created the difficult world in which the player characters live.

Enlightened Knowledge

The oral histories and traditions of most small cultures aboard the *Warden* are much like playing the "telephone game," distorted almost the point where it couldn't easily be reconciled with the truth. But some either inherited a less filtered version of history or pieced it together through a process of discovery. "Enlightenment" reveals some of the truth that most would choose not to believe.

There is no meaning behind the disaster: Most legends create a villain or otherwise cast blame from what ruined the world and killed so many. But whatever the truth behind it all may be, no one figure is responsible. Nothing is more cruel than terrible luck.

Our world is no world: Most of the *Warden's* residents have no idea a "world" isn't supposed to have walls and elevators and ceilings. It's just the way things are. But some have retained or rediscovered the truth that they are still on their ancient journey to a new home, and that they simply live on the vast boat that is taking them there. There might even be an idea of the command deck and how the ship might be brought under someone's control.

Artificial life has somehow gone wrong: There are stories of a time in which computers and robots served those aboard the ship, providing for their needs and obeying commands. An enlightened view realizes there is a fundamental problem, one that could perhaps be repaired and restore order.

The "Truth"

The "truth" of the *Warden's* history is whatever you as the referee would like it to be, and ideally will include your own smaller details that tie into an ongoing campaign. But here are a few details that include standard assumptions.

The world got used up: The ancient home-that-was, Earth, was facing a long-term crisis of diminishing resources, increasing population, and/or unstable climate. Whether it was a forward-thinking solution or one borne of panic, the idea of sending humans and the life of Earth to settle other, habitable worlds was created. The *Warden* was either a unique vessel for this purpose or simply one of many arks sailing through the stars to new homes.

The journey was intended to last many generations: The *Warden* was not built for a short trip, but rather one that would last multiple lifetimes. Traveling shy of the speed of light, it would be forever cut off from Earth and would need to sustain itself and carry the life and cultures of its origin to its new home. It was designed to be a miniature world that reflected the diversity of all life on Earth, assisted by the most sophisticated artificial intelligence and robotic technology of its day. The ship is almost a living thing, able to absorb radiation and cosmic dust and continually repair and renew itself indefinitely.

The disaster was unforeseen: For all technical brilliance, the ancient people who ran the ship and the computer systems that assisted them were caught unprepared for the disaster when it struck. Whether it was a radiation cloud, a mutating virus, or something else entirely, the disaster struck quickly and with no warning. There was so much death and so many malfunctioning systems that only the resilience of the ship's design and life's ability to always find a way that allowed anyone to survive at all.

A new home is still out there: The *Warden* might have already reached its destination, and is patiently orbiting and awaiting instructions to begin the next phase of its mission. Or perhaps the ship still has a century left in its journey. The disaster might have damaged the navigational systems to the point in which it has veered off course until it crashes into a planetoid or into a black hole—or it reversed course and is journeying back to Earth. Either way, at some point in the future the residents may want to finally get off of the boat.

OTHER CAMPAIGN IDEAS

There is endless variety to be found in the "standard" campaign aboard the *Warden*. But if you want to mix things up even more, there are plenty of ideas to choose from. These ideas are often best revealed in the course of an extended campaign.

Tricking the Players

A fun tradition going back to the very first edition of METAMORPHOSIS ALPHA is one in which the players know absolutely nothing about the game in which they are playing. This is tricky to pull off, as it means the referee must help create characters and hand out game information without giving them a copy of the book to speed things up. But it offers some fun surprises and a big reveal to pay off the extra work.

In this setup, you tell the players you are going to run a post-apocalyptic campaign in which they can play primitive mutants. You start them in a simulated environment in which there is no reason for the players to suspect they aren't somewhere on Earth. A few red herrings might even have the players building an idea in their minds about just where the characters are in the "real world," but clues will build up to the moment in which they find the wall at the end of the world, an elevator, or even a porthole looking out into space.

Their blown minds and mouths hanging open can be all the reward a referee needs to manage the setup for this campaign scenario. The group's expectations and understanding of a larger in-game mystery will inform the rest of the campaign as the players become more interested in understanding what happened and how they can "take over" the ship.

A Different Ship

The *Warden* is simply one incarnation of a giant ark in space. You can design an entirely different ship from scratch, map it out, decide how its various zones and decks and regions work and what inhabits them. It could be more modern, more primitive, or include pockets of both. Perhaps computer subsystems (Life Support, Security, Command) broke away from each other with competing interests and have become "gods" that attempt to manipulate life aboard the vessel to accomplish their aims. Maybe there are no pure humans left aboard and those that seem to be are android reconstructions who don't understand their true nature. You can either come up with overriding themes to guide the design of your unique ship or throw figurative spaghetti at the wall and enjoy all the crazy ideas bouncing off each other inside a giant metal box floating through space.

Crashing the *Warden*

This can either be a campaign-starter or a way to change everything in the middle of a long-running game. Crash the ship! If you use this idea as part of

an ongoing game, it will offer the players an entirely new environment to explore and new forms of life to deal with. Whether it's a benign alien world or a huge asteroid housing a hostile form of fungal life, it will instantly generate new goals for the party and new challenges to face.

The flipside of the crash-concept comes by creating characters who live on whatever unlucky world the *Warden* comes crashing down in. Supposing it makes a (somewhat) soft landing means there might be only one small hull breach or accessible hatch by which to enter. Brave explorers might venture inside to discover its secrets and inhabitants and find a chaotic and dangerous environment inside. Just what kind of world the player characters start in determines their approach and tactics, whether they are fantasy adventurers or a modern military.

A Mutant World

A more extreme shift to the assumptions of METAMORPHOSIS ALPHA would be to ditch the spaceship entirely. The rules in this book could easily be adapted for use in a post-apocalyptic science fiction world. Instead of the contained environs of the *Warden*, there is an entire world to be explored and conquered. Part of the fun in games set in a post-apocalypse setting is that you can adventure in your own backyard or include notable landmarks. The clash between character and player knowledge makes for memorable moments and offers easy inspiration for adventures.

WHERE TO NEXT

If you read straight through after *Chapter Seven: Rules* then it's likely time to familiarize yourself with some sample challenges and threats in a METAMORPHOSIS ALPHA campaign, as well as tips on how to create your own: head to *Chapter 9: A Mutant Menagerie*. If you're interested in running an adventure right away, look ahead to our sample adventure: *The Petting Zoo of Death*. If you want to understand the bigger picture of a referee's role before getting into character creation, it's time to head back and understand how it all works in *Chapter Three: Mutants & Mankind*.

A comprehensive list of the mutants and artificial life that one might find aboard the starship *Warden* could easily fill a large volume. And while some stable breeds exist and there are standardized types of robotic life, it is quite rare for two forms of life to be exactly alike.

This chapter provides the referee with easy-to-reference challenges and enemies for a group of characters, and far more importantly serves as inspiration for the thousands of possible variations.

Remember not every entry in this chapter should be presented as a straightforward, bloody battle. Some are challenges best avoided, allies to be won over, or puzzles to be solved.

FORMAT

The entries presented here follow the same structure as player characters, including traits, mutations, and qualities. And many creatures have "breed" notes on how they might be used as a player character type.

Note that the rules for how player characters are generated do not apply to the mutants in this chapter, which is why some might seem "unbalanced" by those standards.

Black One
Medium mutant animal (spider)

Move 25 ft. • **Initiative** 4d
Dodge 5d • **Armor** 2 (natural)
Fatigue / Wounds 15 / 17

Hopeless (–2d):	Influence, Leadership, Performance, Tech
Weak (–1d):	–
Competent (+1d):	Athletics, Constitution, Survival
Good (+2d):	Alertness, Brawn, Stealth, Unarmed Combat
Amazing (+3d):	Artistry (web only), Dexterity

Mutations: Electrical Generation (3d), Multiple Limbs (2d), New Body Parts—Bite (3d), Carapace (2d), Spinnerets* (2d) Poison Bite (2d)

Qualities: Agile Combatant, Talented at Camouflage and Hiding (+1d). +2d bonus for Acrobatics, Climbing, Jumping, Running (multiple limbs mutation).

Attacks
Electric Bolt: 4d attack, +3F electricity.
Unarmed: Grapple, Web (5d), Bite (+2W and paralytic toxin).

Description
Feared predators of dark regions of the ship—dense forests and jungles, or sub-decks where the lights have failed—these spiders the size of adult humans easily disappear inside their shadowy lairs. They appear just as their tiny ancestors but on a terrifyingly large scale, adapted to breathe effectively despite their size. They spin immense webs in their territories up to 100 feet across, which they rarely leave. Even the slightest touch to a strand of web alerts the Black One of the presence of potential prey, and it prefers to use stealth and ambush tactics to gain a meal. They do not plan or think in the traditional sense, but have highly-tuned instincts from millions of years of evolution.

Solitary unless seeking a mate, a Black One dwells in a lair filled with an increasing number of desiccated husks wrapped in silk, with old bones and trinkets littering the ground. It cares nothing for goods and technology, making their lairs attractive for the foolish and greedy.

Spinnerets & Webs
Black Ones and other spiders have several glands on the abdomen that produce webs. They are sticky, breaking away requires a Grapple against the Constitution trait of the creature that produced it—or special measures such as fire, tools, or specific chemicals. A spider can move along its own web as if it was on the ground.

If a spider has a creature in a grapple, it can wrap the victim in a silky cocoon—taking one action for a small creature and an additional action for each size category larger. (Truly small creatures are beneath its notice, and it will avoid huge foes.) Once fully enveloped, a creature must complete a Hard complex action to break free—with required achievements equalling the Constitution trait of the spider who created the web. Outside help can free a trapped creature quickly. Alternately it may attempt to envelope an unwilling target—but cannot take any other actions on that turn—as an unarmed attack. Prey paralyzed by a spider's bite is wrapped up for later consumption.

Variations

The Black One can be used as the basis for many different types of giant spider. In many cases, only the description and one or two changes can be made to create giant tarantulas or black widow spiders. One notable variation is the Brain Spider, below.

Tactics

A Black One stays in its shadowy lair and waits, preferring to strike from the darkness. It will generally stun prey with a burst of electricity and then attempt to use its paralytic bite and wrap it in a silken coffin. If fighting multiple targets it prefers to isolate and carry off the weakest among the group, taking full advantage of its ability to scurry along its massive web.

Notes

Paralytic Toxin: Victim takes 1d Fatigue and must succeed an Average Constitution (Fortitude) check. Failure means the character suffers 2d Trauma and cannot move until it has been recovered.

Arachnid Mind: The nearly-alien arthropod brain makes any attempt to use mental mutations by humans or animals on them is always Hard.

Brain Spider

The normal Black One is effectively mindless. A rare few, however, are demonically clever at the sacrifice of the arachnid mind advantage against psychic attack. The referee can create a Brain Spider with improved mental traits and mental mutations such as telepathy and mental control. Such a creature will dominate prey and lure them into its lair for consumption.

Buzzer

Small mutant animal (bee)

Move 20 ft., fly 40 ft. • **Initiative** 3d
Dodge 4d • **Armor** –
Fatigue / Wounds 8 / 8

Hopeless (–2d):	Deception, Tech
Weak (–1d):	–
Competent (+1d):	Alertness, Unarmed Combat
Good (+2d):	Dexterity, Ranged Weapons
Amazing (+3d):	–

Mutations: New Body Parts—Stinger (2d), Wings (4d), Stunning Blast (2d)

Attacks

Unarmed: Sting (+1W stationary, +2W charging).
Ranged Weapons: Stunning Stinger (Range 10 ft., +2W fire, see below)

Description

Buzzers appear as bees the size of house cats, and represent several enlarged varieties of ancestral bees from Earth. They are sensitive to psychic energies used by outsiders within half a mile of their colony, and the use of mental mutations will summon an angry swarm of buzzers to kill or drive away the offenders. A small group (1d or 2d) will move against those on the outer edge of a buzzer hive's territory, but will send more if the source of the disturbance grows closer.

Buzzer hives are massive and the buzzing from within can be heard from a distance.

Variations

Some buzzers have evolved away from the colonies. They live in small groups (2d individuals) and reproduce more in the manner of normal animals rather than the traditional hive caste structure. These "free buzzers" often exist in symbiosis with plants or small groves, feeding off honey and nectar, and protecting their homes from mental predators.

Buzzer queens are larger and tougher specimens, more intelligent, and have mental mutations.

Tactics

Buzzers evolved to protect the colony from psionic attack, and they focus on the most powerful user of mental mutations in the area. Buzzers will swarm and attempt to stun their intended target and then focus on its allies. They will unhesitatingly sacrifice themselves in their instinctive defense of their hive, and fight to the death. They generally ignore plants unless those are actively attacking or using mental mutations.

Notes

Stunning Stinger: A buzzer has a specialized use of the stunning blast mutation, delivered through its stinger and must be within 10 feet of a single target. A successful attack damages as above, but the target must succeed an Easy Discipline (Mental Resistance) check or additionally take 1d Fatigue damage and be stunned for 2 turns. It may use the stunning blast attack up to once every other turn, but takes 1 Wound for each use. A buzzer may use its stinger as an unarmed attack.

Eyeball Fungus
Medium mutant plant (fungus).

Move 5 ft. • **Initiative** 5d
Dodge 3d • **Armor** 1 (natural)
Fatigue / Wounds 14 / 18

Hopeless (–2d):	Crafting, Performance, Tech
Weak (–1d):	Athletics
Competent (+1d):	Brawn, Dexterity
Good (+2d):	Constitution, Unarmed Combat
Amazing (+3d):	Alertness, Discipline

Mutations: Confusion (4d), Extra Eyes (1d), Hardened Bark (2d), Infravision (2d), Stunning Blast (2d), Vines (2d)

Qualities: Ambidextrous, Unyielding

Attacks
Unarmed: Eyeball Smash (10 foot reach, 4d attack, +2F damage)
Confusion Ray: (5d attack, +1dF psychic damage + confusion, once per combat)
Stunning Blast: (2d attack against all living targets within 50 feet, +1dF damage and possibly stunned for 2 turns, once per combat)

Description
A strange aberration that grows near toxic and radioactive areas throughout the *Warden*, this fungus can survive even on bare metal for extended periods. It is a strange collection of soft fungal tissue and spores with tentacles snaking out that end in large crystal-hard eyes—stolen from consumed victims and grown into both bludgeoning weapons and power sources for its mental mutations. As an eyeball fungus consumes new prey, it grows additional eye stalks and acquires new or enhances its existing mental powers. It cares nothing for gear or technology, and if it dwells in the same area it simply leaves discarded items laying around to be found by others.

Variations
Each eyeball fungus is a unique specimen, as its number of eye stalks and specific mental mutations vary depending on its success as a hunter.

Tactics
Able to see in the dark and shift its body shape as needed, it is a silent and patient hunter who will overwhelm a victim with multiple bludgeoning and grappling attacks, then consumes the decomposing body. After its feasting is done, only the eyes remain—grown unnaturally large and hard as part of a new stalk. Its intelligence is instinctive and quite alien to other forms of life.

Notes
Fungi are not technically plants, and do not share the nourishment requirements of mutant plant characters.

Grabber
Large plant (willow tree)

Move 0 ft. • **Initiative** 5d
Dodge – • **Armor** 2 (mutation)
Fatigue / Wounds 17 / 22

Hopeless (–2d):	Artistry, Tech
Weak (–1d):	–
Competent (+1d):	–
Good (+2d):	–
Amazing (+3d):	Alertness, Discipline, Unarmed Combat
Incredible (+4d):	Brawn, Constitution

Mutations: Hardened Bark, Heightened Physical Trait—Brawn (2d) & Constitution (2d), Thorns (1d), Vines (*)

Qualities: Ambidextrous (1d)

Attacks
Unarmed: Vines (+1W, grapple)
Special: Acidic Maw (1d Fatigue, 1 Wound per turn)

Description
Grabbers are usually found hidden among less aggressive plant life. (Some speculate a grabber spawns many immobile children to surround it and disguise it.) They resemble large willows, with their drooping branches covered in heavy thorns, but are otherwise unremarkable—until they strike. When one attacks, the hundreds of limbs come alive, lashing furiously at anything in range, raking them bloody, then encircling them and dragging them back to its acidic maw.

The area around the base of a grabber is usually rich with discarded weapons, armor, and gear. All organic matter, down to the bones, is digested.

Some animals have evolved pheromones that make the grabber ignore them; this gives them a secure place to stay when sleeping or nesting. A few go further, and lure predators back to the grabber, creating a symbiosis.

Some communities have planted grabbers along likely entrances to their settlements and using a secret path known only to their tribe—creating a living, terrifying trap.

Variations
Particularly dreaded are walking grabbers, which can move at a slow pace (5 or 10 feet movement). While unlikely to chase down an enemy, the fact they can move at all can be a deadly surprise to anyone who thinks they're safe just out of range.

Clubbers are similar to grabbers, but use larger, heavier limbs to smash prey into unconsciousness or death, and then use smaller vines, not suitable for combat, to drag the food in.

Tactics
Grabbers grab. When potential food gets within range, the vine-like limbs lock in on a creature, relying on noise and body heat rather than sight, and simultaneously slash it (to weaken it so it can't fight back) and entangle it. Once a creature is gripped, the grabber hauls it back to its mouth, where it will be digested. It can only eat one creature at a time, so additional enemies will simply be attacked until the first one is fully dissolved.

While they have hundreds of limbs, they can really only coordinate two at a time. It only takes 2 Wounds damage to sever a vine but there are far too many to effectively disarm a Grabber.

Hillfolk
Medium mutated human

Move 15 ft. • **Initiative** 2d
Dodge 2d • **Armor** 2 (Leather)
Fatigue / Wounds 14 / 15

Hopeless (–2d):	Artistry
Weak (–1d):	Discipline, Medicine, Tech
Competent (+1d):	Athletics, Constitution
Good (+2d):	Melee or Ranged Weapons, Survival
Amazing (+3d):	–

Mutations: Kinetic Absorption (2d), New Body Part—Hump (1d)

Qualities: Determined (2d), Unfocused (2d)

Attacks
Unarmed
Melee Weapons: Club (+2F)

Description

Hillfolk are so-named because they're most commonly found in the simulated uplands on some of the *Warden*'s decks, living in huts made from scavenged materials and using their intimate knowledge of the narrow paths, dead ends, and dense forests to waylay travelers. Many of the locals will make a two day detour around a hillfolk stronghold, rather than cut across. They are xenophobic to the extreme, distrusting anyone outside their clan. Rarely, two or three clans will share a territory and work together, but there is always some level of suspicion and a high chance of betrayal. Clans never forgive or forget, and feuds between hillfolk can last for generations.

They appear as mutated humans, in wide variety, but all are twisted and marked in some way. They tend towards oversized teeth, clawed hands, and mental deficiency—though they are also known for brutal cunning and surprising skill at ambushes and trap making. By nature, they are scavengers—not builders—so their clothing, armor, and weapons tend to be battered and worn.

The stats above represent a "standard" warrior member of a hillfolk clan, a baseline that a referee can use to quickly generate several individuals.

Variations

Leaders: Hillfolk leaders are those who've survived twice as long as their kin and learned plenty of tricks. They keep the more rambunctious and violent of their clan in check, and can plan out complex strategies. They usually have higher mental and social traits, as well as mental mutations.

Brutes: Most hillfolk are rather savage, but a brute takes it to the extreme. A clan will do everything it can to keep a brute happy, and will loose them on enemies so they can laugh at the carnage. These folk specialize in combat and physical traits, and have physical mutations that make them terrifying in combat, capable of absorbing or healing massive amounts of damage.

Tactics

Hillfolk hate a fair fight. Their typical tactics are to send out a scout to make sniping attacks from a safe distance, luring the victims into a trap. At this point, the rest of the clan will take out the survivors. They prefer to capture, rather than kill, so they can torture their victims for a few days while devouring them. They will use technological items if they have them on-hand, but they're kept in poor repair and don't see much use.

If forced into an open confrontation, they will seek to escape, or pretend to surrender—but they will never truly submit. However, if they see one of their own killed they will go insane with bloodlust.

Breed

Any mutated human character with the appropriate background could be from a hill folk clan. Such characters would generally be exiles, though, cast out for not following the xenophobic rules of their elders.

Hisser
Medium mutant animal (caiman)

Move 20 ft., swim 30 ft. • **Initiative** 4d
Dodge 2d • **Armor** 2 (natural);
-2W to physical attacks (mutation)
Fatigue / Wounds 15 / 17

Hopeless (–2d):	Tech
Weak (–1d):	–
Competent (+1d):	Athletics, Brawn
Good (+2d):	Alertness, Constitution, Unarmed Combat
Amazing (+3d):	–

Mutations: Achilles Heel (2d), Energy Metamorphosis—Electricity and Fire (4d), Kinetic Absorption (4d), New Body Parts—Bite (3d) & Tentacles (1d), Poison Bite (2d)

Qualities: Talented at Striking (+1d)

Attacks
Unarmed: Bite (+2W)
Unarmed: Paralytic Tentacle (delivery method of poison bite mutation but not other damage)

Description
Resembling small alligators with longer legs, hissers are actually the mutated descendants of caimans from South America. They average four feet in length from nose to tail-tip and on land run with an almost feline gait. Their scales shimmer in odd patterns, hinting both at the protective armor and resistance to energy. They have a vulnerable spot on their lower throat but a hisser instinctively guards it.

Hissers are generally solitary and rarely attack larger prey—but all bets are off during mating season, in which they become aggressive to the point of frenzy. During this time groups of hissers (from a few individuals to more than a dozen) might leave watery areas and rampage. A frenzied hisser swarm will tear through anything even as the males fight each other in nonlethal contests to impress potential mates.

Variations

Spinetail Hissers: These lack the tentacles or poison of their cousins, but instead possess a cluster of spikes on their tail which they can use as a weapon and are even more physically dangerous. (+1d Unarmed Combat, +3W piercing damage).

Brood Hissers: Most hissers lay eggs in sand-covered nests, but a subspecies has evolved that carry their young in skin pouches. For a few weeks the young are able to leave the pouch but rest there, but 1d young will burst out to bite prey. (Treat these as Tiny versions of the adults, with –1d to all physical and combat traits and only +1W damage on all attacks.)

Tactics

Since they lack the intense jaw strength of other crocodilians, hissers use their paralyzing tentacles and then tear prey apart while it's still alive. Whether in water or on land, they prefer to observe a group while perfectly still and then grab a straggler or weaker member. Unless frenzied during mating season, they will quickly withdraw rather than risk serious injury. A frenzied hisser will fight to the death.

Savape
Medium mutant animal (gorilla)

Move 15 ft. • **Initiative** 2d
Dodge 3d • **Armor** –
Fatigue / Wounds 18 / 19

Hopeless (–2d):	Stealth
Weak (–1d):	Deception
Competent (+1d):	Dexterity, Melee Weapons, Survival
Good (+2d):	Athletics, Constitution, Unarmed Combat
Amazing (+3d):	Brawn

Mutations: Confusion (4d), Mental Invisibility (2d), New Body Parts—Bite (3d) & Tentacles (*)

Qualities: Brutal (1d), Vigor (2d)

Attacks
Unarmed: Spiked Tentacles (+2W, reach 10 ft.)
Unarmed: Bite (+2W)

Description
As gorillas are not far behind human intellect, it is not surprising many mutated so as to gain full sapience. But in one place aboard the *Warden* a tribe of intelligent apes found themselves infected with a symbiotic fungus that mutated them into even stranger creatures. The fungus fully integrated itself with the gorillas' bodies, and manifests as a discolored lump just below the back of the head and two long, dark tentacles covered with sharp spikes that grow from the gorilla's shoulders.

Normal gorillas are relatively peaceful creatures, but the infected savapes are aggressive, brutal, and relentless—fully worthy of their name. They live in small villages in jungle and forest regions, or have taken over some abandoned settlements. Scouting parties search the rest of the ship for useful tools; over the decades, some of these groups were cut off and could not return. Now savapes can be found in almost any environment.

Savape hunting grounds often reveal mauled corpses covered in pulsating purple fungus that is normally harmless but could infect any badly wounded human, mutated human, or animal character who touches it—slowing Wound healing by half and causes the character to grow strange discolored patches all over her body. Only advanced medicine tech and expertise can cure the fungal infection.

Variations
Savapes have as much chance of additional mutation as any other creature. A particularly common variant is the Puff Ape, which is covered with fungus growths that look like grey-black boils. When struck in melee, it emits a cloud of spores, a specialized form of Gas Generation. These will be either randomly be one of two types determined by a 1d roll: hallucinogenic (1-3) or toxic (4-6). The nature of the spores won't be known until the Puff Ape is struck.

Tactics

Savapes attack as directed by their fungal symbiote, their first goal being to infect the target with their tentacles. They use mental invisibility to gain surprise and then strike with their tentacles, infecting enemies if they become injured. Once they've inflicted damage with their tentacles, they will revert to whatever tactics bring victory. They like to keep enemies off-guard and then use all their brutality to ensure a kill.

Breed

Savapes who can control their impulses (possibly due to a further mutation) can work as a breed. The fungus is not quite its own character, but it exists almost as a demon whispering in the character's ear—one with its own strange and malicious agenda.

Sword Bush
Medium plant (fern)

Move 15 ft. • **Initiative** 2d
Dodge 3d • **Armor** –
Fatigue / Wounds 14 / 14

Hopeless (–2d):	–
Weak (–1d):	Brawn
Competent (+1d):	Constitution, Dexterity
Good (+2d):	–
Amazing (+3d):	Melee Weapons

Mutations: Force Field Generation (2d), New Body Parts—Blade Fronds (4d*), Photodependent (4d), Precognition (2d), Speech (1d), Teleportation (4d)

Qualities: Agile Combatant (2d), Ambidextrous (1d), Slow Runner (2d)

Attacks
Melee Weapons: Blade Fronds (+2W)

Description

The sword bush appears as a roughly man-sized, vaguely spherical collection of sharp, pointy fronds, capped with a bulbous tuber-like sense organ. Its brain hides within its core, and the creature perceives the world as a mix of temperature, vibration, and "life energy." A number of its leaves have become strong and sharp-edged, making them deadly weapons that it can wield with consummate skill. In addition to those, three flexible vines are placed equidistant around the torso, giving it considerable manipulative skill—it can hold a gun or type on a keypad.

Neither particularly malicious nor friendly, sword bushes are intelligent and capable of speech, and will bargain with, attack, or ignore other creatures as appropriate. Their precognition and teleportation helps them avoid battles they do not wish to join.

Variations

Swordflinger: Some sword bushes have evolved the capacity to telekinetically launch their bladed leaves, giving them a ranged attack (modified version of Quills in the New Body Parts mutation). This is painful to do, causing it 1 Fatigue damage, but it can be worth it to take out an enemy if they can't teleport away or close the distance. They possess dozens of fronds, but are reluctant to fling more than a few.

Tactics

Sword bushes are roughly as clever as humans, which means they may or may not make wise decisions about combat. Generally peaceful, they will attack in self-defense, or to achieve a goal, but will rarely do so without some provocation. (There are exceptions, and "Barleycorn Bob," a sword bush bandit and raider, has earned a fierce reputation on several levels of the ship.) They will use energy weapons if they've found them, but most will not be so lucky, and will attack with the bladed leaves that give them their name, always ready to teleport away if the fight goes against them. When meeting new beings, they will usually keep their force field up until they're sure things are going well. Because they can "play dumb" and pretend to be stationary plants, sword bushes can often overhear valuable information from passers by and use such knowledge as a bargaining chip.

Breed

A sword bush is a workable, if unsual, player character—likely with a less impressive suite of mutations (perhaps Displacement instead of full Teleportation) and will usually vary from the norm in other ways. Its photodependency is a drawback, but one that clever players will not find insurmountable.

Ursoid
Medium mutant animal (bear)

Move 20 ft., bipedal 15 ft. • **Initiative** 2d
Dodge 2d • **Armor** –
Fatigue / Wounds 13 / 17

Hopeless (–2d):	–
Weak (–1d):	Discipline
Competent (+1d):	Constitution, Crafting, Survival, One Combat Trait (Melee Weapons, Ranged Weapons, or Unarmed Combat)
Good (+2d):	Brawn
Amazing (+3d):	–

Mutations: New Body Parts—Claws (2d), Bite (3d), 4d of mental mutations (chosen or rolled randomly)

Qualities: Combat Rage (2d), Inept at Emotional Control (–1d), Talented at Grappling (+1d)

Attacks
Unarmed: Claws (+1W), Bite (+2W)
Melee or Ranged Weapons: Varies

Description
The powerful ursoid is actually a catch-all for a number of bear species that have mutated and thrived on different decks and many climates of the *Warden*. Adaptable and clever, groups and individuals might be found just about anywhere. They strongly resemble their bear ancestors, but with paws much more capable of manipulating weapons and tools and more articulate mouths. Most will have primitive weapons crafted by hand, and might rarely possess scavenged tech.

Ursoids live in family groups or small packs, almost never growing beyond a dozen or so adults. They are ferocious in their loyalty to true (or perceived) family. With enough time to settle and grow, multiple packs may form loose trading and defense alliances—respecting each other's territories for the time being.

Variations
No two ursoids are alike, each prone to individual mutations (often a surprising mental ability). Basic appearance is a function of its ancestral stock (brown, black, or polar bear for instance).

Skinchanger: A small number of ursoids have an inherent, specialized form of the Metamorphosis mutation—allowing them to assume the form of an unmutated human. Some hunt and eat within human society, while others simply live peacefully among them in secret.

Tactics
An ursoid is clever as well as strong, capable of crafting basic weapons and armor. They also use their mental mutations to greatest advantage in a way to surprise an enemy. But they can often lose themselves to the anger in combat and forgo tactics in favor of brute strength.

Breed
An ursoid player character is generally strong, smart, and loyal—with a lack of self-control being a drawback. They can be too literal and easily insulted, going from jovial companion to frothing lunatic in the space of a heartbeat.

20 feet standard movement, bipedal 15 feet
Breed Mutations: New Body Parts—Claws (2d), Bite (3d).
Breed Qualities: Combat Rage (2d), Inept at Emotional Control (–1d), Talented at Grappling (+1d)

Winged Biter
Small mutant animal (coral snake)

Move 15 ft., fly 30 ft. • **Initiative** 2d
Dodge 4d • **Armor** –
Fatigue / Wounds 9 / 8

Hopeless (–2d):	Crafting, Tech
Weak (–1d):	Brawn
Competent (+1d):	Alertness, Deception, Survival
Good (+2d):	Dexterity, Unarmed Combat
Amazing (+3d):	Stealth

Mutations: New Body Parts—Wings (4d), Poison Bite (4d), Precognition (2d)

Qualities: Agile Combatant (2d), Talented at Camouflage (+2d)

Attacks
Unarmed: Bite (+2W, neurotoxin poison)

Description

About three feet long and decorated with brilliantly colored feathers, the winged biter is a common sight in jungle and swamp regions. They rest curled among branches, their features blending with bright flowers, then fly to attack when they spot prey.

Variations

Some winged biters have truly superior camouflage abilities—with either physical or mental mutations that allow them to become invisible for all practical purposes. Rumors persist of others that grow to tremendous size and constrict prey rather than poison.

Tactics

Fly, bite, eat. The winged biter is a straightforward hunter that will attack anything that looks edible but is rarely interested in battle. Medium-sized creatures are too large to be sources of food (since they swallow prey whole) but will attack if frightened. Mated pairs guard their nest until hatching, and baiting winged biters has become custom in some areas because the snakes raised from hatchlings can be trained to guard a specific place.

Wolfoid

Medium mutant animal (gray wolf)

Move 20 ft. • **Initiative** 3d
Dodge 2d • **Armor** –
Fatigue / Wounds 15 / 20

Hopeless (–2d):	Crafting
Weak (–1d):	Influence, Ranged Weapons, Stealth, Tech
Competent (+1d):	Alertness, Athletics, Discipline, Unarmed Combat
Good (+2d):	Brawn, Constitution, Survival
Amazing (+3d):	–

Mutations: Biped (1d), New Body Parts—Claws (2d), Bite (3d), Rapid Recovery (2d)

Qualities: Tough (2d), Unfocused (2d)

Attacks

Unarmed: Claws (+1W), Bite (+2W)

Description

Descended from fierce timber wolves and made strong by weeding out the weak and sick, wolfoids are terrifying foes individually who use pack tactics and teamwork to bring down prey and secure their territory. Most specimens are over seven feet tall, appearing as bipedal wolves with almost humanlike hands. Wolfoids have an inborn hatred of humans and a taste for their flesh. If a wolfoid pack discovers a cryo chamber they will tear it open to get at the sleeping meal inside.

Variations

This entry is an average (and unarmed) member of a wolfoid pack, though there will often be specimens with unique mutations and scavenged weapons and armor. They usually shun utilitarian tech and focus on gear that's useful in the hunt. A pack leader is invariably the strongest, with increased combat-useful traits and mutations. A wolfoid pack might also contain several adolescent cubs that are learning the hunt, with weaker traits.

Tactics

When hunting, wolfoids pick off the weak and the slow to grab the easiest meal. If fighting alone, a wolfoid will spring on the strongest foe—hoping that a brutal victory will demoralize allies. As a pack they use hit and run tactics, aiding each other with instinctive teamwork honed by daily practice, often disabling opponents to reduce their mobility, vision, or anything else that grants an advantage. Even wolfoids who hate each other individually will protect one another against outside threats.

Breed

A wolfoid player character is often a "lone wolf," either rejected from her pack or a sole survivor who must learn to cooperate with other species in order to remain alive—even if her natural tendencies often cause friction. Once trust is earned, however, a wolfoid will be loyal unto death to its new packmates.

20 feet standard movement.

Breed Mutations: Biped (1d), New Body Parts—Claws (2d), Bite (3d)

Breed Qualities: Tough (2d), Unfocused (2d)

Artificial Life

The *Warden* was launched during a period of high technology and artificial intelligence that was self-programming and self-correcting. Overseen by a primary computer system, the ship teemed with robots and androids who were designed to carry out most of the ship's functions so that only minimum crew were required to make decisions and oversee operations.

The rules define constructs—computers, robots, and androids—in much the same way it does living characters, with a few clarifications and additions.

Reasoning

While traits define what dice to roll and give the referee a sense of how strong or weak a particular A.I. might be in a given area, **Reasoning** is included as a short-hand for understanding how capable the robot or android is at interpretation of new information, creative thought, and if it has a personality (whether it is one that is simulated or self-generated). Each "level" of reasoning builds upon the previous one.

Literal A.I. understands everything in terms of hard facts and takes all statements and commands at face value.

Interpretive intelligence allows a robot or android to follow contextual clues to see its current directives through to completion.

Analytical reasoning allows commands to be deconstructed into individual steps and for memories of past explanations and experiences to inform a current goal.

Deductive reasoning enables a thinking machine to combine observation, history, context, and probability to solve problems and succeed.

Rational intelligence expands upon deductive reasoning by allowing logical thought, progressing past the present and anticipating challenges and solutions.

Personality includes motives that go beyond logic, preferences, and a style of communication that seem more life-like to living creatures.

Creative is the ultimate expression of artificial intelligence, capable of making intuitive leaps and the spontaneous creation of new ideas. Artificial intelligence at this level is often hard to distinguish from a living mind.

Movement

Movement is defined for constructs the way it is for other creatures, though a parenthetical notation quickly defines the precise way they are getting around.

Antigrav allows for hovering in place and levitation to any height (using its speed to go in any direction it chooses).

Flight refers in this case to a combination of wings and thrusters that allow the construct to slow before crashing, but only allows one turn of hovering before movement resumes or it's forced to land.

Legs work for artificial life exactly as they do for living creatures, and are suitable for most terrain.

Submersible constructs are sealed and protected against liquid damage, and usually make use of powered jets to propel it quickly through the water.

Tracks allow negotiation of many types of terrain while being less fragile than legs. Only steep angles and impassable obstacles taller than the tracks will stop it.

Wheels are ideal for smooth terrain and are included for artificial life intended for such areas and have a need for speed.

Communication & Sensors

Almost all constructs are capable of sight and hearing through standardized cameras and microphones. They also house sound projection systems for at least basic notifications and warnings while some can synthesize speech with ease, depending on the design and reasoning level of the system. Other modular systems allow for additional "senses" and means of communication.

Air Analysis is effectively a sense of smell, but is capable of breaking down the molecular makeup of an air sample and can identify even trace particles.

Infrared allows it to track heat signatures that stand out as either hot or cold against the baseline temperature.

Microscopic vision allows the construct to see a tiny area in incredible detail, some down to the cellular or atomic levels—generally only seen for scientific and medical robots, or engineering robots designed to monitor nanobots.

Radar uses radio waves and specialized echo-location to determine the location and size of objects outside its visual range.

Telescopic vision uses a sophisticated blend of lenses and digital enhancement to see at great magnifications and distances.

Wireless communication systems use specific radio frequencies to communicate—either to a living creature holding a receiver or (more frequently) other computer-based systems aboard the ship.

Mutations

Some artificial life is given mutation listings. These are functions of tech, not biology, but ultimately work in the same manner as the listed mutation with any exceptions provided in the description.

Faceless One
Medium construct (android)

Move 20 ft. (Legs) • **Initiative** 3d
Dodge 3d • **Armor** 2 (natural)
Fatigue / Wounds 21 / 20

Hopeless (–2d):	Medicine, Melee Weapons, Ranged Weapons
Weak (–1d):	–
Competent (+1d):	Alertness, Dexterity, Tech
Good (+2d):	Athletics
Amazing (+3d):	Brawn, Constitution, Discipline

Reasoning: Literal
Communication & Sensors: Wireless
Qualities: Determined (2d), Fixated (2d), Vigor (2d)

Attacks
Unarmed: Grapple

Description

Androids come in many models, each type intended for a specific purpose or function, and "born" with complete knowledge of how to do that job. Androids were designed with a lifespan of only two years, and hard-coded instincts against ever harming a human (unless their job was security). However, with the *Warden*'s systems badly damaged, the manufacturing facilities that produce androids may give "birth" to some with no built-in death clock or primary laws preventing the harm of humans.

Androids appear as men and women of average size and build, with those intended for highly physical jobs, such as cargo handler or construction worker, being larger. They have the full range of human skin tones and hair colors, but their faces are featureless, with speech coming from a synthesized organ behind the artificial skin. Some androids that are specifically built for human interface (such as those built for diplomacy, childcare, etc.) have a flat screen for a face that projects an uncannily-real face with full range of expression.

Androids were not designed to be creative thinkers, outside of whatever insight or originality might be needed to do their jobs. An engineering android might be brilliant at jury-rigging a broken vehicle, but will be unable to cook a meal given a set of ingredients. Recently produced androids tend to be "defective," and may have surprisingly adaptable minds. (Or particularly limited ones.)

Androids will be given appropriate clothing and tools when they leave the production center, but depending on how long they've been loose on the ship, may be equipped with almost anything.

The above statistics are for a Labor android designed to tirelessly complete repetitive, physical work.

Variations

There are hundreds of different android specialties, broken into broad categories:

Warrior: Android soldiers are strong, agile, and knowledgeable about many weapons and combat styles. They are programmed to do the minimum harm necessary to achieve their goals—but not to hold back if it means failure.

Labor: Labor androids are large, strong, and tireless. Given orders to do some task, such as digging a ditch, they will do it until ordered to stop or they run out of power. This has led to incidents both comical and tragic.

Technical: Technical androids are programmed with a great deal of knowledge about a narrow subject, and the skills needed to perform tasks in that area. They were designed to assist human workers, rather than set their own goals.

Infiltration: These androids shouldn't exist. They were banned decades before the *Warden* left Earth. Somehow, the data for creating them was stored in the *Warden*'s computers, and after the disaster, some systems began to manufacture them. Infiltration androids are indistinguishable from normal humans, and are both creative and clever. They are spies and assassins, and many have come to understand the world they were built to function in does not exist, and have decided to build a place for themselves in the new one.

Mad: A number of androids, confronted with a world totally unlike the one they were built for, simply went insane. Some went catatonic; some became violent berserkers; others somehow transmuted their madness into a form of free will and self awareness, and now travel the ship, pursuing strange goals with the single-minded dedication they were built for.

Tactics

An android's tactics depend on its job. Other than Warrior or Infiltrator types, most will not fight at all, or limit themselves to self-defense.

Warrior Android
Medium construct (android)

Move 20 ft. (Legs) • **Initiative** 3d
Dodge 3d • **Armor** 2 (natural)
Fatigue / Wounds 19 / 20

Hopeless (–2d):	–
Weak (–1d):	Crafting, Medicine
Competent (+1d):	Alertness, Dexterity, Tech
Good (+2d):	Athletics, Brawn, Unarmed Combat
Amazing (+3d):	Constitution, Discipline, Melee Weapons, Ranged Weapons

Reasoning: Analytical
Communication & Sensors: Infrared, Wireless
Mutations: Force Field Generation (4d)
Qualities: Agile Combatant (2d), Tough (2d)

Attacks
Melee Weapons: Duralloy Sword (+2W, integrated)
Ranged Weapons: Laser Rifle (+4W fire, integrated)

Defense Borg
Large construct (robot)

Move 20 ft. (Antigrav) • **Initiative** 4d
Dodge 1d • **Armor** 4 (natural)
Fatigue / Wounds 23 / 23

Hopeless (–2d):	Stealth
Weak (–1d):	Dexterity
Competent (+1d):	Tech
Good (+2d):	Alertness, Discipline
Amazing (+3d):	Constitution, Ranged Weapons

Reasoning: Rational
Communication & Sensors: Infrared, Telescopic, Wireless
Mutations: Telekinesis (5d, twin tractor beams that can function simultaneously and independently)
Qualities: Agile Combatant (2d), Determined (2d), Tough (2d), Vigor (2d)

Attacks
Ranged Weapons: Laser Rifles (+4W fire, 3 placements of 5 rifles each)
Ranged Weapons: Assorted Grenades (5 each; frag, plasma, smoke, stun)

Description

A floating disc 30 feet across and 5 feet thick, a defense borg is placed to guard areas from intrusion or instructed to patrol a specific area on a fixed schedule. Due to its size, it is rarely seen in regions in-between main decks, except in storage or manufacturing areas with plenty of open space. It is bristling with gun emplacements in multiple turrets, and has two pairs of long metal tentacles sprouting from the upper and lower surfaces of its saucer-shaped body. They are among the deadliest beings on the *Warden*, easily capable of slaughtering a small army in short order.

Defense borgs have a synthetic brain at their core—not quite a human brain, but a complex structure of "living" neural tissue that guide their intelligence. Combining this with the speed and accuracy of tech makes them exceptionally dangerous enemies.

Variations

Different weapon load-outs are common. Some truly ancient defense borgs choose to engage in unauthorized self-modification. Very rarely, their organic components may gain mental mutations.

Tactics

A defense borg is direct and to the point. A borg will usually provide a perfunctory warning to leave its protected area, and then attack without a moment's hesitation if the warning is ignored. It is possible, though difficult, to engage one in conversation. A defense borg will continually analyze its enemies, and adapt its tactics moment-by-moment to deal with them. Other than a rare few who have achieved true free will, most will not leave their post even to save themselves.

Depending on its programming, it may first use its tractor beams to push an enemy back, or stun grenades to knock them unconscious … or it might employ lethal measures immediately.

Repair Bot
Medium construct (robot)

Move 10 ft. (Antigrav) • **Initiative** 5d
Dodge 3d • **Armor** 2 (natural)
Fatigue / Wounds 12 / 19

Hopeless (–2d):	–
Weak (–1d):	–
Competent (+1d):	–
Good (+2d):	Brawn, Constitution, Dexterity
Amazing (+3d):	Alertness, Crafting, Tech

Reasoning: Analytical
Communication & Sensors: Microscopic, Wireless
Mutations: Telekinesis (Telekinesis (6d, tractor beam)
Qualities: Talented at Tech Repair (+1d) & Fixing (+1d)

Attacks
Ranged Weapons: Welding Torch (+4W fire)
Melee Weapons: Cutting Tools (+2W) or Tentacle Lashes (+1W, 5 ft. reach)

Note: It may use up to 3 "weapons" simultaneously per turn without penalty.

Description

Repair bots are floating spheres, 10 feet across, fitted with three 8-foot-long manipulative tentacles, and a wide array of retractable and adjustable tools suitable for virtually any routine maintenance task. They have a tractor beam projector which can lift incredible weight, and a short range (5 feet) fusion torch for welding and cutting jobs. Their tentacles end with micro-manipulators that can handle extremely delicate operations on mechanisms as small as a grain of sand. Not intended for human interaction (indeed, they mostly were assigned to regions humans couldn't travel, due to high radiation, vacuum, or extreme temperatures), they seem cold and implacable.

Originally, they had many layers of code designed to keep them from accidentally injuring a human, and would instantly stop work if a fragile creature got in the way of their assignment. Many repair bots still roaming the ship have lost or misinterpreted these directives, and will blithely weld a metal sheet into place right on top of a screaming victim who fell asleep in the wrong nook. Others had their programming twisted to the point where they will "guard" an area, and attack any "vandals" who damage it.

Variations

There are hundreds of specialized models, created to do particular tasks. Normally, they would be disassembled back to raw materials, but now, many still roam the ship, the job they were built for long-forgotten. Some have extra-long arms; others spray powerful adhesive; still others carry swarms of much-smaller "worker bees" that spread out around a damaged area to perform a dozen repair operations concurrently.

A rare few have had full consciousness accidentally uploaded into their systems by the malfunctioning computer network. These self-aware models make their way through the world, doing what they can. Many bargain their ability to fix broken weapons or technological gear for access to power, lubricant, and the raw materials they need to make replacement parts.

Tactics

Normally, repair bots are non-hostile if those nearby do not interfere with it work. If somehow triggered into combat, a repair bot will use its tractor beam to drive back one enemy while using its tentacles to drag another into range of its torch and cutting tools.

Veterinary Bot
Medium construct (robot)

Move 10 ft. (Tracks) • **Initiative** 3d
Dodge 3d • **Armor** 2 (natural)
Fatigue / Wounds 12 / 18

Hopeless (–2d):	–
Weak (–1d):	–
Competent (+1d):	Alertness, Dexterity
Good (+2d):	Brawn, Constitution, Melee Weapons, Tech
Amazing (+3d):	Medicine

Reasoning: Analytical
Communication & Sensors: Infrared, Microscopic, Wireless
Mutations: Electrical Generation (2d, touch only), Poison Bite (2d, injection)
Qualities: Talented at First Aid (+1d) & Surgery (+1d)

Attacks
Brawn: Grapple
Melee Weapons: Laser Scalpel (+1W fire), Electric Prod, Sedative Injector

Description

Veterinary bots were created to assist human animal doctors in everything from routine diagnosis to administering treatments to complicated surgeries. The animal life aboard the *Warden* was considered precious cargo and keeping them healthy was a priority.

They have a vaguely humanoid shape, but move about on 2-foot high treads with a cylindrical body sporting six spindly appendages each capable of fine motor control. Its "head" contains a binocular pair of cameras capable of switching between multiple modes. A veterinary bot understands speech but only directly obeys those with appropriate credentials or an override code, but only communicates in beeps while feeding information to a nearby computer system.

Most veterinary bots are assigned to work in a particular facility, though some will roam a given area looking for animals that are sick or injured. Unfortunately, its programming was not designed to understand heavy mutation and it will generally identify a mutant animal as disfigured and attempt to treat it or surgically alter it in order to restore it to a condition that matches the Earth-normal standards.

Variations

Some veterinary bots were designed to be huge lumbering surgical facilities that will fully engulf a subject, tranquilize it, and perform any needed operations. Others were designed to work on larger creatures or submerge to treat marine life. A rare few have been modified to understand and treat human injuries, though it's dangerous for mutated humans to interact with them.

Tactics

Generally veterinary bots are programmed to do no harm, and will attempt to fulfill their functions in a firm but gentle manner. If badly damaged, the bot will attempt to retreat for recharge and repair. They will use two of their arms to grapple a struggling patient and then tranquilize it before continuing the exam. A creature who does not struggle against an initial exam will suffer various indignities, such as being probed with a rectal thermometer and having various fluids and tissues sampled.

The Petting Zoo of Death

A METAMORPHOSIS ALPHA Adventure
by Jamie Chambers

INTRODUCTION

"The Petting Zoo of Death" is a short adventure for METAMORPHOSIS ALPHA using the SYSTEM 26 roleplaying game rules intended for new players, and can serve as as starting point for campaign play. It quickly establishes some important elements of the setting and the types of action that await on the decks of the starship *Warden*.

The adventure text is intended for the referee only, who should be thoroughly familiar with the basic rules (Chapter Two: Basic Gameplay) and have a passing knowledge of the more detailed rules (Chapter Seven: Rules). Players can jump in completely new to the game, though access to the basic rules is helpful.

Players & Characters

This adventure is intended for 3-6 characters (created using the standard creation rules). The pre-generated characters found earlier in this book would be a perfect fit. The player characters can be human, mutated human, mutant animal, or mutant plant. If playing with a smaller or larger group, the referee should adjust the challenges accordingly.

Refereeing This Adventure

If this is your first time running a roleplaying game, keep a few things in mind. Your primary mission is to host an enjoyable game in which everyone has fun! The job of the referee is to narrate the action, provide descriptions, and answer questions based on what the characters can perceive or understand (which is often quite different than the players).

While a referee plays the mutants and robots the group encounters during the adventure—to sometimes deadly effect—you are not an opponent. Play each encounter logically, using rules and your best judgment, but don't go out of your way to kill characters or stack the desk against the group. A good adventure is challenging but the player characters usually win, or at least survive!

The basic game mechanics are designed to be easy to make judgment calls when a character takes an action. Decide which trait applies to what is being done and then decide if it's of Easy, Average, or Hard difficulty. The dice decide how well a character succeeds, or how spectacularly he fails! This is a game of fast action, so don't be afraid to wing it and make things up to keep things moving. The referee is the final word on what happens at the game table.

Background

The starship *Warden* simultaneously held countless colonists asleep in cryostasis, but also held thousands of active crew, scientists, and support personnel and their families to keep the ship in top repair and its precious cargo of Earth life in good health for the ultimate goal of settling a new world.

Children were born and grew up on the ship, and among the many educational and enrichment activities available to them was the starship Petting Zoo. It was designed to house some of the more harmless animal life and allow young people and families to tour simulated environments to match those once found on Earth—and also hold supply stations with food and veterinary care for animals, and containment for diseased or dangerous creatures. Computer and robotic systems handled most upkeep automatically with human staff overseeing the attraction.

When the disaster wrecked so many things aboard the *Warden*, most life in the Petting Zoo died and the localized computer systems shut down. The entrance was hidden behind debris for an unknown period of time, a darkened tomb memorializing a gentler time.

One day a maintenance bot performing its endless duties cleared away enough debris to reveal the entrance and inspected the facility. It restored power to the Petting Zoo's localized computer system, which within nanoseconds became corrupted by the *Warden's* primary computer core. The Petting Zoo computer defensively cut its network off from the rest of the ship, but it was too late—it now had a fractured understanding of its function and the purpose of the Zoo. The computer took control of the maintenance bot and began "restoring" the Zoo.

While the simulated environments could be repaired easily enough, a Zoo requires living exhibits. The computer instructed the maintenance bot to rebuild itself for the purpose of wrangling living creatures to be placed into the various exhibits. For at least a dozen years, unwilling victims have been brought into a Petting Zoo that is happy to allow visitors in, but will not let "exhibits" escape.

Overview

"The Petting Zoo of Death" is a straightforward location-driven adventure (with some possibility for triggered and random encounters). The player characters find themselves inside a strange place in which the landscape changes quickly and different types of creatures have established territories. A dangerous robot will prevent them from easily leaving.

After the player characters enter the Zoo, they must explore and overcome obstacles, challenges, and inhabitants of the exhibits to find a possible exit.

Establishment

There are a few different ways to introduce a group to "The Petting Zoo of Death," and with different types of characters it's possible to use more than one method at the same time.

Abduction: Each character has only vague memories of blinding white-hot pain, and wake up in Containment (Area 1). The Wrangler stunned them senseless and dragged them to the area. Mutant animals and mutated humans are put in the cages while normal humans are simply tossed on the floor when the computer identified them as such, while mutant plants were unceremoniously tossed in the compost heap.

Every character should roll a Constitution (Fortitude) check to see who wakes up first, with each character still suffering 1 Fatigue damage and not feeling quite 100% at the outset of the adventure.

Accidental Entry: The Wrangler still spends some of its time on system repair, and has recently re-activated the old lift in Administration (Area 3) and sent it to another deck. When the characters step inside, it has been programmed to override other directives and bring them back to the Zoo and then cut the power. They'll have to pry open the doors from the inside, otherwise wait for the Wrangler to return in 1d hours to pull them out and drag them to Containment (Area 1).

The Rescue: In this version (best for an already-established party) it's a close friend or ally of at least one of the characters—or perhaps the character of an absent player—who has been abducted by the Wrangler, as above. They follow the robotic trail back to the entrance to the Zoo and find it easy to gain entrance, and must work their way back to Containment (Area 1) where they might find their friend alive in a cage or already eaten by the mutant that nests in the wall. And though the computer will let anyone into the Zoo, it will take every possible measure to prevent them from leaving.

When the Adventure Begins

Regardless of how you decide to begin the adventure, make sure you give the time for the following:

☣ Have the players describe and introduce their characters if they do not yet know each other.
☣ Make sure you know how each character reacts to the opening situation.
☣ Nudge the players to make short-term goals for their characters, and possibly as a group, to guide their actions.

Encounter 1: Containment

Location. Area 1. This is a holding area for live specimens before they are placed in specific exhibits and a dumping ground for everything else. It's also become the feeding ground for a mutant animal that enjoys having its food delivered.

Note: If using the "Abduction" scenario to establish the adventure, mutant animal and mutant humans will be in spread among the two energy cages (A), humans in the middle of the room (B), and plants dumped unceremoniously in the compost heap (C).

Description: This large room is mostly metal and construction-grade plastic, constantly lit by lights inset in the 15 ft. high ceiling. Two main corners of the room have tiny aligned holes in the floor and ceiling that activate to create energy cages as needed to contain new specimens. A smaller, open side-chamber is used as a compost-heap—containing plants, bones, and random junk. One wall of the main chamber has been carved open by claws to form a small, jagged cave, the den of a dangerous creature.

A. Cages. There are two energy-cages, each 10 ft. x 15 ft., in the corners of the room. Every half hour—or at the touch of a lighted blue button—a section of wall will rotate to offer a basin of purified water (one is malfunctioning and reveals only brownish stains). Every 8 hours another section of wall rotates and reveals a large, shallow bowl filled with a nearly tasteless but nutritional feed appropriate for carnivores and omnivores (one reveals the old, mangled remains of an animal that found its way into feed containment and got caught in the machinery).

The "bars" of the cage are composed of blueish energy and are spaced about 18 inches apart. Large creatures are unable to get out of the bars at all, while Medium can try to squeeze through with a Hard Dexterity (Contortion) action (Average for Small creatures, Easy for Tiny). Success allows the character to escape confinement but they still get singed for 1 Fatigue damage. Failure means 1d Wound fire damage and being driven back inside the cage. A creature simply flinging itself through the bars will suffer 2d Wound fire damage but will be free.

B. Main Room. The room is mostly empty, save for sliding double-doors for exit, requiring either a keycard within 5 feet of the control panel or a code manually entered on the touchpad next to it. A section of wall seems black and glassy, but will activate at a touch to reveal a computer panel that can potentially be used with a Tech (Computer Use) action to deliver food and water to the cages (Easy), open the door (Average), or deactivate the cages (Average). A Botch on any of these actions will shut down power to the entire room,

plunging everything into darkness—but deactivating the cages!—for ten minutes. Without power, the exit door can be pried open manually with a Hard Brawn (Pushing) action.

C. Compost Heap. This is a smelly, bug-ridden heap containing dead plants (mostly mundane, but a few of the sentient variety), garbage, bones (broken bits barely identifiable as human or animal), and miscellaneous garbage. A successful Average Alertness (Searching) will reveal a useful piece of tech from the pile after 20 minutes, with each Enhancement reducing the search time by 5 minutes. It can be anything small—hydrogen power cell, laser fuser, even a grenade.

D. Horror's Den. The **armored horror** (a large mutant armadillo, see Encounter Statistics) has used its claws to carve a hole in the wall and has made itself a small lair. It hides in the den from the Wrangler but takes full advantage of the humans and animals brought here. It will watch the group from the darkness of its den but will eventually find a moment to try and take down a character as its next meal. It will also violently defend its lair if a curious character comes snooping before it makes a move.

Conclusion

Once the threat of the armored horror is dealt with the room can be explored for some time with no further problems. If the group waits a truly long time, however, the Wrangler (see Encounter Statistics) will enter the room and dump a smoking dead corpse of an unintelligent animal into a cage, and if characters are not where it left them it will attempt to subdue or drive them back to those places until they are ready for processing. Other than that, the group is free to rest here if anyone is badly hurt or wants to recover a used mutant power.

There is only one way in or out of this room, leading to Area 2.

Encounter 2: Trip to the Vet

Location. Area 2. This area was used for the examination and care of the animals in the petting zoo, originally with a human veterinary specialist assisted by a robot. Without the human doctor, the VetBot has now taken over and become overzealous in pursuit of its duties.

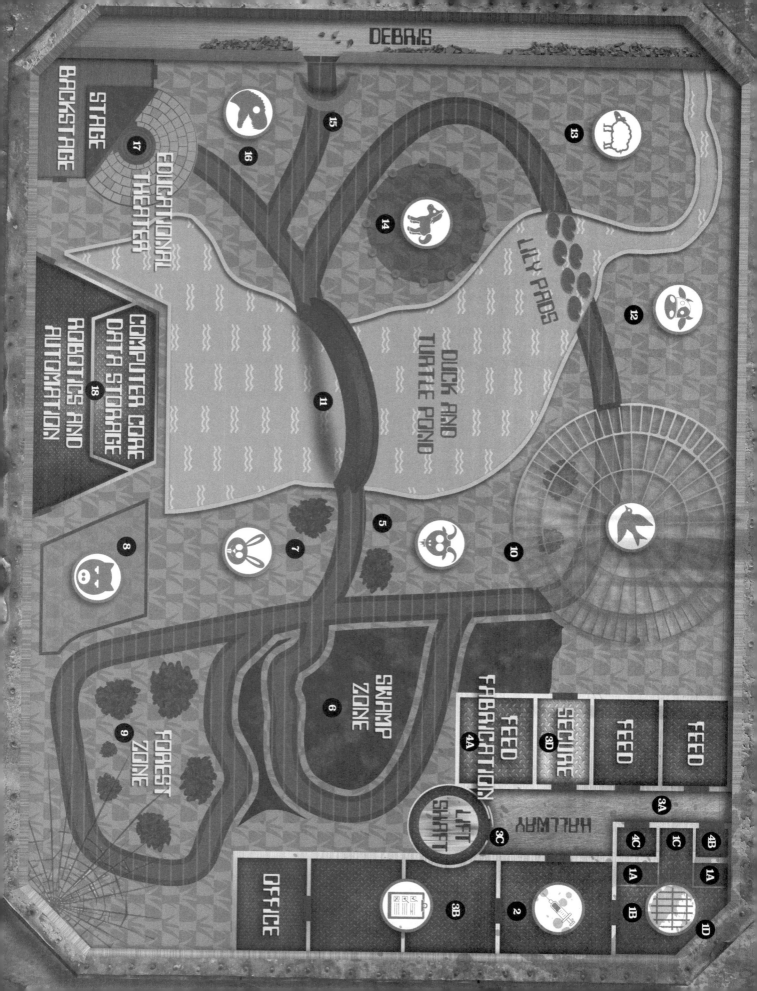

Description: This large room is mostly metal and construction-grade plastic, constantly lit by lights inset in the 15 ft. high ceiling. A large examination table sits 3.5 feet off the floor, and a blue-colored area of the floor near the wall has a readout screen that serves as a scale and takes basic three-dimensional measurements which are displayed on the wall along the computer's best-guess at identifying the specimen. One side of the room has a desk that is built in as part of the wall, and includes a computer terminal, drawers and shelves that are all locked (Average Tech/Tech Infiltration action to open by using the computer terminal, or Hard Brawn/Smashing action to rip things open). If opened, the supplies can be cobbled together for the equivalent of a Doctor's Bag (see Chapter 6). If the exam history of the computer is searched (Easy Tech/Computer Use) they can see many different types of animals that relate to those that can be encountered in this adventure, plus others that didn't survive.

The VetBot

Triggered. If any mutated human or mutant animal steps on the scale, a section of wall slides open, revealing an alcove just big enough to house a Medium robot that rolls out on a small caterpillar track (treads like a tank) and approaches the nearest mutant animal (if in the room) or mutated human (if there are no animals). The **VetBot** (see Veterinary Bot, Chapter 9) completely ignores plants and human characters and tries to go around them. It has a humanoid torso but a flat head with cameras and sensors that can rotate in any direction, and has six spindly "arms" that can be used to manipulate objects and produce more than a few medical instruments.

Without violence, the Vetbot will use Grappling to seize a chosen character and take it to the exam table—if it puts up a fight. A willing subject will be treated with gentle care. Once taken to the examination table, it will begin to study its subject and the main readings will be displayed at the computer terminal on the desk.

☣ The VetBot will conduct a visual inspection, checking the surface area for injuries and imperfections. A terrible wound (if the character is injured) will be cleaned and bandaged immediately, healing 2 Wounds. Otherwise it will simply note the injuries and scars.

☣ It will take a hair sample if available, then swab a moist spot to gather DNA for later analysis.
☣ It will conduct physical measurements using visible but non-harmful lasers to measure the subject's size, mass, and density.
☣ It will produce a thermometer from one of its extremities and take the subject's temperature … rectally.
☣ Using frankly upsetting devices, it will attempt to gain both a urine and stool sample.

If a character willingly undergoes this process, all that is lost is 1 Fatigue and 100% dignity. The VetBot will completely ignore the actions of all other characters during an examination unless they attack it. It is programmed to defend itself only by grappling and avoiding injury. It's an Easy target to attack during examination mode, Average during defensive mode, and it will attempt to grapple the most dangerous assailant. If badly injured (see Chapter 7), the Bot will attempt to retreat to its alcove to repair and recharge, which will require the intervention of the Wrangler (also a repair bot).

Conclusion

Once the VetBot is endured or disabled and the room examined (or plundered) to the group's satisfaction, they can decide which of the two exits they wish to take. One leads into a hallway, the other into the administrative offices.

Encounter 3: Administration & Feed

Locations. Areas 3 & 4. The administrative offices of the zoo are abandoned and sit in ruins, yielding little useful information or items. The lift has been repaired but is controlled by the local Zoo computer. They are briefly described below.

3A. *Hallway.* Once a generic, business-like hallway, marks on the floors and walls might reveal (Hard Alertness/Observation or Easy Survival/Tracking) that many animals were dragged against their will through this area. Any enhancements show that some came from the double doors in the middle of the hallway and go into Area 2, while others come from the Lift. The artwork still hangs on the wall in permanently mounted frames, however—drawings of adorable animals (bunnies and billy goats and cows and such) made with crayon by the hands of young children. An old bloodstain on one picture of a donkey is only slightly disturbing.

3B. *Administrative Offices*. There are a few desks, tables, chairs, and evidence of cracked and ruined computer access panels. It appears that some huge beast raged through here at some point, as there is evidence of damage with a large faded bloodstain on the floor near the executive office and a scorch mark on the wall. (Any character with an electricity-based mutation can identify it as caused by a powerful electrical discharge.)

3C. *Lift*. The cylindrical elevator rotates and the doors are built into its shape and slide outward. It is controlled by the Zoo computer system and currently deactivated and rotated so the door is inaccessible. This can only be changed by deactivating the computer itself (see Encounter 6). Note that the Lift might be a possibly entry point for the adventure.

3D. *Access Hallway*. This hallway leads out to the main portion of the Zoo, both doors easily opened.

4A. *Feed Fabricator, Storage, & Mechanism*. The *Fabricator* chamber has no actual door but can be accessed through a maintenance crawlspace with a Hard Tech/Tech Infiltration action. This machinery converts base compounds into various feeds distributed throughout the Zoo. The *Storage* area is just that, where dry feeds are stored until they are distributed, which is why the access door is locked (locking mechanism broken, requiring a Hard Brawn/Smashing action or Average Crafting/Breaking to trip the mechanical components of the lock itself without power). Nothing inside but food, though. The Mechanism is what sorts, portions, and distributes the food. The door is locked but opened with an Average Tech/Tech Infiltration check, and if a character gets too cozy she might have to dive out of the way before being mangled in the works. It's why safety indicator signs line the room.

4B. *Supplies* contains the leftover cleaning supplies, including a broom, mop, and various solvent chemicals which could possibly be used creatively.

4C. *Bathrooms*. The plumbing is still functional only in the female bathroom. There is a cluster of more than a dozen **plasma bats** chewing on a loose power cable in the male bathroom—tiny mutant bats with green glowing eyes. The lights are on and all is normal unless someone steps too close, then the bats detach and swarm—making hideous high-frequency screeches and fly about the suddenly black room with glowing green eyes. No damage but the referee might make some characters succeed an Average Discipline/Emotional Control check to avoid fleeing or freaking out. The little bats are delicate but agile, Hard to hit but killed by any damage.

Conclusion
The area offers clues, but the real action lies outside.

Encounter 4: The Great Outdoors

Locations. Areas 5 – 9. The same systems that create vast simulated Earth-like environments and entertaining illusions on the rest of the ship are compacted here to make small habitats that combine real and artificial life, holographic visions, and pre-recorded looping sounds to make each area seem both believable and far larger than they truly are. The illusion fades near the edge and the path is always easy to see as long as you don't wander too far. A referee might require some checks or actions if a character decides to go exploring too far on her own.

If any character steps too close to the pond, note that they might make themselves a target for the **hissers** that have claimed it. See Encounter 5 (area 12) if that happens or for a better description of the pond.

Area 5: Billy Goat Turf
This area is ruled with an iron fist and tiny horns by three **gruffoids** … anthropomorphic billy goats that come in three sizes (in game terms): Small, Medium, and Large. A small gruffoid emerges from behind

a boulder and demands the surrender of adequate "treasure" (in his adorable bleating voice) if they wish to pass through the area. He brings out his brothers, one larger and one (apparently) smaller to emphasize the point. While the gruffoids are greedy and always hungry, they might be fooled or negotiated with—otherwise there is a fight on everyone's hands and at least a few surprises waiting.

Area 6: The Marshians

The path leads through a realistic swamp, right down to the noises of bugs and the constant smell of wet rot. While there are some large—but harmless—snakes and other swamp critters who reside in this zone, there is only one event of note. Once fully inside the group will notice (on an Easy Alertness/Awareness check) sharp thwacking sounds and what seems like a low-pitch moan of fear or pain ... more details based on the level of success on the roll.

The source of distress is a mutant **tortoise** with more human-like appendages and the power of speech. He is currently fully retracted inside his shell as a group of 8 small, violent bipedal **dogmen**—imagine a schnauzer standing on two legs at 2 1/2 feet tall. They cannot speak, but seem to enjoy tormenting the tortoise by beating him crude small clubs.

Tommy (Tortoise): Large. Influence +1d, Survival +2d, Tech +1d; Speech; Larger; New *Body Part—Carapace*). He's a fearful pacifist, hiding within his shell.

Schnauzeroids (8): Small. Alertness +1d, Athletics +2d/Swimming +3d, Brawn −1d, Constitution −1d, Discipline −1d. Club +1F. They are initially aggressive but their bark is far worse than their bite. They will gang up on a solo target but will quickly flee at the sign of strength, and they are physically fragile and easy to kill. They are accomplished swimmers, and capable of diving into the swampy water to scatter and hide.

The little mutant dogs will continue to bully the tortoise unless the group intervenes. The little dogs will bark fearsome warnings and shake their sticks threateningly, but any damage/death to one of their own or even an intimidating show of force will cause them to scatter in fear. Non-lethal Wound damage will cause one to fall over, screaming in pain and sounding very much like a hurt little puppy. (The referee is encouraged to have fun with how the group reacts to the schnauzeroids, whether they are a nuisance or even bullied or charmed into service.)

If rescued, the tortoise will thank them but seem cautious as he has been mistreated by every other creature he's come in contact with for at least a dozen years. Good roleplaying and good rolls (Influence and related specialties) might cause him to reveal more, and say that he was brought into this strange place many years ago and has grown. He left the pond when the hissers were brought in. With especially good roleplaying or enhancements, Tommy declares he has "thank you gifts" hidden inside his shell, and produces a protein disruptor pistol with 2 charges left as well and a small passkey that can be used to open any door in the facility—including the exit. The tortoise does not know what either item is or how they work (see Chapter 6 if anyone decides to experiment with the protein disruptor pistol).

Area 7: Bunny Warrens

Near the pond there is a small area with pre-built rabbit nests and soft grass. One small, white **rabbit** nibbles on clover near its shelter. The rabbit is completely ordinary, though at this point paranoid players might make a big deal out of the rabbit and offer obligatory jokes. Other bunnies will emerge from the warrens later—though a Hard Alertness (Observation) check might offer insight that the bunnies are careful not to get closer to the water, nor allow themselves to be within easy line of sight of the water unless they are farther away from the shore.

Area 8: Cleaned-Out Pig Pen

A sign in the shape of a pig indicates the intended occupants of this small enclosure. There is a trough, mud, and a lot of dried feed sitting uneaten, and no evidence of any pigs. The hissers got their fill of ham, pork chops, and bacon long ago, before the survivors fled and dug their way into the Aviary (Encounter 5, Area 11). If the characters go into the pen to investigate and get too close to the water, or try to pass beyond it (an Easy Athletics/Climbing feat) they risk being attacked by the **hissers** lurking in the water (see Encounter 5, Area 12).

Area 9: Hokey Smoke, A Dark Forest!

The "Forest Zone" is really just a grove of trees, but once past the bench and into the treelike it seems impossibly vast and large and exists in perpetual twilight. A few mutant flying squirrels known as **colugoids** that were brought into the area ended up carving out a territory by harassing and driving away other creatures who wander in. They maneuver between the trees and shoot slings and screech awful warnings, their leader uses a fearsome sonic attack.

Colugoid Leader. Identical to the others except Alertness +3d, Leadership +2d; Sonic Blast (4d). His mutation (only usable once) emits a powerful burst of focused sound in a cone 60 feet long and 30 feet wide at the end. 4d attack vs. Constitution/Endurance, all damage is sonic, and any character who takes 2 or more Fatigue are also deafened for 1d turns.

Conclusion

The group may be focused purely on their goal—likely escape—or they may choose to more thoroughly explore the Zoo and get into trouble. But their wanderings will eventually take them near the **pond** (Encounter 5), into the **aviary** (Encounter 6) or to the **Robotics & Automation Center** (Encounter 9).

Encounter 5: Gators, Cows, & Birds—Oh My!

Locations. Areas 10 – 14. The pond and the aviary are two dominant features of the Zoo—intended to showcase animals that glide through the air and swim in the water. The northern section also includes two grazing areas once intended for cows and sheep. The holographic technology here still simulates a cheerful, sunny day but keeps these features of the Zoo open and visible from normal distances.

Area 10: Angry Pigs

The Aviary is essentially a huge dome-shaped cage of plasteel to contain flying critters. Back when the Zoo was functional it only had harmless, chirping examples that would have been well suited to serenading cartoon princesses. But since the computer system's restocking, it now contains a number of predatory mutant avians that have struck up a loose alliance against a common foe. Pigs (and abducted boars brought from the outside) were massacred by the hissers from the pond, and survivors burrowed their way down and inside the aviary. Since then the Aviary has become a battle ground of mutant bird vs. mutant pig—with the hogs stealing and devouring eggs and the birds launching kamikaze assaults on their belly-dragging foes.

The gates to the Aviary are locked with rotating randomly-generated alphanumeric codes by the computer system. Characters could theoretically hack the gates with sufficient Tech, break them by some means, or even tunnel under them—though this encounter is meant as an obstacle and a spectacle rather than a direct encounter. A party skirting the edge of the aviary will be forced to the edge of the pond (see below) and might be ambushed by hissers while gawking at a pig-bird skirmish. Some clever player characters might try to climb the dome, which is only of Average difficulty—though irritated birds might peck and scratch at the climbers to trigger a tumble down the side and into the water filled with hungry reptiles.

Referees are encouraged to flesh out the aviary if inspired, creating a few examples of mutant pigs and raptoroids and deciding just how intruding characters might be caught up in the conflict—a mini-adventure inside the Zoo!

Area 11: On Olden Pond

The pond once sported clear blue waters and a variety of freshwater fish and amphibians. But the filtration systems have degraded it to a murky dark green and the water (up to 8 feet deep) is now home to four **hissers** (see Chapter 9) who survive on maturing fish and the creatures that venture too close to the water—and sometimes leaving the pond to drag prey back to be devoured later. The creatures are Hard to spot, as they are able to float with eyes just barely emerging from the water. The hissers will quietly stalk the group, taking the opportunity to strike anyone who gets close to the water or might arrange an ambush on the bridge (with 1 hisser on each end of the bridge when the party reaches the middle) and then attempting to grapple or shove characters into the water to be eaten by those waiting below. They will attempt to grab anyone on the Lily Pads by dragging them into the water and then tearing them apart.

The Bridge is sturdy and virtually indestructible, but the walls are only four feet high to allow for easy viewing of the water below. The Lily Pads—anchored in place and able to hold virtually any weight—are Easy (Athletics) to cross and the water below is only 3 feet deep, though the hissers might make falling in a much more dangerous proposition.

The stream leading off the north end of the pond has a current that gets increasingly strong (going from Easy to Average to Hard) to swim against before it reaches a grate below the surface that pulls the water and might trap a creature up against it until it drowns. The hissers avoid the stream.

Area 12: Needs More Cowbell

Once a grazing pasture for gentle cows, the hissers made meals of them long ago. Now it's just soft grasses and the illusion of gentle blue sky. A character might find a lone cowbell hidden in the grass attached to a ripped leather thong.

Area 13: Snake in the Grass

Very similar to 13, above, except that it's a handful of gentle hills and slightly taller grass. While the chief predators in the area (the hissers in the pond) have cleared out the sheep this area was intended to house, a venomous snake slithers through the grass. (Use the stats for Winged Biter but without the ability to fly.) It will be an opposed roll against the snake's ability to hide (3d) to spot it, though depending on the circumstances it might be quite Easy for the Snake and Hard for those not looking for it (Average if someone is trying to find something in the grass). It's not interested in being killed, but it may try to take out an edible character with venom and then run and hide, hoping to return later to claim its prize.

Area 14: My Little Sad Pony Corral

A cheerful little tune tune plays from an unknown source in this area as an automated wheel turns in intervals (5 minutes on, 5 minutes off) to pace ponies who have not offered rides in this attraction for a very long time. A sign on the fencepost near the area shows an abstract picture of a young horse being ridden by a small human wearing a cowboy hat.

Conclusion

It's very likely the group will focus on escape, and the arch revealing the primary exit from (and entrance to) the Zoo is within sight of the pony corral. Further "down" on the map are the automated educational attractions and the building that houses the computer and robotic systems that maintain the Zoo.

Encounter 6: Robotic Education

Locations. Areas 15 – 18. If the characters are unable to escape through the exit, isn't distracted by dinosaurs, doesn't stop to take in a play, they might discover the source of the automated systems that have turned the Zoo into a deathtrap.

Area 15: Exit Arch

The archway is decorated with etchings of the various types of animals the Zoo once contained—along with the red-glowing letters **E-X-I-T** that have retained their meaning even for those who don't know how to read. Just beyond the arch is a set of huge double-reinforced doors that can only be opened with a passkey, an override code (rotating and randomly-generated by the computer, much like the doors to the aviary), or if the computer system itself is shut down entirely.

Triggered. If the exit door is opened while the computer system is still active, the Wrangler is summoned and will arrive in short order to subdue the characters and return them to Containment.

Area 16: Cretaceous Playground

This terrifying-looking area is (relatively) harmless. From the path holographic images project a background that appears to go into the far distance, showing huge duck-billed dinosaurs eating from bushes and pterosaurs gliding in lazy patters in the sky. In the immediate area is a triceratops threatening a downy-feathered tyrannosaur, the two foes circling each other but none ever striking. Keeping a safe distance are two squawking velociraptors, the feathered dinosaurs not even reaching the waist of an average human. The scene is intimidating, but a soothing male voice rattles off facts about the ancient, extinct animals and assures visiting children that the exhibit is completely safe. (Spared no expense.)

Triggered. If the computer system has determined that rogue specimens are loose in the Zoo or attempting to escape, it can override the endlessly-repeated pattern of the dinosaurs. The T-Rex will suddenly turn and attempt a bite on a character within reach (which is Hard to avoid, inflicts 1d Fatigue damage from blunted teeth, and is an opposed 5d Grapple to escape). Sufficient damage to the fake dinosaur will cause it to spark and crackle and release the creature caught in its jaws. The other dinosaurs do not change their behavior but can be destroyed if the characters are so inclined.

Area 17: Lair of the Thespians

Curving bench seats orbit an outdoor auditorium. The stage is open, but connected to an enclosed "backstage" area that houses holographic projection equipment, old costumes, and controls for lighting and sound.

Triggered. If at least three individuals occupy the seats for a few minutes a timer will appear on the stage, counting down from 5 minutes to the beginning of the show. Two holographic human children appear on-stage, a boy named Billy and a girl named Susan. Through conversation and song they tell about ponies and bunnies and the other animals that once inhabited the Zoo. The projected-children exhort that some animals are okay to pet, that others are just for looking ("Look with your eyes, not with your hands!") and tell them to ask their Mommy or Daddy if they have questions. To make things extra-creepy, the human children seem speak to someone who is not there on the stage, pausing to listen and agree to unspoken lines. (Human staff once interacted with holographic children during the presentation.) The show ends with a gleeful little song as the children fade into non-existence.

Area 18:
The Bots You're Looking For

This building is in obvious disrepair, as the computer and robotic systems were intended to be maintained by living personnel while the automation attended to the Zoo itself. It is covered in creeping vines and the door shows signs of being dented and clawed. Once protected by a powerful lock that is now broken, it's simply wedged shut and forced open when needed—requiring a Hard Brawn action to open it.

Inside the first room is the robotics facility that includes the non-functional remains of two robots connected to now-useless charging stations. The third station holds the **Wrangler** when not pursuing its duties. (Alternately if the party has disabled the Wrangler in an earlier encounter, another might still be functional here.) There are a number of electronics repair tools in the room, as well as a laser fuser (with 2 hours still available on its power cell, see Chapter Six).

The second room hosts the computer core for the Zoo. Damage to the *Warden* isolated this system from the rest of the ship and its been left to its own devices for centuries. It exists as a dust-covered touchscreen panel overlooking a large desk. Monitors to the side alternate with top-down views of different areas inside the Zoo.

Disabling the computer system using Tech is extremely difficult, a Hard complex action, 1 minute increments, requiring 10 achievements to succeed. Less imaginative means (smashing, breaking) are only of Average difficulty and each increment is only 30 seconds. Either way, the lights, locks, and other systems in the Zoo begin to noticeably shut on and off as the computer system desperately tries to keep itself functional and summon its robotic defense.

Triggered. The computer was never intended to interact directly with humans or communicate with potential exhibits, so it cannot "talk" and has no way to even express its intentions. It can, however, sense the danger of humans and/or animals entering this room and it will summon the Wrangler to defend it.

Optional Encounters

If the characters are having an easy time, the referee might introduce random encounters in different areas to keep up the challenge. A raging ursoid might be roving the Zoo attempting to escape, but will only attempt to murder the party if they don't flee from it immediately. The "empty" cow pasture might hold a hive of buzzers. The computer control room may host an eye fungus that acts as an unwitting guardian.

Encounters can also be used to keep tension and pacing during the course of the adventure. If the group tends to stop, rest, and regroup after each and every time something happens use an existing or improvised encounter to mix things up and encourage the players to keep their characters moving. The Wrangler might patrol looking for escapees from Containment, or any number of mutant animals may go looking for a snack of lounging characters.

Concluding the Adventure

For most groups, simply escaping the Zoo is more than enough victory — though if the Zoo is still functional the Wrangler will continue to abduct creatures from nearby sections of the ship. Perhaps later they will launch a second expedition to explore and shut down the Zoo (providing the referee an opportunity to mix things up to offer new hazards and surprises).

Defeating the Wrangler (or both if the referee introduces a second bot) removes the threat of anyone else being forced into the Zoo against their will, while leaving the Zoo still otherwise functioning in the background. (That doesn't mean the computer might not be able to eventually enlist the assistance of a roving repair bot to put everything back to "normal.")

Complete "victory" means deactivating or destroying the primary computer system. While the computer doesn't sing Daisy, it does indicate its distress as the systems go increasingly haywire before its lights go out forever. Once the computer is gone, a number of things happen immediately:

All electronically controlled doors immediately open as a safety protocol, including the entrance/exit. All automated and holographic systems shut down forever. This means that the feed will no longer be generated, the birds in the aviary can easily escape, the theater and dinosaur exhibits stop functioning, etc.

Shutting down the Zoo makes the starship *Warden* a slightly less terrifying place … though for the player characters it might just be a walk in the park compared to what awaits them in the future.

ENCOUNTER STATISTICS

Armored Horror
Medium mutant animal (armadillo)

Move: 15 ft., burrow 1 ft. • **Initiative:** 2d
Dodge: 1d • **Armor:** 2 (resist electricity 3)
Fatigue / Wounds: 19 / 14

Weak (–1d):	Dexterity, Discipline
Competent (+1d):	Athletics
Good (+2d):	Brawn, Constitution, Unarmed Combat

Mutations: Larger (*), New Body Parts—Carapace & Claws (*), Electrical Generation (3d)

Qualities: Brutal, Burrower, Tough

Attacks
Unarmed: Claws (+1W)
Electric Bolt: 2d ranged attack up to 60 ft, +3F electricity, 1 use only

Description
The "horror" is an oversized armadillo with comically-large and steel-hard front claws and crackling with static electricity with every movement.

Tactics
The creature's primary motivation is hunger, as it's accustomed to food being deposited on a semi-regular basis but it has not fed in some time. Its instincts prefer arthropods (insects) but will gladly eat any animal or human but only attack plant or artificial life defensively.

Watching from its den, it will choose preferred prey—either the weakest-looking or an isolated member of the group. It will then charge and attempt to take it down quickly and then drag it back inside the den, which is small enough to force only one character a time to face it. If the chosen victim looks like it needs to be softened up, it will get just close enough to use its electrical generation mutation and then go in for the take-down. If injured it will retreat to its den and fight only defensively.

Gruffoid, Little
Small mutant animal (goat)

Move: 20 ft. • **Initiative**: 2d
Dodge: 4d • **Armor**: –
Fatigue / Wounds: 13 / 14

Weak (–1d):	Brawn
Competent (+1d):	Deception, Ranged Weapons
Good (+2d):	Dexterity, Melee Weapons, Unarmed Combat
Amazing (+3d):	Leadership

Mutations: Biped (*), Fear Generation (2d), New Body Parts—Horn (*), Smaller (*)

Qualities: Agile Combatant—Melee (2d), Speech (1d)

Attacks
Melee Weapons: Knife (+1W damage if at least one enhancement is rolled)
Ranged Weapons: Sling (+1F damage if at least one enhancement is rolled)
Unarmed: Horns (+1W stationary, +2W if charging)
Fear: 3d psychic attack vs. Discipline/Emotional Control, causes target to flee, 2/day)

Description
A gruffoid is small anthropomorphic goat capable of speech in halting, adorably bleating voices. This is the smallest of the trio, but is actually the leader of the pack by sheer ruthlessness and force of personality … and his mental mutation. He is greedy, his primary motivation being food and "stuff"—the shinier the better.

Tactics
The smallest gruffoid uses its agility and size to inflict wounds and keep moving, keeping opponents off-balance—all while screeching orders to his two larger "brothers" since he is the smartest of the three.

Gruffoid, Bigger
Medium mutant animal (goat)

Move: 20 ft. • **Initiative**: 2d
Dodge: 3d • **Armor**: 1 against physical attacks (mutation)
Fatigue / Wounds: 15 / 15

Weak (–1d):	Discipline
Competent (+1d):	Athletics, Brawn, Dexterity
Good (+2d):	Unarmed Combat
Amazing (+3d):	Melee Weapons

Mutations: Biped (*), Kinetic Absorption (2d), New Body Parts—Horn (*)

Qualities: Speech (1d), Vigor (2d)

Attacks
Melee Weapons: Knife (+1W damage if at least one enhancement is rolled)
Ranged Weapons: Sling (+1F damage if at least one enhancement is rolled)
Unarmed: Horns (+1W stationary, +2W if charging)

Description
The middle brother follows the smallest one's lead.

Tactics
His tactics are solely based on the orders and style of his little brother, and would be unsettled without him. They work in tandem, alternating between ranged and melee to weaken and intimidate enemies, letting the biggest brother be the biggest surprise of them all.

Gruffoid, Biggest
Large mutant animal (goat)

Move: 20 ft. • **Initiative**: 2d
Dodge: 1d • **Armor**: 2 while Small (mutation)
Fatigue / Wounds: 15 / 19

Weak (–1d):	Dexterity
Competent (+1d):	Athletics, Ranged Weapons
Good (+2d):	Constitution, Melee Weapons
Amazing (+3d):	Brawn, Unarmed Combat

Mutations: Biped (*), Density Control—Self (4d) Larger (*), New Body Parts—Horn (*)
Qualities: Speech (1d), Unyielding (2d)

Attacks
Melee Weapons: Long Blade (+2W)
Ranged Weapons: Small Rock (+1F), Large Rock (+1W)
Unarmed: Horns (+1W stationary, +2W if charging)

Description

This is the hulking, largest brother—who uses his ability to shift in density to appear slightly smaller than even the smallest of the trio.

Tactics

Staying "small" until his little brother gives the order, he allows himself to seem the smallest threat—purposefully seeming like less of a threat by not fighting at full potential while small and playing up initial injuries as more serious. Then when the order is given and he's in the middle of opponents who underestimate him, he'll shift to normal size—roughly 8 feet tall of furry, horned muscle and fury.

Colugoids

Medium mutant animal (Asian flying squirrel)

Move: 20 ft. • **Initiative**: 2d
Dodge: 3d • **Armor**: –
Fatigue / Wounds: 15 / 13

Weak (–1d):	Brawn, Constitution
Competent (+1d):	Athletics, Alertness
Good (+2d):	Dexterity, Stealth, Unarmed Combat

Mutations: Larger (*), New Body Parts—Claws (*), Wings

Qualities: Agile Combatant (2d), Mobile (2d)

Attacks

Ranged Weapons: Sling (+1F damage if at least one enhancement is rolled)
Unarmed: Claws (+1W)

Notes

The "wings" (actually just a membrane of skin) granted to this mutant animal allow gliding only. They must climb or catch air currents in order to achieve lift.

Description

Colugoids are mutated descendants of southeast Asian flying squirrels. They can be utterly silent but will begin squealing in a high-pitch cacophony as a group then go quiet, using noise for distraction. Their goal is to drive others out of their forest territory.

Tactics

They will attempt to frighten and harass, not interested in any kind of pitched battle but attempt to drive intruders out of the forest. If badly injured their membranes are torn or limbs broken to where they will fall to the floor, moaning in near-helpless pain. Teamwork tactics are used to isolate, injure, and scare enemies. If presented with an obviously superior foe, they will retreat and hide in the trees.

Wrangler

Medium construct (robot)

Move: 15 ft. (Tracks) • **Initiative**: 5d
Dodge: 2d • **Armor**: 2
Fatigue / Wounds: 12 / 19

Good (+2d):	Constitution, Melee Weapons, Ranged Weapons
Amazing (+3d):	Alertness, Crafting, Tech

Reasoning: Analytical
Communication & Sensors: Telescopic, Wireless
Mutations: Telekinesis (Telekinesis (4d, tractor beam projector)
Qualities: Agile Combatant, Mobile

Attacks

Ranged Weapons: Electric Bolt (+2F electricity), may fire 2 per turn at different targets
Melee Weapons: Stunning Prod (+1dF electricity, target must succeed Hard Constitution check or be stunned for 2d turns, requires 10 minutes to recharge)

Description

A bastardized cross between a repair and veterinary bot on fast-moving treads, the Wranglers are specifically intended to use non-lethal means to stun and relocate animal life. Their nonlethal intent is not apparent in their efficient use of force and lack of caution in the pursuit of their duties.

Tactics

If attempting to subdue multiple targets, the Wrangler attempts to rush the most obvious threat and use its stunning prod to full effect, then use its mobility to fire electric bolts from a distance and even uses its tractor beam to relocate troublesome adversaries. It will defend the computer core to its destruction.

METAMORPHOSIS ALPHA

BIOLOGICAL ANALYSIS

PHYSICAL DESCRIPTION

player

concept

stock

breed

ROUGH APPROXIMATION

OBSERVED TRAITS

amazing
(+3D)

good
(+2D)

competent
(+1D)

weak
(-1D)

hopeless
(-2D)

WOUND CAPACITY

FATIGUE CAPACITY

MOVEMENT

INITIATIVE

DODGE

RAD. RESISTANCE

PERSONAL EFFECTS

NOTES

OBSERVED MUTATIONS

....

....

....

....

....

OBSERVED QUALITIES

....

....

....

....

GAME BASICS

A standard action roll is 2 dice (2d).

Traits modify the number of dice rolled. The normal maximum is 5 dice (5d).

Achievement Thresholds
Easy: 3+   Average: 4+   Hard: 5+

BACKERS